Making the Move to RDA

A Self-Study Primer for Catalogers

Chamya Pompey Kincy with
Sara Shatford Layne

ROWMAN & LITTLEFIELD
Lanham • Boulder • New York • Toronto • Plymouth, UK

Published by Rowman & Littlefield
4501 Forbes Boulevard, Suite 200, Lanham, Maryland 20706
www.rowman.com

10 Thornbury Road, Plymouth PL6 7PP, United Kingdom

British Library Cataloguing in Publication Information Available

Library of Congress Cataloging-in-Publication Data
Kincy, Chamya Pomey, 1976-
  Making the move to RDA : a self-study primer for catalogers / Chamya Pomey Kincy with Sara Shatford Layne.
    pages cm
  Includes bibliographical references and index.
  ISBN 978-0-8108-8769-5 (pbk. : alk. paper) — ISBN 978-0-8108-8770-1 (ebook) 1. Resource description & access—Handbooks, manuals, etc. 2. Descriptive cataloging—Standards—Handbooks, manuals, etc. I. Layne, Sara Shatford. II. Title.
  Z694.15.R47K56 2014
  025.3'2—dc23

                                                                      2013035367

This book is dedicated to Chamya's mother,
Gwendolyn Jean Kincy

In Memoriam

Chamya Pompey Kincy

February 27, 1976–July 20, 2013

Chamya Pompey Kincy had almost finished writing this book when a devastating cancer claimed her at the age of 37. With the assistance of colleagues Luiz Mendes, John Riemer, and Hermine Vermeij, Sara Shatford Layne completed this book following Chamya's untimely passing. Chamya was so very happy when she could help others, and this book was part of her efforts to help other librarians. She is remembered with gratitude for her dedication to her work, her kindness, and her generosity.

Contents

Essential Acronyms
Decoded and Explained

AACR2: *Anglo-American Cataloguing Rules, Second Edition.* A code of cataloging rules prepared by the American Library Association and other organizations, first published in 1978, and widely used beginning in the early 1980s. AACR2 was superseded in 2013 by RDA (*Resource Description and Access*) for cataloging done by many national libraries.

CONSER: *Cooperative Online Serials Program of the PCC.* "CONSER is an authoritative source for bibliographic records, documentation, and training materials for serials cataloging" (http://www.loc.gov/aba/pcc/conser/).

DACS: *Describing Archives: A Content Standard.* DACS was approved by the Society of American Archivists in 2004. "DACS is an output-neutral set of rules for describing archives, personal papers, and manuscript collections, and can be applied to all material types" (http://www.archivists.org/governance/standards/dacs.asp).

FRAD: *Functional Requirements for Authority Data.* This report by the IFLA Working Group on Functional Requirements and Numbering of Authority Records (FRANAR) was first published in 2009. It serves as a conceptual foundation for RDA. http://www.ifla.org/publications/functional-requirements-for-authority-data.

FRBR: *Functional Requirements for Bibliographic Records.* This report of the IFLA Study Group on Functional Requirements for Bibliographic Records was first published in 1998. FRBR serves as a conceptual foundation for RDA. http://www.ifla.org/publications/functional-requirements-for-bibliographic-records.

FRSAD: *Functional Requirements for Subject Authority Data.* This report of the IFLA Working Group on Functional Requirements for Subject Authority Records (FRSAR) was first published in 2011. http://www.ifla.org/publications/ifla-series -on-bibliographic-control-43.

GMD: *General Material Designation.* A term used in AACR2 to describe the general nature of the format of a resource. Examples of GMDs are "microform" and "sound recording."

IFLA: *International Federation of Library Associations and Institutions.* "The International Federation of Library Associations and Institutions (IFLA) is the leading international body representing the interests of library and information services and their users" (http://www.ifla.org/about).

ISBD: *International Standard Bibliographic Description.* A standard developed and maintained by IFLA. A consolidated edition was published in 2011. http://www.ifla .org/publications/international-standard-bibliographic-description.

JSC: *Joint Steering Committee for Development of RDA.* http://www.rda-jsc.org/rda .html.

LC: *Library of Congress.* http://www.loc.gov/index.html.

LCNAF: *Library of Congress Name Authority File.* The common name for what is officially the LC/NACO Authority File, as the records in it are created not just by the Library of Congress but also by NACO participants from many other agencies. It is freely available via the Library of Congress linked data service as *Library of Congress Names* (http://id.loc.gov/authorities/names.html), *Library of Congress Authorities* (http://authorities.loc.gov), and also, for subscribers, via OCLC. "The Library of Congress Name Authority File (NAF) file provides authoritative data for names of persons, organizations, events, places, and titles" (*Library of Congress Names* website).

LC-PCC PS: *Library of Congress-Program for Cooperative Cataloging Policy Statement.* RDA provides many options. These *Policy Statements* reflect decisions made regarding RDA implementation at LC and PCC libraries and others who wish to follow their decisions.

LCSH: *Library of Congress Subject Headings.* A vocabulary for subject access, developed and maintained by the Library of Congress. It is freely available via *Library of Congress Authorities* (http://authorities.loc.gov) and the Library of Congress linked data service as *Library of Congress Subject Headings* (http://id.loc.gov/authorities/ subjects.html).

MARC: *Machine Readable Cataloging.* MARC is a standard developed by Henriette Avram at the Library of Congress in the late 1960s. It is currently maintained by the Network Development and MARC Standards Office at the Library of Congress. "The MARC formats are standards for the representation and communication of bibliographic and related information in machine-readable form" (http://www.loc .gov/marc/).

MeSH: *Medical Subject Headings.* A vocabulary for subject access to medical topics, developed and maintained by the U.S. National Library of Medicine (NLM). MeSH is freely available via the MeSH Browser. http://www.nlm.nih.gov/mesh/.

NACO: *Name Authority Cooperative Program of the PCC.* "Through this program, participants contribute authority records for personal, corporate, and jurisdictional names; uniform titles; and series headings to the LC/NACO Authority File" (http:// www.loc.gov/aba/pcc/naco/).

NLM: *National Library of Medicine.* http://www.nlm.nih.gov/about/.

OCLC: "OCLC" is no longer technically an acronym, but is rather the current name of a not-for-profit organization: "a worldwide library cooperative, owned, governed and sustained by members since 1967 . . . Our public purpose is to establish, maintain and operate a computerized library network" (http://www.oclc.org).

PCC: *Program for Cooperative Cataloging.* "The PCC is an international cooperative effort aimed at expanding access to library collections by providing useful, timely, and cost-effective cataloging that meets mutually-accepted standards of libraries around the world" (http://www.loc.gov/aba/pcc/).

RDA: *Resource Description and Access.* RDA is a cataloging standard implemented widely in 2013. It is available as part of the online product *RDA Toolkit* (http:// www.rdatoolkit.org/).

Preface

As the title *Making the Move to RDA: A Self-Study Primer for Catalogers* suggests, this book is intended as a guide for catalogers new to applying RDA: *Resource Description and Access*. Although this book can be used by catalogers who are completely new to cataloging, it is hoped that it will be particularly useful to experienced catalogers who are familiar with the code of rules that has been widely used for the last thirty years, *Anglo-American Cataloguing Rules, Second Edition*, commonly known as AACR2, but who are less familiar with RDA. Understanding how to use RDA for cataloging can be a daunting prospect. It is hoped that this book will help those who need to understand RDA, particularly those who need to apply it in a MARC environment.

WHAT IS IN THIS BOOK?

This book is divided into three parts. Part I, consisting of chapters 1–3, provides the history of the development of RDA, then explains the underlying models and the resulting organization of RDA, and finishes by examining the major differences between RDA and its predecessor, AACR2. Part II, consisting of chapters 4–7, summarizes RDA itself, explaining the major instructions contained in RDA and giving examples in MARC coding. Part III, consisting of chapters 8–10, shows how RDA plays out in the creation and interpretation of bibliographic and authority records in the MARC environment, using examples of MARC fields and MARC records.

Examples used in part II of this book come primarily from RDA itself. The record examples in part III are based on bibliographic records from the *Library of Congress*

Online Catalog, bibliographic records from the RDA sample set assembled by members of the Program for Cooperative Cataloging (PCC) Standing Committee on Training (SCT) RDA Records Task Group, and authority records from *Library of Congress Authorities*.

The examples assume a basic familiarity with MARC encoding; readers wishing for introductory as well as detailed information about MARC are urged to consult the MARC Standards website. Note that the following conventions are used in this book for the representation of MARC field indicators: # is used when the indicator is defined, but the value is not specified in the example; and either [blank space] or [underscore] is used when the indicator is undefined or it is defined and its value is [blank] in the example. Note also that the MARC examples include ISBD punctuation.

HOW TO USE THIS BOOK

This book can be used in a variety of ways. Part I can be read by those who simply want a basic understanding of the background that led to the development of RDA. Part II can serve as a summary of RDA for someone wanting more knowledge about RDA than is contained in part I. Part II can also be used as a guide to the *RDA Toolkit*, which is the online product containing the full, and most current, version of RDA. Finally, part III can function as a reference for anyone wanting to consult a detailed outline of the instructions in RDA. Part III provides detailed examples that are useful to catalogers who need to create or modify MARC records created using RDA, as well as to anyone who wishes to understand these records. Part III should ideally be used in conjunction with the *RDA Toolkit*.

Although every effort has been made to make this book consistent with RDA instructions as of July 2013, these instructions are subject to almost constant revision and change. Similarly, every effort has been made to ensure that references to the MARC formats are current as of July 2013, but changes are also made from time to time to these formats. Furthermore, RDA is often applied in the United States in accord with *Policy Statements* developed by the Library of Congress in consultation with the Program for Cooperative Cataloging. Referred to as "LC-PCC PS," these *Policy Statements* are also subject to relatively frequent revision; they are freely available as part of the *RDA Toolkit*.

I

UNDERSTANDING RDA'S BACKGROUND AND USE

1

Development, Objectives, and Principles

Many catalogers are familiar with the differences between AACR2 and RDA, but there are also significant similarities between the two standards. Areas of change and continuity may seem arbitrary and often difficult to remember without knowing the context behind them. This chapter details the rationale for RDA's development in order to shed some light on why some guidelines were changed and why some remained the same. It also covers RDA's stated objectives and principles to further elucidate the similarities and differences between the two standards.

HISTORY OF THE DEVELOPMENT

RDA was originally envisioned as the *Anglo-American Cataloguing Rules, 3rd Edition* (AACR3). It was developed by the Joint Steering Committee for Revision of AACR (JSC) in line with its 2005–2009 Strategic Plan for AACR. The Strategic Plan's goals called for structural, conceptual, and terminological changes from AACR2 that would better align the standard with international efforts to improve access to resources within the digital context. The rules would be based on a variety of international cataloging standards and principles, particularly the *Functional Requirements for Bibliographic Records* (FRBR), a conceptual model published in 1998. The rules would also be more compatible with other metadata standards and incorporate the concept of authority control.

The Strategic Plan also aimed to provide instructions that more comprehensively addressed resources of all types and to write the guidelines within a framework that would accommodate emerging formats over time. AACR2 Part I comprises chapters that are devoted to a limited set of format types, which makes it difficult to incorporate rules for new formats into the standard's structure. The rules in AACR2 also do not clearly distinguish between the content and the physical aspects of a resource, often conflating these attributes into one data element. AACR3 would be reorganized and provide special instructions on content and media types to address these concerns. This would eliminate many of the redundancies found across the format-based chapters of AACR2 Part I, which was another aim of AACR3.

AACR3 was projected to comprise three parts offering guidelines similar to AACR2, but within a different organizational framework. Part I would provide instructions similar to AACR2 Part I, but would be organized into three sections: general rules, supplementary rules for specific types of content, and supplementary rules for specific types of media. Part II would be based on AACR2 Chapter 21 ("Choice of Access Points") and would provide guidelines for adding access points that represent relationships among resources and relationships between resources and the entities responsible for them. Part III would incorporate authority control principles. As such, it would provide guidelines for formulating authorized and variant access points for persons, corporate bodies, titles, and other entities along lines similar to those in Chapters 22–26 of AACR2. Part III would also provide guidelines for recording the attributes of these entities.

The draft of AACR3 Part I was submitted for constituency review in December 2004, and the JSC deliberated on the constituencies' comments during its April 2005 meeting. The constituencies agreed with the goals of the JSC's Strategic Plan, but they expressed dissatisfaction with Part I's organization and with the language of the text, which some considered to be abstruse and rife with library jargon. The constituencies also believed that the code should be modeled on metadata standards used by other communities beyond the library context.

Based on constituency feedback, the JSC decided to embark on a new direction for revising AACR. The committee argued that the current digital environment is different from the one in which AACR2 was developed, and that it posed new challenges that would be more adequately addressed by a new standard for resource description and access. This new standard would be based on AACR2. However, the structure would be more aligned with the two conceptual models that define the functional requirements for bibliographic and authority records: FRBR and *Functional Requirements for Authority Data* (FRAD). The new standard would also separate the instructions for recording data from the instructions for displaying data and would have a more "user-friendly" layout and format. To signify this change in direction, the new standard was renamed *Resource Description and Access*, or RDA.

After its 2005 meeting, the JSC rewrote and reorganized the standard and issued drafts of the text from December 2005 through November 2008 for constituency review. Throughout the review period, the JSC met twice a year to deliberate on constituency responses and make decisions on revision proposals. In June 2009, the JSC delivered the full text of the new standard to the publishers of RDA. In 2010, the text was released as part of an online product called *RDA Toolkit*.

THE CURRENT TEXT OF RDA

RDA emerged from the development and review process as a cataloging standard framed within the theoretical context of FRBR and FRAD, yet brimming with instructions that were carried over from AACR2. Many of the instructions are similar, if not identical, to AACR2, which facilitates coexistence of records described using both standards. However, there are some significant differences that have resulted from the effort to make RDA more responsive to the end user's needs and to make it more extensible and adaptable by other communities. The instructions were written to be simpler to understand and with terminology more in keeping with other metadata standards. The instructions also encourage avoiding esoteric terminology in the recording of data to make this data more understandable to today's users.

AACR3 was originally envisioned as a loose-leaf product, similar to AACR2. However, RDA was the result of the JSC's fundamental shift in direction toward a standard created within the digital context. Thus, RDA was written to be operable in a web-based environment, and its primary format is an online product—the *RDA Toolkit*—with print derivatives issued periodically.

For RDA's ultimate organization, the JSC abandoned the three-part precept and divided RDA into thirty-seven chapters in ten sections, each tied inextricably to FRBR and FRAD concepts. Two of the chapters provide extensive guidelines for addressing a variety of formats (including digital formats) and offer instructions for describing the physical aspects of a resource, the formatting and encoding of information stored in the resource, and the content of the resource. Several other chapters provide guidelines that address the recording of authority data, which was not explicitly addressed in AACR2. In addition to the main chapters, appendices were added to provide guidance on the presentation of data and other supplemental instructions.

The resulting text is substantially different from AACR2, yet grounded in many of AACR2's cataloging tenets. Even with a firm understanding of RDA's development and rationale, it may still be difficult to tease out, let alone understand, areas of change and of continuity. To further elucidate this, RDA includes a list of four objectives and eight principles that may help contextualize the similarities and differences.

RDA OBJECTIVES

Responsiveness to User Needs

The first objective of RDA is *responsiveness to user needs*, which means that the data describing resources should enable the user to carry out a variety of tasks. First, the data should help users find all relevant resources in response to their search criteria. To this end, the instructions are written so that catalogers will record all the attributes and relationships that thoroughly connect users with their desired resources.

The data should also help users find all resources that embody a work; all resources associated with a person, family, or corporate body; persons, families, and corporate bodies associated with other persons, families, or corporate bodies; and all resources on a given subject. In meeting this aim, RDA provides an extensive set of instructions for describing various types of relationships. Recording primary relationships helps organize resources for better navigability for the user. Recording responsibility relationships helps users find all the resources created or produced by a particular entity. Recording subject relationships helps users find all the resources on a given topic.

The data should help users identify resources and the entities responsible for the creation or production of those resources. This often means recording data in a way that helps users confirm that the resource or responsible entity found in a search result corresponds to the one that was sought. To facilitate this, RDA instructions encourage transcription of data that faithfully represent the unique attributes of a particular resource to better ensure unambiguous identification. Helping users identify resources and the entities responsible for them sometimes means providing data that help them distinguish between similarly named entities. Thus, RDA provides guidelines on recording additional data in access points that help users readily differentiate between two or more entities within a browse list. It also provides guidelines for recording additional attributes in bibliographic and authority records that can give the user further confirmation that the entity found corresponds with the one that was sought.

The data should help users select a resource based on its physical characteristics, intended audience, language, or other attributes. One of the main aims for RDA was to tease out the characteristics related to carrier from those related to content. In meeting this aim, RDA provides a chapter of instructions that has as its goal the recording of data that will help users select a resource based on carrier attributes and a separate chapter that has the same goal for content attributes.

The data should help users obtain a resource by purchase, loan, or accession via the Internet. RDA provides instructions for recording data to facilitate this user task.

Finally, RDA states that the data should help users understand the relationship between entities, the relationship between different forms of names for the same entity, and the reason that a name or title was chosen as the preferred form for an entity. In meeting this aim, RDA provides specific instructions on authority control that encourage catalogers to record information that helps users understand the rationale behind why authorized and variant forms of names and titles are chosen and to document any relevant relationships they may have.

Cost Efficiency

The second objective, *cost efficiency*, means that *the data should meet functional requirements for the support of user tasks in a cost-efficient manner.* RDA instructions lack many of the cataloging-specific conventions prescribed in AACR2, such as how data should be abbreviated and when data should be omitted. Moreover, when there is more than one of the same type of data element listed for a resource, RDA allows for omission of all but the first. The end result is a set of instructions that can be learned more quickly and that facilitate the streamlining of workflows, both of which can lead to cost savings.

Flexibility

Flexibility, the third objective, means that *the data should function independently of the format, medium, or system used to store or communicate the data. They should be amenable to use in a variety of environments.* Unlike AACR2, RDA was written outside of the card catalog context. Thus, the instructions do not prescribe truncation or omission of data along the same space-saving conventions as AACR2. Moreover, the card catalog–based terminology of main and added entry is absent from RDA. Furthermore, the instructions are not written within the MARC-centric dichotomy of bibliographic and authority records. They are written in terms of the attributes of and relationships among resources and the entities associated with them. RDA instructions prescribe the recording of data that can be encoded into the MARC record. However, the instructions are flexible enough to be applied in the non-MARC context as well.

Continuity

Finally, *Continuity* means that *the data should be amenable to integration into existing databases (particularly those developed using AACR and related standards).* Though most catalogers tend to focus on the differences between AACR2 and RDA, they have more similarities. This is because RDA is based on AACR2, with many of the latter's rules carried over into RDA with little, if any, modification (save for a difference in the wording of the instructions). This facilitates the coexistence of AACR2 and RDA records within the same database. Many catalogers will find that the same information is coded in many of the same fields in the same manner, but with a few changes in abbreviation conventions or other differences.

For example, if users wanted to check the record for the presence of a bibliography, they would find this information in the 504 field, regardless of the cataloging standard used for describing the data. They might even see similar wording, such as "Includes bibliographical references." The only difference would be if there were a page span involved; an AACR2 record would precede the page span with the abbreviation "p.," whereas an RDA record would precede it with the spelled-out form of the word "page." This would at most create inconsistency for the user, in terms of seeing the abbreviated form sometimes and the spelled-out form at other times. However, the meaning of the data, their location in the record, and the general wording in which they are conveyed is the same, so that users can rely on this information, whether it is in an AACR2 record or an RDA record.

RDA PRINCIPLES

Differentiation

Differentiation means that *the data should differentiate one resource from another. The data describing an entity associated with a resource should differentiate that entity from other entities.* To help meet the objective of responsiveness to users' needs, RDA instructions encourage addition of data beyond the core set of elements needed to describe a resource or an entity associated with a resource, if the cataloger feels this is necessary for distinguishing that resource or entity from others. One example of this is the addition of a note explaining the unique characteristics of a particular resource. Another is the addition of a term of profession or occupation to the authorized access point representing a person, to distinguish that person from another similarly named person.

Sufficiency

Sufficiency means that *the data should be sufficient to meet the user's needs with respect to selection of an appropriate resource.* To further meet its objective of responsiveness to users' needs, RDA parses out attributes related to the content from those related to the carrier and provides a plethora of guidelines for recording both sets of attributes. This facilitates a more comprehensive, granular description of the data, so that a user can choose, for example, a resource that is an unmediated English-language text with illustrations, an online bilingual text without illustrations, or a spoken-word Spanish narrative on audiocassette.

Relationships

Relationships means that *the data should indicate significant relationships between a resource and other resources and entities associated with it.* RDA places a greater emphasis on relationships than AACR2 did. Indeed, twenty-one out of thirty-seven chapters in RDA are devoted to providing instructions for recording various types of relationships. Moreover, RDA provides instructions on recording relationship designators that clarify the nature of the relationship and provides appendices with an open list of specific terms and phrases that can be used. For example, a person responsible for the creation of a work could have the designator "author" added to specify the nature of that person's relationship with the work. Likewise, a translation or a revision of a resource could have the designators "translation of" and "revision of" added, respectively.

Representation

Representation means that *the data describing a resource should reflect the resource's representation of itself.* Application of this principle can often result in the most commonly recognizable changes from AACR2 to RDA. AACR2 prescribes the alteration of data in many ways. It requires the cataloger to apply specific capitalization and ab-

breviation conventions, instructs the cataloger to truncate or omit data in the statement of responsibility, and prescribes abbreviation of data in the edition statement
and the publication statement. AACR2 also directs the cataloger to correct inaccuracies in the title proper and the series statement, among other prescribed practices.

RDA encourages catalogers to apply what has come to be known as the "take what
you see" approach, in which data are faithfully transcribed into the record as they
appear on the resource. As a result, catalogers will see inaccuracies in titles proper
corrected in notes rather than in situ. They may also see edition statements and
publication data spelled out, fuller statements of responsibility, and even data that
are transcribed in all uppercase letters.

Attribution

Attribution means that *the data should reflect attributions of responsibility made either
in the resource itself or in reference sources, irrespective of whether the attribution of responsibility is accurate.* AACR2 discourages false attribution and directs the cataloger to
record information that correctly attributes responsibility for a resource. For example,
if a fictitious character was cited on the resource as an author, AACR2 rules prescribed
against attributing this responsibility through the provision of an access point for that
character. However, RDA encourages faithful recording of the relationship between a
fictitious character and the resource it is purported to have created or produced.

Common Usage or Practice

Common usage or practice means that *data not transcribed from the resource itself
should reflect common usage in the language and script preferred by the agency creating
the data.* As with representation, application of this principle often results in the recording of data that are recognizably different from AACR2. This can be seen most
in cases in which AACR2 prescribes Latin abbreviations, for example *s.n.* and *ca.*,
whereas RDA prescribes the spelled-out equivalents in the language of the cataloging
agency. For English-language cataloging agencies, this would mean recording *publisher not identified* and *approximately*, respectively. Also, because of its international
scope, an increasing number of translations of RDA will provide instructions that
allow agencies beyond the Anglo-American context to record data in their own languages and scripts. Finally, common usage or practice can be seen in certain RDA
instructions that allow common usage terms, such as *DVD*, to be recorded in the
extent, rather than the RDA vocabulary term, *videodisc*.

Uniformity

Uniformity means that *the appendices on capitalization, abbreviations, order of elements,
punctuation, etc., should serve to promote uniformity in the presentation of data describing
a resource or an entity associated with a resource.* To extend the reach of RDA beyond
the library community, the JSC strategically separated the instructions for recording

data from those for displaying data. To benefit traditional catalogers within the library context, instructions for display are still present in RDA, but they are relegated to appendices. This means that the guidelines for punctuation and the order of elements, as outlined in the *International Standard Bibliographic Description* (ISBD), are not present in the main instructions to provide visual cues for the cataloger to replicate in the MARC record, as is the case with AACR2. Although this may make it more difficult for catalogers who regularly record data in accord with the ISBD standard, it does make the information more standard-neutral for those not applying ISBD specifications. And regardless of their location within the standard, these display guidelines ensure uniformity in the presentation of data for the network of cataloging agencies that apply them.

Accuracy

Accuracy means that *the data should provide supplementary information to correct or clarify ambiguous, unintelligible, or misleading representations appearing in the resource itself.* As AACR2 did, RDA provides guidelines for correcting or clarifying information. For recorded data, both standards instruct the cataloger to add this information immediately after the "faulty" data. For transcribed data, both standards prescribe the same method for *clarifying* information. However, for *correcting* information in transcribed data, RDA differs from AACR2 in that it instructs catalogers to describe the correction in a note rather than inserting the correction immediately following the inaccuracy.

CONCLUSION

This chapter explores the history of RDA's development, the rationale for its original incarnation as the third edition of AACR, and the evolution of that rationale, which changed the direction of its development and shaped the current text. This historical overview, in conjunction with an explanation of RDA objectives and principles, attempts to contextualize the similarities and differences between AACR2 and RDA so that catalogers can understand them, learn them more quickly, and transition to RDA more smoothly.

Chapter 3 covers the differences between AACR2 and RDA in more detail. However, in order to know whether an AACR2 rule was carried over into RDA, one must know how to find the analogous instruction in RDA. Indeed, if the corresponding instruction is not located in RDA, a cataloger may not be sure if this was because the AACR2 rule was not carried over into RDA or because he or she failed to locate it within RDA's new structure. Therefore, understanding RDA's organization is crucial if catalogers are to successfully locate the instructions they need to inform them of changes in cataloging practice. The structure of RDA is inextricably linked to the conceptual models underlying the new standard. Therefore, chapter 2 explains these underlying models in detail and illustrates how they affect the organization of RDA.

2

Underlying Models and Organization

Chapter 1 covered the history of RDA's development and its objectives and principles in an attempt to contextualize its similarities to and differences from AACR2. One of the main differences from AACR2 is the theoretical framework upon which RDA was written and organized. The text of the June 2010 release of RDA was based on two underlying conceptual models: FRBR and FRAD. A third model, *Functional Requirements for Subject Authority Data* (FRSAD), will form the basis for subject-related content in future iterations of RDA. Together these three models form the "FR Family" of conceptual models, which encourage the recording of bibliographic and authority data in a way that optimizes search and retrieval of resources. This chapter introduces the basic concepts of all three models, but focuses on FRBR and FRAD and their influence on the current structure, organization, and content of RDA.

FRBR

FRBR forms the foundation upon which the other two models are built, so it helps to understand its basic premise. The FRBR model defines the key objects of interest to users of bibliographic data as *entities* and divides the entities into three groups. Group 1 entities are the primary objects of interest to users: *works, expressions, manifestations*, and *items*. These entities provide categories into which specific aspects of bibliographic data can be placed for optimal organization and navigation of resources. Those responsible for Group 1 entities are categorized as Group 2 entities and comprise *persons* and *corporate bodies*. Group 3 entities are the subjects of works, which can include *concepts, objects, events*, and *places*. Group 3 entities can also include Group 1 and Group 2 entities, because those entities can also be the subjects of works.

To optimize the end users' search and retrieval of resources, four types of user tasks must be addressed. First, users must be able to *find* entities that meet their specified search criteria. Second, they must be able to *identify* an entity or distinguish one entity from other similarly named entities. Third, users must be able to *select* from among resources with similar characteristics. Finally, they must be able to *obtain* their desired resources.

To help users accomplish these tasks, there are two types of bibliographic information with respect to entities that must be recorded. First, the entities' *attributes* (or "characteristics") must be recorded in order to provide the bibliographic details that help users identify their desired resources, select from among similar resources, and obtain the resources they need. Second, the *relationships* among the entities must be recorded in order to help users find related resources, find all the resources associated with a particular person or corporate body, or find all the resources on a particular subject.

The FRBR model defines the relevant attributes and relationships with respect to each entity and maps them to the corresponding user tasks. RDA's structure and terminology are heavily influenced by this conceptualization of bibliographic data. It is therefore imperative that catalogers familiarize themselves with FRBR concepts in order to understand and navigate RDA.

FRAD

The FRBR model conceptualizes how to record data of interest to users of bibliographic data. As such, it focuses on the attributes and relationships of Group 1 entities. It defines a limited number of attributes for Group 2 and Group 3 entities and does not address relationships outside of those that involve Group 1 entities. FRAD conceptualizes how to record authority data, and it expands upon the original FRBR model in several important ways.

First, FRAD defines two classes of entities: bibliographic entities and authority entities. Bibliographic entities comprise the ten entities defined by the FRBR model plus a new entity introduced by FRAD: *family*. Authority entities include *name*, *identifier*, *controlled access point*, *rules*, and *agency*. According to FRAD, bibliographic entities are known by *names* and/or *identifiers*, which form the basis for *controlled access points*. *Rules* as applied by (a cataloging) *agency* govern the content and form of the controlled access points. The FRAD model also introduces many new attributes for Group 2 entities and defines relationships between Group 2 entities that are not addressed in the original FRBR model.

The FRAD model further expands upon the FRBR model by defining four user tasks for authority data. The first two—*find* and *identify*—are similar to those defined in FRBR, but the last two—*contextualize* and *justify*—are unique to FRAD. The *contextualize* user task necessitates placing an entity into context or clarifying a relationship between entities. The *justify* user task necessitates documenting the reason for the choice of a name used as the basis for a controlled access point.

Because FRAD focuses on authority data, its influence on RDA's content can be seen in the chapters containing instructions for recording data traditionally found in authority records. This is particularly true for instructions on identifying Group 2 entities, but also, to a lesser extent, for instructions on identifying works and expressions. FRAD's influence on RDA can also be found in the chapters containing instructions for recording relationships between Group 2 entities. With these influences on RDA's content, FRAD fleshes out the conceptual gaps in the FRBR model and provides the theoretical basis for a more comprehensive set of RDA instructions that address both bibliographic and authority data.

FRSAD

FRSAD was developed as an extension of the FRBR and FRAD models to focus on subject authority data. According to the original FRBR model, all bibliographic entities can be the subject of a work and can therefore be classed under the Group 3 entities. Building on this, the FRSAD model groups all of the bibliographic entities under a superclass of entities known as *thema*. Not surprisingly then, a thema is defined as "an entity used as a subject of a work." Thema is one of two entities introduced by the FRSAD model. The second entity is *nomen*, which is defined as "any sign or sequence of signs (alphanumeric characters, symbols, sound, etc.) that a thema is known by, referred to, or addressed as."

According to the FRSAD model, a work has as a subject a *thema*—which could be any one of the eleven bibliographic entities—and that thema has an appellation referred to as a *nomen*. The FRSAD model defines a new set of attributes and relationships for thema and nomen, the recording of which aims to address four user tasks. The first three tasks—*find*, *identify*, and *select*—are similar to the FRBR user tasks, except that they pertain to subject information. The fourth user task—*explore*—is unique to FRSAD and is aimed at allowing the user to explore a subject domain, its terminology, and the relationships among themas.

FRSAD was published in 2011, more than a year after the first release of the *RDA Toolkit*. Its theoretical concepts have yet to make their way into the chapters involving Group 3 entities, which—with the exception of RDA Chapter 16 ("Identifying Places")—currently serve as placeholders. Since the content of RDA involving Group 3 attributes and relationships has yet to be developed, this chapter only lightly touches on them, focusing more on the attributes and relationships of Group 1 and Group 2 entities.

UNDERSTANDING GROUP 1 ENTITIES

One of the most challenging tasks with respect to the FRBR model is understanding the differences among works, expressions, manifestations, and items. The FRBR model defines a *work* as *a distinct intellectual or artistic creation*. An *expression* is defined as *the intellectual or artistic realization of a work in the form of alpha-numeric, musical, or choreographic notation, sound, image, object, movement, etc., or any combination of such forms*. A *manifestation* is *the physical embodiment of an expression of a work*. Finally, an *item* is defined as *a single exemplar of a manifestation*.

To understand how these definitions apply in practice, consider a hypothetical resource that compares various types of forestry data across the major regions of the United States. The *work* would be the intellectual idea of comparing regional forestry phenomena along specifically chosen parameters. The details of this work would be held in the mind of the creator who conceived them. In order for others to have insight into the ideas in the creator's mind, the details would have to be realized through some form of communication or *expression* to the outside world.

There are a variety of ways in which these ideas could be expressed. One is to convey the statistical details purely in the alphanumeric form of a text. For the visually impaired, such information could be rendered into braille. Another way is to visually communicate the information using a series of statistical charts, graphs, or other still images. Because the comparisons are across geographical regions, an alternate way is to represent the statistical phenomena cartographically. Still another way is to share these details in the audio context of an oral lecture. Finally, the information could be conveyed in any combination of the above (e.g., a PowerPoint lecture presentation using charts, maps, and text). (See Figure 2.1.)

Forestry statistical data across U.S. regions can be expressed or communicated in a variety of ways:
- Alpha-numerically (*text*)
- In braille (*tactile text*)
- Using statistical charts and graphs (*still image*)
- Using maps (*cartographic image*)
- In an oral lecture (*spoken word*)

Text

Braille

Still image

Cartographic image

Spoken word

Figure 2.1.

If the expression is meant for sharing on a wider scale, it needs to be embodied in a physical carrier that can be mass produced and disseminated to a broader audience. This embodiment represents the *manifestation*, and this can be done in a variety of ways. If the original work was expressed as a text, a series of cartographic or other images, or a combination of these, then the manifestation could be in the form of a book, a packet of sheets, a web document, or microfiche. If the details of the work were conveyed in an oral lecture, then the audio could be captured on a cassette tape, a compact disc, or an mp3 file. If the oral lecture were accompanied with visuals (e.g., in a PowerPoint presentation), then it could be filmed and embodied in a VHS cassette, a videodisc, or a streamed video. (See Figure 2.2.)

If the manifestation is meant for mass production, it can serve as a template for the physical details of each copy that gets produced. In this way, every copy of the same manifestation should be fabricated to have the same layout, the same number of pages, and the same dimensions. A newly produced copy of this mass production would exemplify the intended details of the manifestation. However, over time this exemplar might get damaged or eventually bear handwriting, inscriptions, or other annotations. The exemplification of a manifestation is called an *item*, and it will bear details specific to its own unique history.

To further understand works, expressions, manifestations, and items, it may help to consider how changes in the content of a resource or the carrier embodying the content would result in a different work, expression, manifestation, or item.

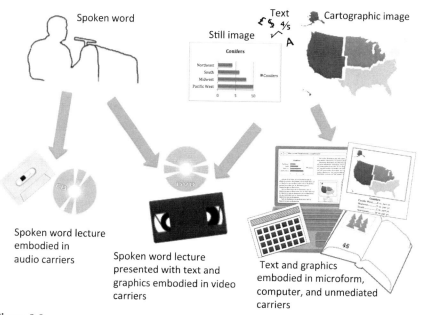

Figure 2.2.

If the content of a resource changes so much that it substantially alters the nature or intent of the original work, then it is a new work. Examples of this include derivative works, such as film adaptations of novels and television adaptations of films. Other examples include sequels, prequels, commentaries, critical analyses, and abridgments.

If the content of a resource changes in a way that leaves the original intent of the work intact, then it is a different expression of the same work. One way to imagine this is to picture two readers using different expressions of the same work. (See Figure 2.3, top.) As they read along with each other, one might encounter something in the text that could contextualize the content in a way that would give that reader a better understanding of the work. Minor examples include an index to help the first reader find concepts within the text, revisions that could keep the first reader up to date on specific topics, illustrations that could facilitate a greater understanding of certain concepts, and a foreword to contextualize the content for the reader. Major examples include whether the content is read as a text or heard as a spoken-word narrative and whether the content is rendered in the person's native language or in a foreign-language version. Each of these differences represents a change that could affect the person's understanding of the content but leaves the overall intent of the work intact.

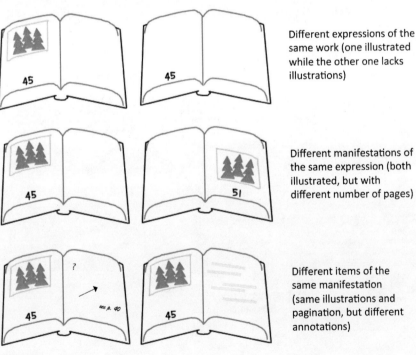

Different expressions of the same work (one illustrated while the other one lacks illustrations)

Different manifestations of the same expression (both illustrated, but with different number of pages)

Different items of the same manifestation (same illustrations and pagination, but different annotations)

Figure 2.3.

If there is no change in the content of a resource, but the carrier (or packaging) differs, then it is a different manifestation of the same expression. Let's imagine our two readers using two different resources again, but this time the content of both resources is exactly the same. (See Figure 2.3, center.) However, the first reader has a 25 cm book with 500 pages, whereas the second has a 29 cm book with 300 pages. It would at first be difficult for both to read the text together if the first reader informed the second that he was on the fourth paragraph of page 30. However, once the second reader oriented herself and located the analogous text in her book, she could read along with the first reader without ever encountering a different illustration, a newly revised section of a chapter, or any other difference in content. The only difference would be the packaging of the content: its size, its extent, its carrier type (physical volume vs. online resource), its publisher, or some other carrier-specific attribute.

If there is no change in the carrier of a resource, but it is a different physical copy from another resource, then it is a different item of the same manifestation. In this case, our first reader should be able to state which page and paragraph he is on, and the other should be able to orient herself very quickly. However, the first reader's copy may be dog-eared, with heavy highlighting, whereas the second reader's copy may be nearly pristine, save for a few annotations in pencil here and there. (See Figure 2.3, bottom.)

ATTRIBUTES OF GROUP 1 ENTITIES

To keep track of the various details of a resource that help distinguish it from other resources, it is important to record its *attributes*. And to keep resources organized in a way that helps users navigate among the different entity levels, the attributes of resources must be recorded at the appropriate entity level. Each entity has its own set of attributes that helps users distinguish one work from all other works, one expression from all other expressions, and so forth.

Because the work is at a highly conceptual level, many of its attributes involve general details about the content (e.g., *intended audience*), details that help identify the work (e.g., *title of work*), and details that help distinguish it from other similarly named works (e.g., *form of work* and *date of work*).

With the realization of a work through an expression come attributes that provide more specific details about the content. One important attribute is the *form of expression* (referred to as *content type* in RDA terminology) in which the user experiences the content, such as alphanumeric notation (or text), cartographic images, still images, moving images, spoken word, or performed music. For language-based resources, it would be helpful to record the *language of the expression*. Other expression-related attributes, such as the presence or absence of illustrations, bibliographies, indexes, color content, and sound content, can help users select the precise expression that meets their specific needs.

Manifestation-level attributes describe details related to the carrier embodying the expression or to the production or publication of the manifestation. These include *title of the manifestation, statement of responsibility, edition statement, place of publication, name of publisher, date of publication, identifier for the manifestation, extent, dimensions*, and *form of carrier* (referred to as *carrier type* in RDA terminology).

Finally, item-level attributes describe details related to a single copy, such as *identifier for the item* (e.g., a barcode) and *access restrictions*.

ATTRIBUTES OF GROUP 2 ENTITIES

Just as Group 1 entities have attributes that help users identify, select, and obtain resources, Group 2 entities have attributes that help users identify entities responsible for those resources. The original FRBR model focuses on the types of information about persons and corporate bodies typically found in their access points on bibliographic records and defines these as attributes. For persons this includes *name of person, dates of person, titles of person*, and *other designation associated with the person*. For corporate bodies this includes *name of the corporate body, number associated with the corporate body, place associated with the corporate body, date associated with the corporate body*, and *other designation associated with the corporate body*.

FRAD builds on this and introduces an array of new attributes that—along with the attributes defined in FRBR—can be recorded in authority records. For persons this includes *gender, place of birth, place of death, country, place of residence, affiliation, address, language of the person, field of activity, profession/occupation*, and *biography/history*. For corporate bodies this includes *language of the corporate body, address, field of activity*, and *history*.

ATTRIBUTES OF GROUP 3 ENTITIES

The FRBR model defines only one attribute for each of the four Group 3 entities, namely *term for the concept, term for the object, term for the event*, and *term for the place*. The FRAD model does not address attributes of Group 3 entities at all. Interestingly, the FRSAD model also fails to address attributes of Group 3 entities, instead introducing two attributes for thema and eleven attributes for nomen. The current version of RDA provides instructions for recording the attributes of places, but of no other Group 3 entities (in large part because AACR2 included essentially the same chapter), and defines these attributes as *Name of the Place* and *Identifier for the Place*. It remains to be seen how the chapters on recording attributes of Group 3 entities will ultimately materialize and how FRBR, FRSAD, and the current scheme of Chapter 16 will influence the content of this set of instructions.

RELATIONSHIPS BETWEEN WORK, EXPRESSION, MANIFESTATION, AND ITEM

The FRBR model details the various types of bibliographic relationships that each entity can have. The set of relationships most central to the model are the inherent relationships among the Group 1 entities, or the *primary relationships*. First, a work is realized through an expression. Then an expression is embodied in a manifestation. Finally, a manifestation is exemplified by an item. Reviewing the section "Understanding Group 1 Entities" in this chapter may help elucidate the meanings of these relationships.

RELATIONSHIPS BETWEEN GROUP 1 ENTITIES AND GROUP 2 ENTITIES

Because Group 2 entities are responsible for Group 1 entities, the relationships between these two entity groups are referred to as *responsibility relationships*. Any of the Group 2 entities—persons, families, and corporate bodies—can be responsible for a Group 1 entity, and their level of responsibility depends on the Group 1 entity involved.

A Group 2 entity—person, family, or corporate body—can create a work. For example, a person can write a novel or compose a musical piece, and a corporate body can create a catalog of its inventory of artworks. A Group 2 entity can contribute to the realization of an expression. For example, a person can translate or illustrate a novel, and a corporate body, such as an orchestra, can perform a musical piece. A Group 2 entity can produce a manifestation. For example, a corporate body can publish a book. Finally, a Group 2 entity can own an item. For example, a person can be the former owner of a book that he or she donates to a corporate body, such as a library.

RELATIONSHIPS BETWEEN WORKS AND GROUP 3 ENTITIES

The relationship between a work and a Group 3 entity constitutes a *subject relationship*. A work can have as its subject matter a concept (e.g., "philosophy"), an object (e.g., "pollen"), an event (e.g., "World War II"), or a place (e.g., "Argentina"). It can also have as its subject matter a Group 1 or Group 2 entity. For example, a work can be about another work, such as Shakespeare's *Romeo and Juliet*, or it can be about a person, such as Mozart.

The FRSAD model defines four types of relationships: work-to-thema, thema-to-nomen, thema-to-thema, and nomen-to-nomen. Work-to-thema relationships involve the association of a work to its subject matter and are thus the most likely to influence the RDA instructions on relationships between works and Group 3 entities. However, it remains to be seen if these theoretical underpinnings will be incorporated into future versions of RDA and how they will influence the content of the instructions.

OTHER RELATIONSHIPS BETWEEN GROUP 1 ENTITIES

The FRBR model outlines the possible relationships between two different works, two different expressions, two different manifestations, and two different items. The possible relationships between two different works include derivative relationships, such as adaptations (e.g., the film *The Wizard of Oz*, adapted from the novel); successive relationships, such as sequels (e.g., *Mrs. Rochester: The Sequel to Jane Eyre*); and whole-part relationships, such as journal articles within a serial, monographs within a series, and chapters within a book. The possible relationships between two expressions include translations (e.g., the English translation of the original Spanish text of *Don Quixote*) and revisions (e.g., the New American Edition of *Gray's Anatomy*). The possible relationships between two manifestations include reproductions, facsimiles, and alternate formats (e.g., a PDF version of a print resource). The possible relationships between two items include reproductions and resources comprising one item bound with another item.

RELATIONSHIPS BETWEEN PERSONS, FAMILIES, AND CORPORATE BODIES

Recording the relationship between a Group 2 entity and another Group 2 entity is traditionally done in the authority environment. As a result, such relationships are not defined in the original FRBR model but are introduced in FRAD.

A person can be related to another person in the form of an alternate identity (e.g., Lewis Carroll vs. Charles Dodgson). A person can be related to a family in the form of a membership (e.g., Marcel Duchamp, member of the Duchamp Family). Likewise, a person can be related to a corporate body in the form of a membership (e.g., Mick Jagger, member of the musical group The Rolling Stones).

A family can be related to another family through a progenitor-descendant relationship (e.g., the House of Conde, descendant family of the House of Conti). A family can be related to a corporate body through a founding relationship (e.g., the McMahon Family, founder of World Wrestling Entertainment, Inc.).

A corporate body can be related to another corporate body in the form of a hierarchical relationship (e.g., the Women in Physiology Committee, subunit of the American Physiological Society) or a sequential relationship (e.g., American Veterinary Medical Association, successor to the United States Veterinary Medical Association).

RELATIONSHIPS BETWEEN CONCEPTS, OBJECTS, EVENTS, AND PLACES

FRSAD describes thema-to-thema relationships as those that are hierarchical (e.g., "sculpture" being a narrower category of "art") or associative (e.g., "forestry" vs. "forests"). The model also describes nomen-to-nomen relationships as those that are equivalence relationships, which can include authorized and variant forms of the same concept within the same system. Nomen-to-nomen relationships can also include equivalent terms across different languages or schemes (e.g., the Library of Congress's "Medical Policy" versus the National Library of Medicine's "Health Policy"). It is likely that the RDA instructions on the relationships between concepts, objects, events, and places may draw from these FRSAD concepts. However, it remains to be seen how this will actually materialize in the ultimate text of RDA.

THE PROMISE OF THE "FR" FAMILY OF MODELS

The attributes and relationships of the entities defined in the "FR" Family of Models encourage the recording of data that organize and describe bibliographic and authority information in a way that helps users meet their needs. Recording the relationships between Group 1 and Group 2 entities can help a user find all the resources associated with a person, family, or corporate body (e.g., all the works written by George Orwell). Similarly, recording the relationships between works and Group 3 entities can help users find all the resources on a given subject (e.g., all the works about the concept "political fiction"). Recording relationships between two different works can help users find related works of which they may have been unaware (e.g., movie adaptations and critical analyses of the novel *1984*).

Once a work has been located, the inherent relationships between works, expressions, manifestations, and items can help gather together all resources that are related to a given work and organize them in a way that facilitates easier navigation for the user. The details of each resource, recorded in the form of attributes, can help a user find, identify, and select the manifestation best suited to his or her needs, as can be seen in the following example.

The novel *1984* can be found on George Orwell's name because a relationship was made between him (the creator) and this novel (the work).

---

p1: George Orwell
w1: Nineteen Eighty-Four (Novel)
w2: Road to Wigan Pier (Treatise)
w3: Animal Farm (Novel)
w4: Homage to Catalonia (Autobiography)

The novel can also be found through a search on "political fiction" because a relationship was made between that concept and this work.

> c1: Political fiction
> **w1: Nineteen Eighty-Four (Novel) by George Orwell**
> w2: Camel Club (Novel) by David Baladicci
> w3: Man in full (Novel) by Tom Wolfe

Once the work is found, the user can burrow down to the English-language expression to identify and select the volume published by New American Library in 1977. Alternatively, the user can peruse through the spoken word expression in order to identify and select the audiocassette version published by BBC Audiobooks in 2006. This identification and selection is made possible because attributes such as language, content type, carrier type, publisher, and date of publication were assigned to these resources at their respective levels.

> w1: Nineteen Eighty-Four (Novel) by George Orwell
>   e1: Original English-language text
>   m: Secker and Warburg's 1949 volume
>   **m: New American Library's 1977 volume**
>   m: 1st World Library's 1996 online resource
>   e2: French translation in text
>   m: Gallimard's 1950 volume
>   e3: English text in braille
>   m: New American Library's 1983 volume
>   m: American Printing House for the Blind's 1992 volume
>   e4: English spoken word
>   **m: BBC Audiobooks' 2006 audiocassette**
>   m: Blackstone Audiobooks' 2009 online resource

If the user prefers to watch the movie version of *1984* in English, he or she can search for the English-language expression of the moving image work, navigate through the manifestations listed under that expression, and choose between the MCA Distributing Corporation's videocassette published in 1984 and the MGM Home Entertainment's videodisc published in 2003.

> w1: Nineteen Eighty-Four (Motion Picture)
>   e1: English-language two-dimensional moving image
>   **m1: MCA Distributing Corporation's 1984 videocassette**
>   **m2: MGM Home Entertainment's 2003 videodisc**

ORGANIZATION OF RDA

RDA contains thirty-seven chapters divided into ten sections and includes an intro-duction, twelve appendices that provide supplementary instructions, a glossary, and an index. RDA's organization is heavily tied to the concepts outlined in the "FR" Family of Models. Each of the ten sections is devoted to recording information about one of the entity groups, and the order follows that of the FR models: that is, first the instructions for Group 1 entities are provided, then the Group 2 entities, and then the Group 3 entities. The first four sections provide instructions for recording attributes of the entities, while the last six provide instructions for recording relation-ships among the entities.

RDA Sections 1 and 2 provide instructions on recording attributes of Group 1 entities. RDA Section 1 (Chapters 1–4) addresses attributes of manifestations and items, while RDA Section 2 (Chapters 5–7) addresses attributes of works and expres-sions. RDA Section 3 (Chapters 8–11) addresses attributes of the Group 2 entities—persons, families, and corporate bodies. RDA Section 4 (Chapters 12–16) addresses attributes of the Group 3 entities—concepts, objects, events, and places. Most of the instructions for Group 3 entities—namely concepts, objects, and events—are still under development, so the relevant RDA chapters (Chapters 12–15) currently serve as placeholders for future instructions. However, the instructions for identifying places (RDA Chapter 16) are provided.

RDA Section 5 (Chapter 17) provides instructions for recording the primary relationships among Group 1 entities. RDA Section 6 (Chapters 18–22) addresses relationships between Group 1 and Group 2 entities. RDA Section 7 (Chapter 23) comprises a placeholder chapter that will address relationships between works and the Group 3 entities in future versions of RDA. RDA Section 8 (Chapters 24–28) addresses relationships between Group 1 entities of the same type (e.g., related works, related expressions, etc.). RDA Section 9 (Chapters 29–32) addresses re-lationships between Group 2 entities (e.g., related persons, related families, etc.). Finally, RDA Section 10 (Chapters 33–37) comprises placeholder chapters that will address the relationships between Group 3 entities of the same type in future versions of RDA (e.g., related concepts, related objects, etc.).

As outlined in RDA's introductory chapter at instruction 0.5, the organization is further broken down by user tasks. RDA Sections 3–10 involve only one user task and are thus easier to explain. RDA Section 3 provides instructions on *identifying* persons, families, and corporate bodies, whereas RDA Section 4 will provide instruc-tions for *identifying* concepts, objects, and events, and currently provides instruc-tions for *identifying* places. RDA Sections 5–10 provide instructions for recording relationships, which all meet the *find* user task.

RDA Sections 1 and 2 are a little more complicated and contain chapters that ad-dress different user tasks. In RDA Section 1, RDA Chapter 2 addresses the *identify* user task, RDA Chapter 3 addresses the *select* user task, and RDA Chapter 4 ad-dresses the *obtain* user task. In RDA Section 2, RDA Chapter 6 addresses the *identify* user task, and RDA Chapter 7 addresses the *select* user task. As shown in chapter 3 of this book, this often causes data in adjacent MARC fields and subfields to be found in different areas of RDA, because they address different user tasks. Indeed, if catalogers followed the order of the MARC bibliographic record, they would feel as if they were jumping around in RDA in an attempt to find the analogous instructions.

Tying the organization to attributes, relationships, and user tasks can be a real source of confusion for catalogers working with MARC fields and trying to find the corresponding instructions in RDA. A firm handle on the concepts involving the entities, their attributes and relationships, and the various user tasks will help catalogers understand the rationale for the placement of instructions for certain bibliographic data and may ultimately help them predict where to find the instructions they need for a given MARC field or subfield.

CONCLUSION

The current version of RDA is based on two underlying models, FRBR and FRAD, which heavily influence its organization. The eleven bibliographic entities—*works, expressions, manifestations, items, persons, families, corporate bodies, concepts, objects, events,* and *places*—have specific attributes and relationships. The recording of these attributes and relationships helps users meet specific bibliographic tasks (*find, identify, select,* and *obtain*) and specific authority tasks (*find, identify, contextualize,* and *justify*). The organization of RDA is heavily based on these concepts, which often results in a disconnect between the instructions and the order of MARC fields and subfields. It is therefore imperative that catalogers familiarize themselves with the conceptual models underlying RDA so that they can more easily locate and apply RDA instructions.

In the next chapter we look at some of the major differences between RDA and AACR2 and discuss some generalities that catalogers can apply in specific situations to help them make the move to cataloging with RDA.

3

Major Differences between RDA and AACR2

The first two chapters provided an overview of RDA's development, its objectives and principles, and the underlying models that shaped its structure and much of its terminology. This chapter details some of the common differences between AACR2 and RDA, pulling from many of the issues covered in the previous chapters to contextualize these changes.

Because RDA records are expected to coexist in the same databases as AACR2 records, RDA instructions were written to be compatible with AACR2. Thus, there are many similarities between the two standards. Some stem from carrying AACR2 rules over into RDA with no alteration. Others arise from application of an RDA objective or principle, which renders similar looking data with a few cosmetic differences.

There are, however, many differences that result from either significantly changing an AACR2 rule, not carrying an AACR2 rule over into RDA, or introducing an RDA instruction that did not exist in AACR2. Any combination of these intricate factors can provide the rationale for a difference—be it major or minor—between the two standards. This chapter attempts to synthesize the complexities involved to offer a more simplified, predictable way to anticipate these changes.

CHANGES IN ORGANIZATION

When the JSC shifted the direction from writing the third edition of AACR to creating the standard that became RDA, the committee modified their strategic plan and developed a set of long-term goals. One of these goals was to "provide a consistent, flexible and extensible framework for both the technical and content description of all types of resources and all types of content." One way that the JSC aimed to meet this goal was to "[a]lign the structure, concepts and terminology of the instructions more directly with the FRBR and FRAD models." This has resulted in a radical difference in the organization of RDA instructions compared with AACR2.

Whereas AACR2 chapters are organized, roughly, by type of format (AACR2 Part I) and type of heading (AACR2 Part II), RDA chapters are organized by bibliographic entities, the attributes and relationships of these entities, and user tasks. The chapters in Part I of AACR2 are further broken down by ISBD area, whereas RDA chapters are further broken down by elements. Thus, catalogers accustomed to using AACR2 in the MARC environment will have to suppress the impulse to look for RDA instructions based on format, ISBD area, and type of heading. Instead, they will have to think about how the MARC data elements relate to the FRBR and FRAD models and search for the analogous instructions within this framework.

Another goal of the JSC was to "ensure that descriptions and access points produced through the application of RDA meet the goals for functionality." Therefore the committee aimed to "[d]irectly relate the elements of the description and access points to the user tasks that they support." In RDA, this materialized into the objective *responsiveness to users' needs*.

As mentioned in chapter 2 of this book, RDA Sections 3 and 4 address the *identify* user task, and RDA Sections 5–10 address the *find* user task. However, RDA Sections 1 and 2 address more than one user task. RDA Section 1, Chapter 2 contains instructions that address the *identify* task; RDA Section 1, Chapter 3 addresses the *select* task; and RDA Section 1, Chapter 4 addresses the *obtain* task. RDA Section 2, Chapter 6 addresses the *identify* task, and RDA Section 2, Chapter 7 addresses the *select* task.

It is important to understand how the user tasks are tied to chapters within RDA Sections 1 and 2, because this often explains why two adjacent MARC fields and subfields are in two different areas of RDA. For example, many of the 2XX fields in MARC bibliographic records correspond to instructions in RDA Chapter 2, because these 2XX fields encode information that helps users *identify* a manifestation. For books, many of the MARC 3XX fields in bibliographic records correspond to instructions in RDA Chapter 3, because these 3XX fields encode information that helps users *select* a manifestation. However, the instructions for recording data encoded in the MARC 336 field are found in RDA Chapter 6, because this information helps users *identify* an expression, and the instructions for recording illustrative content that is encoded in the MARC 300 $b are found in RDA Chapter 7, because this information helps users *select* an expression.

In the format-based structure of AACR2, much of this information would be contained in one or two chapters. For example, all of the AACR2 rules that apply to a book and that correspond to the MARC bibliographic fields 2XX through 5XX (often referred to as the *description*) can be found in the "General Rules for Description" and the "Books, Pamphlets, and Printed Sheets" chapters of AACR2. In contrast, to find the analogous instructions in RDA, catalogers will really have to know which entity is involved, whether or not it is an attribute or a relationship, and which user task is being addressed.

CHANGES IN TERMINOLOGY

Another goal of the JSC was to create instructions that would be "usable primarily within the library community, but be capable of adaptation to meet the specific needs of other communities." To this end, the JSC aimed to "[r]evise and modernise terminology to eliminate unnecessary library jargon, and eliminate ambiguous and inconsistent terminology." Therefore, although many AACR concepts were carried over into RDA, terminology was changed. For example, the term "heading," though the concept was carried over into RDA, was altered to "access point." Taking this further, "authorized heading" was changed to "authorized access point"; "personal name heading" was changed to "authorized access point representing the person"; and "uniform title" was changed to "preferred title" for the work or expression. Other terms, like "see reference" and "see also reference," were brought over to RDA as "variant access point" and "authorized access point representing the related [entity]," respectively.

Terms like "entry" introduce complications when comparing terminology between AACR2 and RDA. The terminology of main and added entry was not carried over into RDA. However, there are some RDA elements that, by and large, fill the same roles as main and added entries. Thus, catalogers working in the MARC environment who are familiar with the AACR2 instruction to "enter a work . . . under the heading for . . . [a person or corporate body]" will, when using RDA, generally construct an authorized access point for the first (or only) named creator and encode it in the 100 or 110 or 111 field of the MARC record, as well as using that access point when formulating the "authorized access point for a work." Along similar lines, "added entries" in AACR2 have become "access points for other persons, families, or corporate bodies associated with a work" or "access points for contributors" in RDA. And the AACR2 "series added entry" has become an "access point for the related work" in RDA.

CONCEPTUAL DIFFERENCES

Just as there are differences in terminology, there are conceptual differences from AACR2 that, when understood, will better guide the cataloger in the use of RDA. First is the conceptual difference of "rules" versus "instructions." AACR2 has stricter guidelines—referred to as "rules"—that often direct the cataloger to alter or omit data, and it provides fewer options for recording data. RDA guidelines are seen as "instructions" that are more flexible and allow more room for the cataloger's judgment. For example, in many cases AACR2 directs the cataloger to omit all but the first of more than three of the same data elements. While RDA allows this omission, it does not *require* it.

Another conceptual difference can be seen in that AACR2 provides guidelines for three levels of description, whereas RDA provides a set of core and "beyond core" elements that are required to meet the basic needs of users. Whereas AACR2's levels of description are rooted in the card catalog and record-based context of the library community, RDA's core elements transcend this idea of "packaging data" and are terminologically more in line with non-MARC metadata standards.

Finally, there are differences in how "sources of information" are conceptualized. RDA does away with AACR2's dual concept of "chief source of information" versus "prescribed source of information" and simply offers the concept of "preferred source of information." There are further differences between the standards in terms of sources of information, which have implications for the choice of data that get recorded and the manner in which they are recorded. These differences are detailed later in this chapter.

DIFFERENCES IN GRANULARITY

There are many instances in which RDA is more granular than AACR2. One example involves the replacement of AACR2's *general material designation*—which encompasses one element—with three new data elements in RDA: *content type, media type,* and *carrier type*. In the MARC context, this means eliminating the 245 $h and replacing it with three new fields that were added in MARC to accommodate RDA: the 336 field for *content type*, the 337 field for *media type*, and the 338 field for *carrier type*. As discussed later, this allows for more consistent and more comprehensive treatment of data related to a resource's technical and content description.

Another example of how RDA is more granular is in the parsing out of AACR2's *Publication, Distribution, Etc. Area* with five discrete data elements: *Production Statement, Publication Statement, Distribution Statement, Manufacture Statement,* and *Copyright Date*. In MARC terms, this has meant the creation of a new field—the 264 field—with specific second indicator values for each of the different elements. For *Production Statement*, the second indicator value is 0; for *Publication Statement*, the second indicator value is 1; for *Distribution Statement*, the second indicator value is 2; and so forth.

Another example is the parsing out of *Dissertation or Thesis Information* into three separate elements—thus introducing three new subfields in MARC field 502. Likewise, many of the physical details of carriers, which in AACR2 were all coded in the 300 $b, now have newly created fields—namely, 344, 345, 346, and 347—and subfields in the 340 field. A final example of RDA's greater granularity can be seen in the many new MARC fields created to accommodate attributes for authority entities that were nonexistent in AACR2.

DIFFERENCES IN TRANSCRIBING DATA

As mentioned in chapter 1 of this book, RDA's *principle of representation* results in substantially less alteration of data than AACR2. This means that inaccuracies in the title proper and the series numbering will not be followed by *sic* or by the correction in brackets. It also means that terms like "Mr." and "Ph. D," institutional affiliations, and creators and contributors numbering more than three will generally be included in the statement of responsibility. It further means that edition statements, publication data that include states and provinces, and terms used with series numbering will be spelled out, unless abbreviated on the source of information. Finally, it means that some records may reflect capitalization conventions that follow what appears on the source. This may result in data that show all letters in uppercase or the first letter of each functional word in uppercase.

DIFFERENCES IN RECORDING DATA

Chapter 1 of this book mentioned that RDA's principle of *common usage or practice* will result in the recording of data that are spelled out in English (for English-language cataloging agencies). One example of this is recording the phrase "and others" (along with the specific number) in a truncated statement of responsibility rather than recording AACR2's "et al." Another example is recording "that is" to clarify or correct pagination information rather than AACR2's "i.e." Yet another example is recording *Place of publication not identified* and *Publisher not identified* rather than AACR2's "S.l." and "s.n.," respectively. A final example is recording "approximately" in the pagination or in an access point rather than AACR2's "ca."

DIFFERENCES IN THE SOURCE OF INFORMATION

As mentioned previously, RDA does not continue the concept of *chief* versus *prescribed source of information* in AACR2, but simply uses *preferred source of information*. In addition, AACR2 and RDA sometimes differ on what constitutes the preferred (or prescribed) source of information. As we saw with the difference between the organization of the two standards, AACR2 chapters on description are broken down by ISBD area, whereas RDA chapters are broken down by element. Along these lines, prescribed sources of information are broken down by ISBD area in AACR2, but by element in RDA. Since the MARC format largely follows the ISBD areas, this means that, for catalogers using RDA and encoding data in MARC, different preferred sources of information may be specified for sources of data encoded within a single MARC field.

One example of this difference between RDA and AACR2 is publication information for a book. In RDA, the preferred source of information for all resources *Place of Publication* is the same source as the *Publisher's Name*, and the preferred source for the *Publisher's Name* and the *Date of Publication* is the same source as the title proper. Though slightly convoluted, the result is that the preferred source for all three of these elements is the same source as the title proper. In AACR2, the prescribed source for a printed book encompasses three options, with no one source preferred over the others: *title page*, *other preliminaries*, and *colophon*. Publication data on the title page sometimes differ from those in other areas on the resource. With the less precise directives from AACR2, the source of information can be chosen inconsistently from cataloger to cataloger, yielding a variety of possible renderings of the data. RDA's more precise and granular directive may yield more consistent choices for sources of information that will better identify a resource and distinguish it from similar resources.

CONTENT, CARRIER, AND REPLACEMENT OF THE GMD

The JSC had as a goal to "provide a consistent, flexible and extensible framework for both the technical and content description of all types of resources and all types of content." In addition to aligning RDA with FRBR and FRAD, another way that the committee aimed to meet this goal was to "[r]esolve problems associated with the class of materials concept and the related issue of GMDs." They also sought to "[e]xtend consistency within the technical and content description, and eliminate unnecessary redundancy."

The general material designation (GMD) in AACR2 posed problems, because it inconsistently used terms related to the content description (such as "cartographic material" and "sound recording") and the technical description (such as "microform" and "videorecording"). It sometimes provided one term that could describe a variety of resources. For example, any resource accessed via the Internet would be given the GMD "electronic resource," regardless of whether it was textual, cartographic, or audiovisual. To address this, the RDA divides the aspects of different classes of materials into three elements: *content type*, *media type*, and *carrier type*.

Content type details the form in which a resource is expressed, such as *text, still image, spoken word, two-dimensional moving image*, and *three-dimensional object*. *Media type* is an aspect of the physical description that details the type of intermediation device needed to access the content. Some examples are *audio, computer*, and *video*. If no intermediation device is needed to access the content—as would be the case with a book—then the media type is *unmediated*. Finally, *carrier type* details the physical form in which the content is embodied, such as *audiocassette, online resource, videodisc*, and *volume*. Together, these three elements successfully separate aspects of the content from those of the carrier and provide more granular information about the format of a resource than the GMD. Because of this, the GMD concept was carried over into RDA but significantly altered so that it was replaced collectively by *content type, media type*, and *carrier type*.

In addressing the aim to eliminate redundancy, the JSC abandoned the AACR2 approach of relegating similar instructions for the technical and content description of resources to the GMD and physical description area (ISBD areas 2 and 5) of each chapter in Part I. Instead, the committee introduced two chapters in RDA: one for describing carriers (Chapter 3) and another for describing content (Chapter 7). In these chapters, the instructions are provided in one location rather than repeatedly, as was done across analogous areas of AACR2 Part I chapters.

For example, AACR2 guidelines for describing color content can be found in "Area 5" of the general instructions in AACR2 Chapter 1. Additional guidelines for describing color content can also be found in the same area of AACR2 Chapter 2 ("Books, Pamphlets, and Printed Sheets"), AACR2 Chapter 3 ("Cartographic Materials"), AACR2 Chapter 7 ("Motion Pictures and Videorecordings"), AACR2 Chapter 8 ("Graphic Materials"), AACR2 Chapter 9 ("Electronic Resources"), and AACR2 Chapter 12 ("Continuing Resources"). In RDA the guidelines for describing color content are found only in RDA Chapter 7, at instruction 7.17. Instructions for describing color content for specific types of resources are found in subsections within this instruction.

To understand where RDA instructions are for the physical description area and for data that used to be in the GMD area, catalogers need to develop a better understanding of which bibliographic elements carry "content" information versus "carrier" information. For example, if the MARC 300 $a contains information about pagination, then this is an aspect of the carrier, so the relevant instructions are found in RDA Chapter 3. However, if the MARC300 $a contains information about duration, then this is an aspect of the content, so the relevant instructions are found in RDA Chapter 7. Likewise, if the MARC 300 $b contains information about illustrative, sound, or color content, then these are aspects of the content, and the relevant instructions are in RDA Chapter 7. However, if the MARC 300 $b contains information about the type of recording or the configuration of playback channels, then these are aspects of the carrier, so the relevant instructions are in RDA Chapter 3.

ELIMINATION OF THE "RULE OF THREE"

A long-term goal of the JSC was to provide instructions for recording access points that met the general objectives of functionality and adaptability. To meet this goal, the JSC aimed to "[r]evise the instructions relating to the choice of access points to address issues associated with the concept of 'authorship' as it is currently reflected in AACR2 and restrictions imposed by the 'rule of three.'" In short, the AACR2 "rule of three" was not carried over into RDA.

In AACR2, if up to three authors or contributors are associated with a resource, then access points would be provided for all of them. However, if there were more than three authors or contributors, then only the first one named would have an access point added to the record. Moreover, if a resource had three or fewer authors, then the first author would be entered as the main entry (or in the 1XX field of a bibliographic record). However, if there were more than three authors, then the first would be recorded as an added entry (or in the 7XX field of a record). This has implications for the identification of works, where if three or few authors are associated with a work, then the AACR2 entry for the work includes the name of the first author. However, if there are more than three authors, then the AACR2 entry for the work omits the first author's name and consists only of the title of the work.

In RDA, catalogers have the option of recording only the first named principal author or contributor, or they can record as many of the other authors as they choose, regardless of the number. Also, the first named principal author is always recorded in the 1XX field of the bibliographic record, if a cataloger is working in the MARC environment. Moreover, if an authorized access point for the work is constructed, it always includes the name of the first named principal author, regardless of how many other authors are involved.

ISBD PRESENTATION OF DATA

Another aim of the JSC was to provide instructions for recording descriptive data that met the goal of making RDA adaptable to other metadata environments, while meeting the RDA objective of *uniformity*. The committee addressed this by separating the instructions on recording data from those on presenting data. This means that catalogers consulting RDA instructions will not have the benefit of seeing examples of how to record data elements in a particular order using specific ISBD punctuation, as they are accustomed to seeing in AACR2.

For instance, in AACR2 an example for transcribing other title information would appear after an example for the title proper, and both elements would be separated by the correct ISBD punctuation, as follows: *Title proper: other title information.* In RDA, the example for transcribing other title information would appear in isolation, with no punctuation at all, such as: *other title information.* The cataloger would then have to consult RDA Appendix D for guidance on how to present data within the context of that particular ISBD area.

RDA is often described as a "content standard rather than a display standard." Catalogers will have to adjust to seeing guidelines on the content of bibliographic data in one location in RDA and guidelines on the ISBD display of the data in another location, whereas they were all in the same location in AACR2.

NEW INSTRUCTIONS

The differences between AACR2 and RDA mentioned thus far involve situations in which there were radical changes between the two different standards, something in AACR2 was carried over into RDA with minor or major alteration, and something from AACR2 was not carried over into RDA at all. In some cases, a difference in RDA can stem from the fact that there are no analogous concepts in AACR2.

Among its various goals, the JSC aimed to create guidelines that "facilitate collocation at the FRBR work and expression levels." This led to the creation of RDA Chapter 17, which offers guidelines for recording primary relationships, a chapter for which there is no exact equivalent in AACR2. The JSC also supported the inclusion of explicit and detailed instructions for authority work in RDA. Therefore, in the RDA chapter that provides general guidelines on recording works and expressions (RDA Chapter 5) and the chapter that provides general guidelines on recording names (RDA Chapter 8), there are certain authority data elements that were not included in AACR2. These include *Scope of Usage*, *Date of Usage*, and *Cataloguer's Note*, all three of which map to MARC authority field 667. Other elements are *Undifferentiated Name Indicator* (MARC authority field 008 byte 32), *Status of Identification* (MARC authority field 008 byte 33), and *Source Consulted* (MARC authority fields 670 and 675).

Additional instructions introduced in RDA that are absent in AACR2 involve relationship designators. In RDA, Sections 5, 6, 8, and 9 have introductory chapters that include instructions on recording relationship designators. These instructions point the cataloger to several appendices (I, J, and K) that provide open lists of relationship designator terms or phrases from which the cataloger can choose to clarify or explain the nature of a relationship. All of these instructions are absent from AACR2 but are crucial in RDA, which places a heavier emphasis on explicit relationships.

CONCLUSION

The differences between AACR2 and RDA mentioned in this chapter involve several types of situations. In one case there have been radical changes, such as in the organization of the two different standards. In other cases there is something from AACR2 that has been altered in a minor way. For example, the term "heading" in AACR2 has become "access point" in RDA, and many Latin abbreviations in AACR2 have been replaced by the spelled-out modern form due to the principle of *common usage or practice*. In yet other cases there is something from AACR2 that has changed in a major way. For example, the ISBD display of information has been carried over into RDA but relegated to the appendices, and the GMD has been replaced by three new elements.

There are also some cases in which something from AACR2 has not been carried over into RDA at all. These include the "rule of three" and the terminology "main entry" and "added entries." Also not carried over are the various AACR2 rules that prescribed the abbreviation, omission, and in situ correction of data, which were not carried over into RDA because of the principle of *representation*. Finally, there are cases in which RDA introduces new instructions that have no counterpart in AACR2, such as the instructions for recording certain kinds of authority data, explicit instructions for collocation at the FRBR work and expression levels, and the greatly expanded use of relationship designators.

Part III of this book revisits many of the differences outlined in this chapter, but within a field-specific scope that provides basic guidance for how to create and interpret MARC bibliographic and authority records using RDA. First, however, part II takes a closer look at RDA's structure, examining the specific elements, then maps these elements to specific MARC fields and subfields.

II

MASTERING RDA BASICS

4

Attributes of Manifestations and Items

The first section of RDA contains four chapters (1–4) that provide instructions for recording and transcribing attributes of manifestations and items. Specifically:

- RDA Chapter 1, "General Guidelines on Recording Attributes of Manifestations and Items," provides the context for the terminology and other concepts covered in RDA Chapters 2–4. It also provides guidelines for transcribing many of the elements covered in the other chapters, particularly Chapter 2.
- RDA Chapter 2, "Identifying Manifestations and Items," provides instructions for transcribing and recording attributes that support the "identify" user task.
- RDA Chapter 3, "Describing Carriers," provides instructions for recording attributes that mainly support the "select" user task.
- RDA Chapter 4, "Providing Acquisition and Access Information," provides instructions for recording attributes that support the "obtain" user task.

This chapter highlights some of the RDA Chapter 1 guidelines that frame how the data covered in the other RDA chapters should be input into the bibliographic record. It then details the data elements covered in RDA Chapters 2–4, noting if the element is core and, for many of the elements, providing the source of information and the relevant MARC fields. The information is not meant to be exhaustive, but merely to spotlight some of the more important guidelines in RDA. We revisit these guidelines in Part III of this book, in which we compare them with AACR2 rules in order to understand the similarities and differences with respect to how data are recorded in MARC using either content standard.

RDA CHAPTER 1: GENERAL GUIDELINES ON RECORDING ATTRIBUTES OF MANIFESTATIONS AND ITEMS

RDA Chapter 1 provides general guidelines on how to transcribe and record the elements outlined in RDA Chapters 2–4. The chapter's contents include its scope, an explanation of the terminology used throughout RDA Section 1, the functional objectives and principles addressed by Chapters 2–4, a list of the core elements, and another list of the elements that should be transcribed in the language and script in which they appear on the resource. This RDA chapter also delineates the different types of resource description, explains the changes in bibliographic data that necessitate a new description, and provides guidelines on transcribing and recording various types of information. The following discussion focuses on the guidelines for transcribing and recording data.

RDA 1.7 Transcription

For transcribing data, RDA provides instructions on the following: capitalization, punctuation, diacritical marks, symbols, spacing of initials and acronyms, letters or words intended to be read more than once, abbreviations, and inaccuracies. RDA provides an alternative instruction, however, that allows cataloging agencies to use other sources for their transcription guidelines. The alternative also allows catalogers to accept data derived through automated means. Following is a summary of RDA's transcription guidelines for those who elect to follow them.

Capitalize data following the conventions outlined in Appendix A.

    245   #4 $a The HMO salary survey.

Transcribe punctuation as it appears on the resource. If the resource contains information that will be transcribed in separate elements, and this information bears intervening punctuation, omit the punctuation.

    Title page verso:
      Medical Library Association, Chicago
    Transcription:
      264 _1 $a Chicago : $b Medical Library Association

However, add punctuation if necessary for clarity.

    Title page:
            by
      Thomas Hadjistavropoulos
      Heather D. Hadjistavropoulos
    Transcription:
      245   ## / $c by Thomas Hadjistavropoulos, Heather D.
             Hadjistavropoulos

Transcribe diacritical marks as they appear on the source. Optionally, add them even if absent from the resource and follow the standard usage for the language.

> Title page: LES MISERABLES
> Transcription: 245   #4 $a Les misérables

If a symbol cannot be reproduced using the available facilities, provide a brief description of the symbol in brackets and, if necessary, an explanatory note.

> Title page: Spanakopita, the little Greek π
> Transcription: Spanakopita, the little Greek [pie]
> Explanatory note: On the title page "[pie]" is represented by the Greek letter "pi"

Transcribe acronyms and initials without spaces, even if there is spacing on the resource.

> Title page: by J. D. Salinger
> Transcription: 245   ## / $c by J.D. Salinger.

If a letter or word appears once, but is designed to be read more than once, repeat the letter or word.

> Title page: Canadian CITATIONS canadiennes
> Transcription: 245   #0 $a Canadian citations = $b Citations canadiennes

Abbreviate data following the conventions outlined in Appendix B, which contains instructions to abbreviate data in transcribed elements only if the information is already abbreviated on the source.

> 250 $a Fourth edition.
> 250 $a 2nd ed., revised and enlarged.

Transcribe inaccuracies as they appear on the resource, unless instructed otherwise. Make a note correcting the data if necessary.

> 245   #0 $a Statisical methods in bioinformatics
> 246   1_ $i Title should read: $a Statistical methods in bioinformatics

Numbers Expressed as Numerals or as Words

In transcription fields, transcribe numbers as they appear on the source.
In other fields, record numbers when numerals are expressed as words.

> 245   #0 $a Twenty-first century women
> 300 $a 55 pages (*last page number appears as "Page Fifty-five"*)

When numerals are expressed as numbers, record the data in the form preferred by the cataloging agency. If preferred, substitute Arabic numerals for the form found on the resource.

> 246 1_ $i Volume 2 has title: $a . . .
> 264 ## $c 2013

As an alternative, record the number as it appears on the resource.

> 246   1_ $i Volume II has title: $a . . .
> 264   ## $c MMXIIIM

As a second alternative, record the number as it appears, followed by the Arabic equivalent in brackets.

> 246   1_ $i Volume II [2] has title: $a . . .
> 264   ## $c MMXIII [2013]

Record the first and last number in full when recording inclusive dates.

> 100   1_ $a Barrett, William J., $d active 1916–1943

Record ordinal numbers in English—whether they appear as numerals or words—as 1st, 2nd, 3rd, etc. Record ordinal numbers in Chinese, Japanese, and Korean with the symbol for the number, followed by the symbol indicating that it is an ordinal number. Record ordinal numbers in all other languages according to the usage of the language.

> 1o, 1a, 2o, 2a, 3o, 3a, etc. for Italian

If usage cannot be readily ascertained, record the ordinal numbers as 1., 2., 3., etc.

Dates

When supplying a date for *date of production, date of publication, date of distribution,* and *date of manufacture,* record the data in brackets. If the actual year is known, record it as shown in the following example: [1976]. If the date is either one of two consecutive years, record it as shown in the following example: [1934 or 1935]. When approximating the date, record the probable year as shown in the following example: [2009?]. When supplying the probable range of years, record it as shown in the following example: [between 1963 and 1968?]. When supplying the earliest or latest possible date, record it as shown in the following example: [not after November 4, 1950].

Notes

The same capitalization guidelines and alternatives listed under transcription apply to transcribed notes. If quoting from the resource, place the passage in quotation marks and state the source of information if the quote is not taken from the preferred source.

> 500 $a "A publication of the Northeast Asia Seminar"—
> Page facing title page.

Make references to passages in the text if needed to support other descriptive information or obviate repetition of information readily available from other sources.

> 500 $a Introduction (page xiv–xvi) refutes attribution to Anacreon.

If information in the note does not apply to every part or iteration of a resource, indicate the applicable part or iteration.

> 246   1_ $i Title on accompanying CD-ROM:
> $a Anexos conomía de la papa en Bolivia, 1998–2007

RDA CHAPTER 2: IDENTIFYING MANIFESTATIONS AND ITEMS

RDA Chapter 2 provides guidelines on how to transcribe and record elements that help users identify resources. The chapter's contents include its purpose and scope, guidelines for determining the basis for identification of a resource, guidelines on sources of information, and detailed guidelines on the eighteen major elements contained within the chapter.

Basis for Identification of the Resource

Comprehensive Description

For comprehensive description of a single unit resource (such as a novel issued in one volume), choose a source of information that identifies the resource as a whole. If no such source exists, treat the sources of information that identify the individual components as the collective source of information.

For comprehensive description of a multipart monograph or serial, choose the following as the basis for identifying the resource as a whole: the source of information from the lowest numbered part or issue; the earliest part or issue; some other source that identifies the resource as a whole; the main part (if applicable) of a resource that has no ordered parts; or the collective source of information gleaned from sources that identify the individual parts or issues.

For comprehensive description of an integrating resource, choose a source of information that identifies the current iteration of the resource as a whole. If no such source exists, treat the sources of information that identify the current iterations of the individual components as the collective source of information.

Analytical Description

For analytical description of a single part (e.g., a journal article, one volume in a multipart set, a special issue of a journal, etc.) choose a source of information that identifies the individual part. For analytical description of more than one part, follow the guidelines for comprehensive description of a multipart monograph or serial. For analytical description of one or more parts issued as an integrating resource, choose the source or sources of information that identify the current iterations of the individual part or parts.

RDA 2.2 Sources of Information

RDA 2.2.2 Preferred Source of Information

When choosing a source of information, first determine the basis for identification of the resource, as outlined above. Specifically, decide first which type of description is intended: comprehensive or analytical. Next, determine the mode of issuance involved: single part, multipart monograph, serial, or integrating resource. Once the basis for identification has been discerned, determine which presentation format is involved. Does the resource consist of pages, leaves, sheets, or cards (or images thereof); is it a moving image resource; or is it some other type of resource?

For a resource that comprises one or more pages, leaves, sheets, or cards (e.g., print books and cartographic sheet maps) or images thereof (e.g., PDF documents and microfiches), the preferred source of information is the title page, title sheet, or title card (or image thereof). For microforms and computer resources, alternatively use a permanently affixed label as the preferred source of information. If the resource lacks a title page, title sheet, or title card (or image thereof), use the following as the preferred source of information (in order of preference): cover (or image thereof), caption (or image thereof), masthead (or image thereof), colophon (or image thereof), or some other source within the resource that bears the title. For early printed resources, the preferred order is colophon, cover, and caption.

For moving image resources, the preferred source of information is the title frame or frames, or the title screen or screens. Alternatively, use a permanently affixed label as the preferred source of information. If the resource lacks a title frame or title screen, use a permanently affixed label, embedded metadata that carry the title, or some other source within the resource as the preferred source of information. For other types of resources, use a permanently affixed label, embedded metadata that carry the title, or some other source within the resource as the preferred source of information.

RDA 2.2.3 More Than One Source of Information

If there is more than one preferred source of information in different languages or scripts, choose the source that corresponds to the predominant language or script, the language or script of the translation, the original language or script (if identified in the resource), or the first occurring of the sources. For resources other than multipart monographs and serials that bear differing dates, use the latest date as the preferred source of information. For facsimiles and reproductions that have sources of information for both the original and the reproduction, use the source for the reproduction.

Other Sources of Information

If information needs to be taken outside of the resource for the purposes of identification, take it from the following sources (in order of preference): accompanying material, a container not issued as part of the resource itself, other published descriptions of the resource, or any other available source. If information taken from outside the resource is used for recording information in certain elements, indicate this by making a note or by placing the information in brackets. The elements that require this include *title proper, parallel title proper, other title information, parallel other title information*, and all the subelements under *statement of responsibility, edition statement, numbering of serials, production statement, publication statement, distribution statement, manufacture statement*, and *series statement*. If, however, the resource is the type that does not usually bear information, such as a naturally occurring object, omit the note or other means of stating that information was taken from outside the resource.

RDA 2.3 Title

Title is defined as *a word, character, or group of words and/or characters that names a resource or a work contained in it*. It has the following subelements: *title proper, parallel title proper, other title information, parallel other title information, variant title, earlier title proper, later title proper, key title*, and *abbreviated title*.

A title can be abridged as long as the first five meaningful words are retained and essential information is preserved.

```
245   #2 $a A defence of the late Lord Russel's innocency :
         $b by way of answer or confutation of a libellous pamphlet
         intituled, An antidote against poyson . . .
```

For monographs, transcribe a title as it appears on the source of information, even if there are inaccuracies.

```
245   #0 $a Breif history of Cambodia
```

For serials and integrating resources, record the title proper by correcting typographical errors and add a note that shows the inaccuracies.

> 245   #0 $a Boletín estadístico anual
> 246   1_ $i Title appears on issue for 1985 as: $a Boletín estadística anual

Omit introductory words not intended to be part of the title. If considered important for identification, add a note transcribing the title with the introductory words.

> 245   #0 $a Ocala, Marion County, Florida
> 246   1_ $i Title appears as: $a Welcome to beautiful Ocala, Marion County, Florida

Title Proper

Title proper is a core element defined as *the chief name of a resource.* The source of information for the title proper is determined from the guidelines in RDA 2.2.2–2.2.4. The title proper is transcribed in MARC field 245 subfield $a.

> 245   #4 $a The HMO salary survey
> 245   #0 $a Lacan and Lévi-Strauss, or The return to Freud, 1951–1957

A musical title may consist solely of the name or names of one or more types of composition.

> 245   #0 $a Symphony

In addition, one or more of the following may appear with such a title: medium of performance, key, date of composition, and number. If so, treat all elements together in the order they appear and transcribe them as the title proper.

> 245   #0 $a Sonata in A minor for piano, op. 11 (1918)

In all other cases, treat additional information on the medium of performance, key, date of composition, or number as other title information.

> 245   #0 $a Moonlight sonata : $b opus 27, no. 2 (complete)

For cartographic resources, treat statements of scale as part of the title proper.

> 245   #0 $a Namibia 1:50,000

Parallel Title Proper

Parallel title proper is the title proper in a different language or script. The parallel title proper can be taken from any source within the resource. The parallel title proper is transcribed in the 245 preceded by either "=" or "= $b."

245   #0 $a Edad de la tentación = $b **The age of temptation**
245   #0 $a Ligne de vie : $b récits électriques = **Life line** : electric tales

Other Title Information

Other title information appears with, but is subordinate to, the title proper. It is taken from the same source as the title proper and is transcribed in MARC field 245 subfield $b.

245   #0 $a Auditing and assurance services : $b **an integrated approach**

For cartographic resources, if the relevant geographic region is not indicated in the title proper or in other title information, record it as other title information in brackets.

245   #0 $a Wildlife & wet lands : $b [India]

For moving images, if the fact that a resource is a trailer is not indicated in the title proper, add the word "trailer" in brackets as other title information.

245   #0 $a Location Hong Kong with Enter the dragon : $b [trailer]

Parallel Other Title Information

Parallel other title information is other title information in a different language or script. It is taken from the same source as the corresponding parallel title proper (if present). Otherwise, take from the same source as the title proper. Parallel other title information is transcribed in MARC field 245 and preceded by a colon.

245   #0 $a Ligne de vie : $b récits électriques = Life line : **electric tales**

Variant Title

Variant title is any title that does not fall into any of the other subelement categories. It can be taken from any source and is transcribed or recorded in MARC field 246.

246   1_ $i Title should read: $a Brief history of Cambodia
246   31 $a Age of temptation

Earlier Title Proper

Earlier title proper is the title proper of an earlier iteration of an integrating resource that differs from the current iteration's title proper. It is taken from sources in earlier iterations of an integrating resource and is transcribed in MARC field 247.

When transcribing earlier title proper, also record the applicable date of publication or the last date viewed.

>   247   10 $a Lime guide to radio on the Internet $f <September 1, 2000>

Later Title Proper

Later title proper is the title proper of a later serial issue or multipart monographic part that differs from the earliest issue or part. It is taken from a later issue or part that bears a different title proper from the earliest issue or part, and it is transcribed in MARC field 246. Record the numbers or dates of publication applicable to the later title proper in a note.

>   246   1_ $i **Volume 2 has title:** $a Contemporain en scène

Key Title

Key title is the resource's unique title as assigned by an ISSN registration agency. It is taken from the following sources (in order of preference): the ISSN register, any source within the resource, or any source. Record the key title in MARC field 222.

>   222   _0 $a Accounting history review

Abbreviated Title

Abbreviated title results when a cataloging agency, an abstracting and indexing service, or an ISSN registration agency abbreviates the title of a resource for indexing or identification purposes. It can be taken from any source and is recorded in MARC field 210.

>   210   0_ $a Account. hist. rev.

RDA 2.4 Statement of Responsibility

Statement of responsibility is defined as a *statement relating to the identification and/ or function of any persons, families, or corporate bodies responsible for the creation of, or contributing to the realization of, the intellectual or artistic content of a resource.* Statement of responsibility has two subelements: *statement of responsibility relating to title proper* and *parallel statement of responsibility relating to title proper.* Other types of statement of responsibility are subelements of other elements. These include statements of responsibility associated with a designation of an edition, a designation of a named revision of an edition, the title of a series, and the title of a subseries. Statements of responsibility associated with the titles proper are transcribed in MARC field 245 subfield $c.

Generally, transcribe a statement of responsibility as it appears on the source. Optionally, abridge a statement of responsibility as long as the first name appearing in the statement is retained and essential information is preserved. Examples of data that can be omitted include titles of address, institutional affiliations, and other intervening data. Thus, an unabridged statement of responsibility might appear as follows:

> 245　## $c / edited by Carlos D. Garcia, Ph.D.,
> University of Texas at San Antonio,
> Karin Y. Chumbimuni-Torres, Ph.D., University of Texas at
> San Antonio, Emanuel Carrilho, Ph.D., University of Sao Paulo.

while the abridged version would appear as follows:

> 245　## $c / edited by Carlos D. Garcia,
> Karin Y. Chumbimuni-Torres, Emanuel Carrilho.

Another optional omission allows for all but the first named entity to be omitted from a statement of responsibility. When omitting names beyond the first, record (as a word and in brackets) the number being omitted using the construction: [and # others]. When the optional omission is not applied, a statement could appear as:

> 245　## $c / Paul Cornell, Axel Giménez,
> Pete Woods, Kenneth Rocafort, Jesús Merino.

When the optional omission *is* applied, the statement would appear as:

> 245　## $c / Paul Cornell [and four others].

If needed, clarify the role of the person, family, or corporate body responsible for the resource by explaining the nature of their relationship as a word or short phrase placed in brackets.

> 245　#0 $a Piers Plowman / $c [edited by] Elizabeth Salter.

Treat nouns and noun phrases occurring in conjunction with the statement of responsibility as part of the statement of responsibility.

> 245　10 $a Dickens & Dickens / $c a novel by Mary Camp.

Statement of Responsibility Relating to Title Proper

Statements of responsibility relating to title proper is a core element. The preferred source of information is the same as the title proper. Otherwise, follow the guidelines in RDA 2.2.2 and 2.2.4.

> 245　14 $a The catcher in the rye / $c **J.D. Salinger**.

Parallel Statement of Responsibility Relating to Title Proper

Parallel statement of responsibility relating to title proper is the statement of responsibility relating to title proper in a different language or script. It is taken from the
same source as the corresponding parallel title proper.

> 245   #0 $a Gio Ponti : $b il fascino della ceramica /
> $c a cura di Dario Matteoni = Gio Ponti :
>   fascination for ceramics / **edited by Dario Matteoni**.

RDA 2.5 Edition Statement

Edition statement is defined as *a statement identifying the edition to which a
resource belongs.* It includes eight subelements: *designation of edition, parallel designation of edition, statement of responsibility relating to edition, parallel statement of
responsibility relating to edition, designation of named revision of an edition, parallel
designation of named revision of an edition, statement of responsibility relating to a
named revision of an edition,* and *parallel statement of responsibility relating to a
named revision of an edition.* Edition statement is recorded in MARC field 250.
Designation of edition is transcribed in subfield $a. All other subelements are
transcribed in subfield $b.

Transcribe edition statements as they appear on the source of information.

> 250 $a Fourth ed.
> 250 $a 1st American edition.

If the resource lacks an edition statement, but it is known to be significantly different from other editions, RDA offers the option of supplying an edition statement
if such a statement is considered important for identification or access. Indicate that
such a statement was taken from outside the resource.

> 250 $a [Hand-coloured and corrected edition]

Designation of Edition

Designation of edition is a core element comprising one or more words and/or
characters that identify the edition of a resource. The preferred source of information is the same as the title proper. Otherwise, follow the guidelines in RDA 2.2.2
and 2.2.4.

> 250 $a 9th edition.
> 250 $a *** edition.

Parallel Designation of Edition

Parallel designation of edition is the designation of edition in a different language or script. The preferred source of information is the same as the designation of edition. Otherwise, follow the guidelines in RDA 2.2.2 and 2.2.4.

> 250 $a Segunda edición = $b **Second edition**.

Statement of Responsibility Relating to the Edition

Statement of responsibility relating to the edition is used for identifying the entities responsible for the edition being described, which may differ from other editions. The preferred source of information is the same as the designation of edition.

> 250 $a 4th edition / $b **edited by John Black,**
> **Nigar Hashimzade, Gareth Myles**.

Parallel Statement of Responsibility Relating to the Edition

A parallel statement of responsibility relating to the edition is the statement of responsibility relating to the edition in a different language or script. The source of information is the same as the corresponding parallel designation of edition (if present). Otherwise, take from the same source as the designation of edition.

> 250 $a Deutsch/Englische Ausgabe /
> **$b** herausgegeben von Giles R. Hoyt = German/English edition /
> **edited by Giles R. Hoyt**.

Designation of a Named Revision of an Edition

Designation of a named revision of an edition is a core element comprising one or more words and/or characters that identify a specific revision of a named edition. The source of information is the same as the designation of edition. Otherwise, follow the guidelines in RDA 2.2.2 and 2.2.4.

> 250 $a 1st American edition, **new enlarged revision**.

Parallel Designation of a Named Revision of an Edition

Parallel designation of a named revision of an edition is the designation of a named revision of an edition in a different language or script. The source of information is the same as the designation of a named revision. Otherwise, follow the guidelines in RDA 2.2.2 and 2.2.4.

> 250 $a Sixth edition, second revision = $b Sixième édition, **deux-**
> **ième revision**.

Statement of Responsibility Relating to a Named Revision of an Edition

Statement of responsibility relating to a named revision of an edition is used for identifying the entities responsible for a named revision of an edition. The source of information is the same as the designation of a named revision of an edition.

> 250 $a 1st American edition, new enlarged revision / $b **revision by Donald Sears**.

Parallel Statement of Responsibility Relating to a Named Revision of an Edition

Parallel statement of responsibility relating to a named revision of an edition is the statement of responsibility relating to a named revision of an edition in a different language or script. The source of information is the corresponding parallel designation of a named revision of an edition (if present). Otherwise, take from the same source as the designation of a named revision.

> 250 $a Segunda edición, tercera revisión / **$b** revisado y aprobado
> por el Instituto Costarricense de Turismo = Second edition,
> third revision / **revised and approved by the Costa Rican
> Tourism Institute**.

RDA 2.6 Numbering of Serials

Numbering of serials is defined as *the identification of each of the issues or parts of a serial*. Numbering of serials is generally transcribed in MARC field 362, but it can also be recorded in MARC 363. The numbering is to be recorded in other fields when applicable.

Numbering of serials can include any combination of the following: a numeral, a letter, or any other character.

> 8
> RP 21

It may also contain a caption, such as "volume" or "number."

> Volume 4, number 9
> Issue #07

It may also contain a chronological designation.

> March/April 2000
> Vol. 1 (Winter 1999)

Numeric and/or Alphabetic Designation of First Issue or Part of Sequence

Numeric and/or alphabetic designation of first issue or part of sequence is a core element. The preferred source of information is the source on the first issue or part of the sequence that bears the title proper. Otherwise, follow the guidelines in RDA 2.2.2 and 2.2.4.

> 362   0_ $a v. 1–
> 362   0_ $a New series, no. 1–

Chronological Designation of First Issue or Part of Sequence

Chronological designation of first issue or part of sequence is a core element. A chronological designation includes numbering that appears as a date. The preferred source of information is the source on the first issue or part of the sequence that bears the title proper. Otherwise, follow the guidelines in RDA 2.2.2 and 2.2.4.

> 362   0_ $a 1992–
> 362   0_ $a Vol. 1, issue 1 (**Spring 2003**)-

Numeric and/or Alphabetic Designation of Last Issue or Part of Sequence

Numeric and/or alphabetic designation of last issue or part of sequence is a core element. The preferred source of information is the source on the last issue or part of the sequence that bears the title proper. Otherwise, follow the guidelines in RDA 2.2.2 and 2.2.4.

> 362   0_ $a vol. 1, no.1 (April 1980)-**vol. 11, no. 4** (July 1990)
> 362   0_ $a 78/1–**93/16.**

Chronological Designation of Last Issue or Part of Sequence

Chronological designation of last issue or part of sequence is a core element. The preferred source of information is the source on the last issue or part of the sequence that bears the title proper. Otherwise, follow the guidelines in RDA 2.2.2 and 2.2.4.

> 362   0_ $a 1992–**2005.**
> 362   0_ $a vol. 1 (Spring 1992)-vol. 11 (**Fall 1994**)

Alternative Numeric and/or Alphabetic Designation of First Issue or Part of Sequence

Record alternative numeric, alphabetic, or chronological designation information whenever there is a second or subsequent numbering system. The preferred source of information for *alternative numeric and/or alphabetic designation of first issue or part of sequence* is the source on the first issue or part of the sequence that bears the title proper. Otherwise, follow the guidelines in RDA 2.2.2 and 2.2.4.

> 362   0_ $a Vol. 1, no. 1 (May 1997)-v. 5, no. 12 (December 2001);
> **new series, v. 1, number 1** (January 2002)-

Alternative Chronological Designation of First Issue or Part of Sequence

The preferred source of information for *alternative chronological designation of first issue or part of sequence* is the source on the first issue or part of the sequence that bears the title proper. Otherwise, follow the guidelines in RDA 2.2.2 and 2.2.4.

> 362   0_ $a Vol. 1, no. 1 (May 1997)-v. 5, no. 12 (December 2001);
> new series, v. 1, number 1 (**2002**)-

Alternative Numeric and/or Alphabetic Designation of Last Issue or Part of Sequence

The preferred source of information for *alternative numeric and/or alphabetic designation of last issue or part of sequence* is the source on the last issue or part of the sequence that bears the title proper. Otherwise, follow the guidelines in RDA 2.2.2 and 2.2.4.

> 362   0_ $a Vol. 1, no. 1 (May 1997)-v. 5, no. 12 (December 2001);
> new series, v. 1, number 1 (2002)-**new series, v. 3, number 7** (2004)

Alternative Chronological Designation of Last Issue or Part of Sequence

The preferred source of information for *alternative chronological designation of last issue or part of sequence* is the source on the last issue or part of the sequence that bears the title proper. Otherwise, follow the guidelines in RDA 2.2.2 and 2.2.4.

> 362   0_ $a Vol. 1, no. 1 (May 1997)-v. 5, no. 12 (December 2001);
> new series, v. 1, number 1 (2002)- new series, v. 3, number 7 (**2004**)

Production, Publication, Distribution, Manufacture, and Copyright

Production statement, publication statement, distribution statement, manufacture statement, and *copyright date* are separate elements in RDA. Accordingly, a new MARC field, 264, was created to accommodate these discrete data elements. Field 264 has five different indicator values—0, 1, 2, 3, and 4—to address each element. *Production statement, publication statement, distribution statement,* and *manufacture statement* each have subelements that address the place, name, and the date relating the function involved. These subelements occupy the same subfields—$a, $b, and $c, respectively—for all of the main elements.

Though the main elements each hold specific bibliographic information, their analogous subelements share commonalities. Places and names of producers, publishers, distributors, and manufacturers are transcribed as they appear on the source of information, with the exception of the optional omission of levels in a corporate hierarchy. Dates are recorded according to the guidelines in RDA instruction 1.8.

Another commonality across the elements involves the transcription of larger jurisdictions that appear on the source and the in situ recording in brackets of such jurisdictions that are absent from the source but needed for clarification.

    264   ## $a Portland, Oregon, USA
    264   ## $a Portland [Arkansas]

Though clarification of a place is allowed within the same element, correction is only allowed in a note.

    264   _1 $a Belfast
    500      $a Actually published in Oslo.

Along the same lines, fictitious and incorrect dates are corrected in notes.

Known places and probable places are recorded in brackets, the latter followed by a question mark.

    264   _1 $a [Australia]
    264   _1 $a [Chicago?]

If places, names, or dates are absent from the source and cannot be approximated, the name of the subelement is recorded, followed by the phrase "not identified," and the entire phrase is bracketed.

    264   _1 $a [Baltimore] : $b [publisher not identified],
          $c [date of publication not identified]
    264   _2 $a [Place of distribution not identified] :
          $b Distributed by Mansfield Incorporated, $c 2003.

A statement of function beyond solely publishing is transcribed as it appears on the source. If such a statement is absent and is needed for clarification, it can be recorded in brackets within that element.

    264   _1 $a . . . : $b SAGE Publications on behalf of McGill University
    264   _2 $a . . . : $b Johnson Brothers, Inc. [distributor]

For dates, the default instruction is to record dates in the Gregorian or Julian calendar.

    264   ## $a . . . : $b . . . , $c 1975.

Optionally, dates not of the Gregorian or Julian calendar can be recorded followed by their bracketed Gregorian or Julian counterpart.

> 264   ## $a . . . : $b . . . , $c 4308 [1975]

A chronogram can be transcribed as it appears on the source.

> 264   ## $a . . . : $b . . . , $c Ipso anno tertlo saeCVLarl
> typographlae DIVIno aVXILIo a gerManIs InVentae.

As an alternative, it can be transcribed with its bracketed numerical counterpart following afterward.

> 264   ## $a . . . : $b . . . , $c Ipso anno tertlo saeCVLarl
> typographlae DIVIno aVXILIo a gerManIs InVentae [1740]

As a second alternative, the chronogram's numerical counterpart can be recorded in brackets without the chronogram.

> 264   ## $a . . . : $b . . . , $c [1740]

RDA 2.7 Production Statement

Production statement is defined as *a statement identifying the place or places of production, producer or producers, and date or dates of production of a resource in an unpublished form*. It includes statements relating to the inscription, fabrication, and construction of unpublished resources like manuscripts, paintings, sculptures, and locally made recordings. *Production statement* has five subelements: *place of production, parallel place of production, producer's name, parallel producer's name*, and *date of production*. It is recorded in MARC field 264 with a second indicator value of 0.

Place of Production

Take the *place of production* from the same source as the producer's name. Otherwise, follow the guidelines in RDA 2.2.2 and 2.2.4. Transcribe place of production in the subfield $a of MARC field 264 with a second indicator value of 0.

Parallel Place of Production

Take the *parallel place of production* from the same source as the place of production. Otherwise, follow the guidelines in RDA 2.2.2 and 2.2.4. Transcribe parallel place of production in the subfield $a of MARC field 264 with a second indicator value of 0.

Producer's Name

Take the *producer's name* from the same source as the title proper. Otherwise, follow the guidelines in RDA 2.2.2 and 2.2.4. Transcribe producer's name in the subfield $b of MARC field 264 with a second indicator value of 0.

Parallel Producer's Name

Take the *parallel producer's name* from the same source as the *producer's name*. Otherwise, follow the guidelines in RDA 2.2.2 and 2.2.4. Transcribe parallel producer's name in the subfield $b of MARC field 264 with a second indicator value of 0.

Date of Production

Date of production is a core element. Take the date of production from any source. Record date of production in the subfield $c of MARC field 264 with a second indicator value of 0.

Examples of Full Production Statements

> 264 _0 $a Pittsburgh, Pennsylvania : $b McDouglas & Company, $c 1998.
> 264 _0 $a [Place of production not identified] : $b [producer not identified], $c 2012.

RDA 2.8 Publication Statement

Publication statement is defined as *a statement identifying the place or places of publication, publisher or publishers, and date or dates of publication of a resource.* It includes statements relating to the publication, release, or issuance of resources. *Publication statement* has five subelements: *place of publication, parallel place of publication, publisher's name, parallel publisher's name,* and *date of publication.* It is recorded in MARC field 264 with a second indicator value of 1.

Place of Publication

The first named *place of publication* is a core element. Take place of publication from the same source as the publisher's name. Otherwise, follow the guidelines in RDA 2.2.2 and 2.2.4. Transcribe place of publication in the subfield $a of MARC field 264 with a second indicator value of 1.

Parallel Place of Publication

Take the *parallel place of publication* from the same source as the place of publication. Otherwise, follow the guidelines in RDA 2.2.2 and 2.2.4. Transcribe parallel place of publication in the subfield $a of MARC field 264 with a second indicator value of 1.

Publisher's Name

The first named *publisher* is a core element. Take publisher's name from the same source as the title proper. Otherwise, follow the guidelines in RDA 2.2.2 and 2.2.4. Transcribe publisher's name in the subfield $b of MARC field 264 with a second indicator value of 1.

Parallel Publisher's Name

Take the *parallel publisher's name* from the same source as the *publisher's name*. Otherwise, follow the guidelines in RDA 2.2.2 and 2.2.4. Transcribe parallel publisher's name in the subfield $b of MARC field 264 with a second indicator value of 1.

Date of Publication

Date of publication is a core element. Take the date of publication from the same source as the title proper. Otherwise, follow the guidelines in RDA 2.2.2 and 2.2.4. Record date of publication in the subfield $c of MARC field 264 with a second indicator value of 0.

Examples of Full Publication Statements

> 264　_1 $a [Mumbai?] : $b Department of Food Science & Nutrition, S.N.D.T. Women's University, $c [1996]
>
> 264　_1 $a Hoboken, N.J. : $b John Wiley & Sons, Inc., $c 2008.

RDA 2.9 Distribution Statement

Distribution statement is defined as *a statement identifying the place or places of distribution, distributor or distributors, and date or dates of distribution of a resource*. It has five subelements: *place of distribution, parallel place of distribution, distributor's name, parallel distributor's name,* and *date of distribution*. It is recorded in MARC field 264 with a second indicator value of 2.

Place of Distribution

The first named *place of distribution* is a core element if the place of publication is not identified. Take place of distribution from the same source as the distributor's name. Otherwise, follow the guidelines in RDA 2.2.2 and 2.2.4. Transcribe place of distribution in the subfield $a of MARC field 264 with a second indicator value of 2.

Parallel Place of Distribution

Take the *parallel place of distribution* from the same source as the place of distribution. Otherwise, follow the guidelines in RDA 2.2.2 and 2.2.4. Transcribe parallel place of distribution in the subfield $a of MARC field 264 with a second indicator value of 2.

Distributor's Name

The first named *distributor* is a core element if the publisher's name is not identified. Take distributor's name from the same source as the title proper. Otherwise, follow the guidelines in RDA 2.2.2 and 2.2.4. Transcribe distributor's name in the subfield $b of MARC field 264 with a second indicator value of 2.

Parallel Distributor's Name

Take the *parallel distributor's name* from the same source as the *distributor's name*. Otherwise, follow the guidelines in RDA 2.2.2 and 2.2.4. Transcribe parallel distributor's name in the subfield $b of MARC field 264 with a second indicator value of 2.

Date of Distribution

Date of distribution is a core element if the date of publication is not identified. Take the date of distribution from the same source as the title proper. Otherwise, follow the guidelines in RDA 2.2.2 and 2.2.4. Record date of distribution in the subfield $c of MARC field 264 with a second indicator value of 2.

Examples of Full Distribution Statements

> 264 _2 $a Naples [Florida] : $b Distributed by Mansfield Incorporated, $c 1982.
> 264 _2 $a [Dublin, Ohio?] : $b Casemate [distributor], $c [date of distribution not identified]

RDA 2.10 Manufacture Statement

Manufacture statement is defined as *statement identifying the place or places of manufacture, manufacturer or manufacturers, and date or dates of manufacture of a resource in a published form*. It includes statements relating to the printing, duplication, and casting of a published resource. Manufacture statement has five subelements: *place of manufacture, parallel place of manufacture, manufacturer's name, parallel manufacturer's name*, and *date of manufacture*. It is recorded in MARC field 264 with a second indicator value of 3.

Place of Manufacture

The first named *place of manufacture* is a core element if neither the place of publication nor the place of distribution is identified. Take place of manufacture from the same source as the manufacturer's name. Otherwise, follow the guidelines in RDA 2.2.2 and 2.2.4. Transcribe place of manufacture in the subfield $a of MARC field 264 with a second indicator value of 3.

Parallel Place of Manufacturer

Take the *parallel place of manufacture* from the same source as the place of manufacture. Otherwise, follow the guidelines in RDA 2.2.2 and 2.2.4. Transcribe parallel place of manufacture in the subfield $a of MARC field 264 with a second indicator value of 3.

Manufacturer's Name

The first named *manufacturer* is a core element if neither the publisher's name nor the distributor's name is identified. Take manufacturer's name from the same source as the title proper. Otherwise, follow the guidelines in RDA 2.2.2 and 2.2.4. Transcribe manufacturer's name in the subfield $b of MARC field 264 with a second indicator value of 3.

Parallel Manufacturer's Name

Take the *parallel manufacturer's name* from the same source as the *manufacturer's name*. Otherwise, follow the guidelines in RDA 2.2.2 and 2.2.4. Transcribe parallel manufacturer's name in the subfield $b of MARC field 264 with a second indicator value of 3.

Date of Manufacturer

Date of manufacturer is a core element if neither the date of publication nor the date of distribution is identified. Take the date of manufacture from any source. Record date of manufacture in the subfield $c of MARC field 264 with a second indicator value of 3.

Examples of Full Manufacture Statements

> 264   _3 $a Berlin : $b Lexikon Verlag, $c 2005.
> 264   _3 $a [London] : $b Commonwealth Printing Office, $c 1952.

RDA 2.11 Copyright Date

Copyright date is a core element if neither the date of publication nor the date of manufacture is identified. It is defined as *a date associated with a claim of protection under copyright or a similar regime* and includes phonogram dates. Take information on copyright dates from any source, and record the information in $c of MARC field 264 with a second indicator value of 4.

When recoding copyright and phonogram dates, precede the dates with their respective symbols. If the symbols cannot be reproduced, record the spelled-out word instead.

264	_4	$c ©2005	OR	264	_4	$c copyright 2005
264	_4	$c ®1983	OR	264	_4	$c phonogram 1983

RDA 2.12 Series Statement

Series statement is defined as *a statement identifying a series to which a resource belongs and the numbering of the resource within the series.* It has sixteen subelements: *title proper of series, parallel title proper of series, other title information of series, parallel other title information of series, statement of responsibility relating to series, parallel statement of responsibility relating to series, ISSN of series, numbering within series, title proper of subseries, parallel title proper of subseries, other title information of subseries, parallel other title information of subseries, statement of responsibility relating to subseries, parallel statement of responsibility relating to subseries, ISSN of subseries,* and *numbering within subseries.* Record series statement in MARC field 490.

Title Proper of Series

Title proper of series is a core element and is defined as the *chief name of a series.* The preferred source of information is the series title page. Otherwise, follow the guidelines in RDA 2.2.2 and 2.2.4.

490 ## $a How the health are you?

Parallel Title Proper of Series

Parallel title proper of series is a title proper of series in a different language or script. Take parallel title proper of series from any source within the resource.

490 ## $a Etudes et travaux = $a Studies and working papers

Other Title Information of Series

Transcribe *other title information of series* only if considered necessary for identification of the series. Take from the same source as the title proper of the series.

490 ## $a Insurrections: **critical studies in religion, politics, and culture**

Parallel Other Title Information of Series

Take *parallel other title information of series* from the same source as the corresponding parallel title proper of series (if present). Otherwise, take from the same source as the title proper of series.

> 490   ## $a Art and artists : conversations among the experts =
> $a L'Art et les artistes : **conversations parmi les experts**

Statement of Responsibility Relating to Series

Transcribe *statement of responsibility relating to series* only if considered necessary for identification of the series. Take from the same source as the title proper of the series.

> 490   ## $a Critical perspectives in the history of environmental design /
> **edited by Daniel J. Nadenicek**

Parallel Statement of Responsibility Relating to Series

Take the *parallel statement of responsibility relating to a series* from the same source as the corresponding parallel title proper of the series (if present). Otherwise, take from same source as the title proper.

> 490   ## $a Classical music / edited by Jeanne Cors = $a Musique
> classique / **sous la direction de Jeanne Cors**.

ISSN of Series

Take *ISSN (International Standard Serial Number) of series*, the identifier assigned to a series by an ISSN registration agency, from any source.

> 490   ## $a Studien und Texte zur Byzantinistik, $x **0944–7709** ; $v 7

Numbering within Series

Numbering within series is a core element that designates the sequencing of parts within a series. It may include any combination of a numeral, letter, or another character, and it may also include an accompanying caption (e.g., "volume," "number," etc.) and/or a chronological designation. Take numbering within series from anywhere within the resource.

> 490   ## $a Studies in Slavic and general linguistics ; $v volume 4

Title Proper of Subseries

Title proper of subseries is a core element defined as *the chief name of a subseries*. The preferred source of information is the series title page. Otherwise, follow the guidelines in RDA 2.2.2 and 2.2.4.

> 490　## $a Veterinary clinics of North America. **Equine practice**
> 490　## $a C.I.E.R.E.C Travaux ; $v 157. $a **Musique et musicologie**

Parallel Title Proper of Subseries

Take the *parallel title proper of subseries* from anywhere within the resource.

> 490　## $a Papers and documents of the I.C.I. Series F, Monographs ; $v no. 8 = $a Travaux et documents de l'I.C.I. **Série F, Monographies** ; $v no 8

Other Title Information of Subseries

Take the *other title information of subseries* from the same source as the title proper of the subseries.

> 490　## $a Information and health. Bioinformatics : **applications in biomedicine**

Parallel Other Title Information of Subseries

Take *parallel other title information of subseries* from the same source as the corresponding parallel title proper of the subseries, if present. Otherwise, take from the same source as the title proper of the subseries.

> 490　## $a Modern gallery. Sculpture : modernist movements and artists = $a Galerie d'art moderne. Sculpture : **mouvements modernistes et des artistes**

Statement of Responsibility Relating to Subseries

Transcribe the *statement of responsibility relating to subseries* only if considered necessary for identification of the series. Take from the same source as the title proper of the subseries.

> 490　## $a Women in STEM. Engineering / **edited by Grace Strauss**.

Parallel Statement of Responsibility Relating to Subseries

Take the *parallel statement of responsibility relating to subseries* from the same source as the corresponding parallel title proper of the subseries, if present. Otherwise, take from the same source as the title proper of the subseries.

> 490   ## $a La historia y cultura de latinoamericana / editado
> por Consuelo Vargas = $a Latin American history and
> culture series. Guatemala / **edited by Consuelo Vargas**.

ISSN of Subseries

Take the *ISSN (International Standard Serial Number) of subseries* from anywhere within the resource.

> 490   ## $a Janua linuarum, $x 0446–4796. $a Series maior,
> $x **0075–3114**

Optionally, omit ISSN for the main series if the subseries has an ISSN.

> 490   ## $a Janua linuarum. $a Series maior, $x **0075–3114**

Numbering within Subseries

Numbering within subseries is a core element. Take numbering within subseries from anywhere within the source.

> 490   ## $a Temas actuales ; $v 3. $a Bolsillo ; $v **número 7**

RDA 2.13 Mode of Issuance

Mode of issuance is defined as *a categorization reflecting whether a resource is issued in one or more parts, the way it is updated, and its intended termination.* The source of information for mode of issuance can be determined from evidence presented by the resource itself (or on accompanying matter). If desired, additional evidence can be taken from any source. Record the mode of issuance as *single unit, multipart monograph*, *series*, or *integrating resource*.

In the MARC record, the mode of issuance element is mapped to the Bibliographic Level (Leader position 07). For both single units and multipart monographs, record the value "m" (for "Monograph/Item"). For serials, record the value "s" (for "Serial"). For integrating resources, record the value "i" (for "Integrating resource").

RDA 2.14 Frequency

Frequency is defined as *the intervals at which the issues or parts of a serial or the updates to an integrating resource are issued.* Take information on frequency from any source, and record the information in MARC field 310. For frequency, record one of the following: *daily, three times a week, biweekly, weekly, semiweekly, three times a month, bimonthly, monthly, semimonthly, quarterly, three times a year, semiannual, annual, biennial, triennial,* or *irregular.* If none of these terms is sufficient, give the frequency details in a note.

RDA 2.15 Identifier for the Manifestation

Identifier for the manifestation is a core element defined as *a character string associated with a manifestation that serves to differentiate that manifestation from other manifestations.* An identifier for the manifestation can be assigned by an international body (e.g., ISBN and ISSN) or by a publisher, government publications agency, or some other body (e.g., music publishers' numbers and plate numbers). An identifier for the manifestation can be taken from any source.

```
016   7_ $a 101560044 $2 DNLM
020      $a 9781435459632
022   0_ $a 1918–123X
500      $a Supt of Docs. no.: ED 1.328/3:Sa 3
```

Publisher's Number for Music

Publisher's number for music is assigned by a music publisher. It appears on the title page, cover, or first page of music and may include words, initials, or abbreviations that identify the publisher. Take the publisher's number for music from any source.

```
028   00 $a 72009
```

Plate Number for Music

Plate number for music is assigned by a music publisher and is usually printed at the bottom of each page (and sometimes also on the title page). It may include words, initials, or abbreviations that identify the publisher, and it may also be followed by a number representing the number of pages or plates. Take the plate number for music from any source.

```
028   02 $a R2 72815
```

RDA 2.16 Preferred Citation

Preferred citation is defined as *a citation for a resource in the form preferred by a creator, publisher, custodian, indexing or abstracting service, etc.* It can be taken from any source and is transcribed in MARC field 524.

```
524      $a Phineas Indritz Papers, Special Collections and Archives
         Division, Howard University Law Library.
```

RDA 2.17 Custodial History of Item

Custodial history of item is defined as *a record of previous ownership or custodianship of an item*. It can be taken from any source and is recorded in MARC field 561.

> 561 $a From a collection that was first owned by Walter L. Gordon, Jr., later given to William C. Beverly, Jr. in 2002, and ultimately donated to UCLA in 2010.

RDA 2.18 Immediate Source of Acquisition of Item

Immediate source of acquisition of item is the source from which the agency directly acquired an item and the circumstances under which it was received. It can be taken from any source and it maps to MARC field 541.

> 541 $c Gift; $a Terry Belanger; $d 2012.

RDA 2.19 Identifier for the Item

Identifier for the item is defined as *a character string associated with an item that serves to differentiate that item from other items*. It can be taken from any source.

RDA 2.20 Note

Note on manifestation or item is defined as *an annotation providing additional information relating to manifestation or item attributes*. It can be taken from any source. Note on manifestation or item has twelve subelements *note on title, note on statement of responsibility, note on edition statement, note on numbering of serials, note on production statement, note on publication statement, note on distribution statement, note on manufacture statement, note on copyright date, note on series statement, note on frequency*, and *note on issue, part, or iteration used as the basis for identification of the resource*.

Note on Title

> 246   1_ $i Commonly known as: $a AACR2
> 500 $a Cover title.
> 500 $a Title varies.
> 500 $a The symbol for chemical equilibrium appears between the words "bioscience" and "society" on the title page.

Note on Statement of Responsibility

> 500 $a Editor varies.

Note on Edition Statement

500      $a Edition statement from jacket.

Note on Numbering of Serials

362   1_ $a Began with May 2011.
362   1_ $a Ceased with vol. 85 (Fall 1994).
515      $a Issues for August 2007- also called Vol. 11-
515      $a Volume 11, no. 1- Volume 18, no. 9 also called issue 1
          (1991)- issue 293 (1998)

Note on Production Statement

500      $a Probable year of production based on date range in which
          the producer was active.

Note on Publication Statement

362   1_ $a Began in 1985; ceased in 2004.
500      $a Name of publisher varies.

Note on Distribution Statement

500      $a Volumes 1–5 distributed by Bell & Sanford;
          volumes 6 and 7 distributed by Aimsworth Limited.

Note on Manufacture Statement

500      $a Updates previous to 2001 bear the imprint:
          Editora Leo Antillas, S.A.

Note on Copyright Date

500      $a Copyright on title page verso is 2003; copyright next to
          running title is 2004.

Note on Series Statement

500      $a Series numbering should read: vol. 421.

Note on Frequency

321      $a Semiannual, $b 2005–2007
500      $a Frequency varies.

Note on Issue, Part, or Iteration Used as the Basis for Identification of the Resource

> 588 $a Identification of the resource based on: Volume 1, no. 3 (August 1999).
> 588 $a Description based on: Vol. 14, no. 18 (Jan. 5, 2009); title from title page.
> 588 $a Latest issue consulted: Vol. 2, issue 1 (January 2006).
> 588 $a Description based on resource; title from PDF title page (viewed on January 28, 2011).

RDA CHAPTER 3: DESCRIBING CARRIERS

RDA Chapter 3 provides guidelines on how to record elements that mainly help users select resources, although there are some elements that can be recorded to aid in the identification of a resource. The chapter's contents include its purpose and scope, general guidelines on describing carriers, and detailed guidelines on the twenty major elements covered in the chapter. For all elements in Chapter 3, the source of information can be determined from evidence presented by the resource itself (or on accompanying matter). If desired, additional evidence can be taken from any source.

RDA 3.2 Media Type

Media type is defined as *a categorization reflecting the general type of intermediation device required to view, play, run, etc., the content of a resource.* For media type record one or more of the following terms: *audio, computer, microform, microscopic, projected, stereographic, unmediated,* or *video.* If none of the terms applies, record *other.* If the media type cannot be determined record *unspecified.* The MARC field for media type is field 337 subfield $a.

> 337 $a audio
> 337 $a unmediated

RDA 3.3 Carrier Type

Carrier type is a core element defined as *a categorization reflecting the format of the storage medium and housing of a carrier in combination with the type of intermediation device required to view, play, run, etc., the content of a resource.* For carrier type record one or more terms like *audiocasette, computer disc, online resource, microfiche, object, volume, videodisc,* or some other term from the closed list of carrier types. If none of the terms applies, record *other.* If the carrier type cannot be determined record *unspecified.* The MARC field for carrier type is field 338 subfield $a.

> 338 $a audio disc
> 338 $a volume

RDA 3.4 Extent

Extent is a core element when it is complete and its totality is known. It is defined as *the number and type of units and/or subunits making up a resource*. A unit, in turn, is a *physical or logical constituent of a resource*, and a subunit is a *physical or logical subdivision of a unit*. An example of an extent would be the following: *1 online resource (556 pages)*, where "online resource" would be the unit and "pages" would be the subunit.

RDA provides extensive instructions for recording *extent* for a variety of carrier types. The default method for describing *extent* is to record the number of units followed by the carrier type term, such as *1 videodisc* or *3 microscope slides*. The exceptions to this are cartographic resources, notated music, still images, text, and three-dimensional forms, which each have their own conventions (described later). Extent is generally recorded in MARC field 300 subfield $a.

> 300 $a 1 computer disc
> 300 $a 5 microfiches

In lieu of using a carrier type term that is defined in RDA's vocabulary, catalogers have the option of using a term in common usage.

> 300 $a 1 videodisc OR 300 $a 1 DVD

When adding the number of subunits, record it in parentheses following the number of units.

> 300 $a 1 flipchart (14 sheets)
> 300 $a 7 microfiches (approximately 800 frames)
> 300 $a 1 online resource (3 audio files)

Comprehensive vs. Analytical Description

For a comprehensive description of a collection, either record the number of items, containers, or volumes, record the storage space, or record the number and type of unit, depending on what is most appropriate for the resource.

> 300 $a 18 $f boxes
> 300 $a 20 $f linear ft.

For an analytical description of a part, either record the number of units and/or subunits in the part or record the location of the part within the larger resource

> 300 $a 400 pages
> 300 $a pages 545–730
> 300 $a on cassette 5 of 8 audio cassettes

RDA 3.4.2 Extent of Cartographic Resource

For *extent of a cartographic resource* record *atlas, diagram, globe, map, model, profile, remote-sensing image, section, view,* or some other concise term (e.g., *wall charts*). Precede the term with the appropriate number. If applicable, precede the number and term with the word "approximately."

300	$a 1 globe
300	$a 3 wall charts
300	$a approximately 350 maps

For atlases, record the number of volumes and/or pages.

300	$a 1 atlas (5 volumes)
300	$a 1 atlas (vii, 62 pages)

RDA 3.4.3 Extent of Notated Music

To record *extent of notated music,* use a term from the list under *Format of Notated Music* (RDA instruction 7.20), precede the term with the appropriate number, follow the term with the number of units or subunits as instructed for texts (RDA 3.4.5), and place the number of units or subunits in parentheses.

300	$a 1 score (ii, 70 pages)
300	$a 1 piano conductor part (10 leaves)

RDA 3.4.4 Extent of Still Image

For *extent of still image,* record one or more terms like *chart, drawing, flash card, painting, photograph, picture, postcard, poster,* or some other term from the list in instruction RDA 3.4.4.2. If no term applies, use another that would describe it concisely (e.g., *flannel board pieces*). Precede the term with the appropriate number. If applicable, precede the number and term with the word "approximately."

300	$a 1 painting
300	$a approximately 300 posters

For albums, portfolios, or cases that contain drawings, prints, and other still images, record the number of albums, portfolios, or cases and the appropriate term. Optionally, add the number of still images within the container.

300	$a 2 portfolios
300	$a 2 portfolios (80 prints)

RDA 3.4.5 Extent of Text

For single volume texts, record the number of pages, leaves, or columns based on the numbered or lettered sequences in the resource.

      300        $a iv, 42 pages
      300        $a 78 columns

If the resource consists solely of unnumbered pages, leaves, or columns, either record the exact number, record the approximate number, or record *1 volume (unpaged)*.

      300        $a 45 unnumbered pages
      300        $a approximately 200 leaves
      300        $a 1 volume (unpaged)

If recording numbered and unnumbered sequences, either record the exact number of unnumbered pages, record the approximate number of unnumbered pages, or record *unnumbered sequences of pages*.

      300        $a 28 leaves, 96 unnumbered pages
      300        $a xi, approximately 200, 12 pages
      300        $a 84 pages, unnumbered sequences of leaves

Correct misleading or incorrect pagination by following the number with "that is" and the corrected number.

      300        $a 731, that is, 713 pages

If the resource has complicated or irregular paging, foliation, or numbering of columns, either record the total number followed by "in various pagings" (or "in various foliations" or "in various numberings"), record the exact numbering within each sequence, or record *1 volume (various pagings)*.

      300        $a 200 leaves in various foliations
      300        $a 64 pages, 270 pages, 20 unnumbered pages
      300        $a 1 volume (various pagings)

For a resource with numbered plates that are separate from the sequence of pages or leaves of text, record the number of plates at the end of the sequence.

      300        $a iii, 27, 84 pages, 21 leaves of plates

If a parallel text has duplicated paging, record both pagings.

      300        $a iv, 84, 84 pages

If a resource has two different pagings numbered in opposite directions, record each sequence of lettered and numbered pages in order, starting from the title page selected for the description.

        300        $a ix, 52, 55, ix pages

For resources comprising a single sheet, record *1 sheet*. If the sheet is designed to be folded and read as pages, record 1 folded sheet, followed by the number of imposed pages in parentheses, such as *1 folded sheet (8 pages)*.

If there is more than one volume and the total number is known or the set is complete, record the number of units followed by the word "volumes."

        300        $a 5 volumes

For incomplete resources, either omit the number and simply record *volumes* or omit the extent altogether.

If there is continuous paging across multiple volumes, record the number of volumes followed by the total number of pages in parentheses, ignoring preliminary pages in all but the first volume.

        300        $a 5 volumes (xi, 858 pages)

For resources comprising one or more updating loose-leafs, record the number followed by the phrase "volume (loose-leaf)" or "volumes (loose-leaf)."

        300        $a 1 volume (loose-leaf)
        300        $a 8 volumes (loose-leaf)

For resources comprising more than one sheet, precede the word "sheets" with the appropriate number.

        300        $a 20 sheets

RDA 3.4.6 *Extent of Three-Dimensional Form*

For *extent of three-dimensional form*, record one or more terms like *coin, diorama, game, jigsaw puzzle, medal, model, sculpture, specimen, toy*, or some other concise term (e.g., *feather headbands*). Precede the term with the appropriate number. If applicable, precede the number and term with the word "approximately."

        300        $a 4 jigsaw puzzles
        300        $a approximately 200 coins

When appropriate, specify the number of components in parentheses following the number of units.

> 300 $a 1 game (1 board, 100 cards, 8 counters, 2 dice)

RDA 3.5 Dimensions

Dimensions is defined as *the measurements of the carrier or carriers and/or the container of a resource* and includes *height, width, depth, length, gauge, and diameter.*

The default method for recording dimensions is to record the number of centimeters followed by the metric symbol *cm*, rounding to the nearest whole centimeter. However, cataloging agencies are given the option to use a different system of measurement, as long as they follow the abbreviation conventions outlined in Appendix B. Exceptions to the default method are detailed where applicable. The MARC field for extent is field 300 subfield $c.

Dimensions of Resources Other Than Maps and Still Images

300	$c 10 × 7 cm, 4 mm tape *(for the gauge of an audiocassette)*[1]
300	$c standard 8 mm *(for the gauge of a videocassette)*[2]
300	$c 30 cm *(for the diameter of an analog audio disc)*[3]
300	$c 12 cm *(for the diameter of a digital audio disc)*[4]
300	$c 21 cm *(for the diameter of a videodisc)*[5]
300	$c 12 cm *(for the diameter of a computer disc)*[6]
300	$c 28 × 10 cm *(for the dimensions of a flash card)*
300	$c 35 mm *(for a filmstrip 35 mm)*
300	$c 11 × 15 cm *(for microfiches)*
300	$c 28 × 22 cm *(for a sheet)*
300	$c 48 × 30 cm folded to 24 × 15 cm *(for a folded sheet)*
300	$c 12 cm *(for the diameter of a globe)*
300	$c 25 cm *(for a volume over 10 centimeters in height)*
300	$c 90 mm *(for a volume below 10 centimeters in height)*
300	$c 20 × 32 cm *(for a volume with width greater than the height)*
300	$c 30 × 12 cm *(for a volume with height more than twice the width)*

If the dimensions of a multipart monograph or serial changes, record the range from the smallest to the largest.

> 300 $c 27–32 cm

---

1. In practice, measurements in inches may be the more common convention.
2. In practice, "1/2 in." may be the more common convention.
3. In practice, "12 in." may be the more common convention.
4. In practice, "4 3/4 in." may be the more common convention.
5. In practice, "4 3/4 in." may be the more common convention.
6. In practice, "4 3/4 in." may be the more common convention.

If the dimensions of an integrating resource change, adjust the data to reflect the current iteration and make a note, if considered necessary.

RDA 3.5.2 Dimensions of Map, Etc.

Record the dimensions of sheet maps, measured within the neat line, as height × width or as diameter, as appropriate.

    300        $c 25 × 35 cm
    300        $c 45 cm in diameter

If the cartographic content measures less than half the size of the sheet, or if the sheet contains substantial content that is not cartographic (e.g., text), apply the convention in the following example:

    300        $c 20 × 31 cm, on sheet 42 × 50 cm

If a map is printed on both sides of a sheet at a consistent scale, record the total dimensions of the map followed by the dimensions of the sheet.

    300        $c 45 × 80 cm, on sheet 50 × 44 cm

RDA 3.5.3 Dimensions of Still Image

Describe *dimensions of still image* by recording the pictorial area in height × width, diameter, or other dimensions, as appropriate.

    300        $c 33 × 25 cm
    300        $c 6 cm in diameter
    300        $c 7 × 5 cm oval

If the still image measures less than half the size of the sheet or if the sheet contains substantial content that is not pictorial (e.g., text), apply the convention in the following example:

    300        $c 20 × 31 cm, on sheet 42 × 50 cm

RDA 3.6 Base Material

Base material is defined as *the underlying physical material of a resource.* For the base material, record one or more terms like *canvas, ceramic, glass, metal, paper, porcelain, stone, textile, wood,* or some other concise term. The new MARC tag for base material is 340 subfield $a.

    340        $a canvas

Record the base material for microfilm, microfiche, photographic film, and motion picture using one or more of the following terms: *acetate, diacetate, nitrate, polyester, safety base,* and *triacetate.*

RDA 3.7 Applied Material

Applied material is defined as *a physical or chemical substance applied to a base material of a resource.* For applied material, record one or more terms like *acrylic paint, chalk, charcoal, dye, ink, oil paint, pastel, watercolor,* or some other concise term. The new MARC tag for applied material is field 340 subfield $c.

        340        $c charcoal

For the emulsion on microfilm and microfiche, record one or more terms like *diazo, mixed, silver halide, vesicular,* or some other concise term.

RDA 3.8 Mount

Mount is defined as *the physical material used for the support or backing to which the base material of a resource has been attached.* Record the mount using one or more terms from the same list of base material terms (e.g., *Bristol board* and *wood*). If none of the terms applies, use another term that would describe it concisely. The new MARC tag for mount is field 340 subfield $e.

        340        $e wood

RDA 3.9 Production Method

Production method is defined as *the process used to produce a resource.* For the production method of resources other than manuscripts and tactile resources, record one or more terms like *blueprint, etching, lithograph, photocopy, photoengraving, print, pastel, woodcut,* or some other concise term. The new MARC tag for production method is field 340 subfield $d.

        340        $d etching

For the production method of a manuscript, record *holograph, manuscript, printout, typescript,* or some other concise term. If the manuscript is a copy, add *carbon copy, photocopy,* or *transcript* in parentheses. Add *handwritten, typewritten,* or *printout* in parentheses to *transcript.* If none of the terms applies, use another that would describe it concisely.

        340        $d holograph (carbon copy)
        340        $d manuscript (transcript, handwritten)

For the production method of a tactile resource, record *embossed, solid dot, swell paper, thermoform,* or some other concise term.

> 340 $d solid dot

RDA 3.10 Generation

Generation is defined as *the relationship between an original carrier and the carrier of a reproduction made from the original.* For the generation of an audio recording, record *master tape, tape duplication master, disc master, mother, stamper, test pressing,* or some other concise term. For the generation of a digital resource, record *original, master, derivative master,* or some other concise term. For the generation of a microform, record *first generation, printing master, service copy, mixed generation,* or some other concise term. For the generation of a motion picture film, record *original, master, duplicate, reference print, viewing copy,* or some other concise term. For the generation of a videotape, record *first generation, second generation, master copy, second generation, show copy,* or some other concise term. The new MARC tag for generation is field 340 subfield $j.

> 340 $j master tape, tape duplication
> 340 $j mixed generation

RDA 3.11 Layout

Layout is defined as *the arrangement of text, images, tactile notation, etc., in a resource.* For the layout of sheets other than cartographic images and tactile text, record *single sided* or *double sided.* The new MARC tag for layout is field 340 subfield $k.

> 340 $k double sided

For the layout of cartographic images, record *both sides* if the image is continued on the other side of a sheet. Record *back to back* if the same image is represented on each side of the sheet in different languages.

For layout of musical notation, record one or more of the following terms: *bar by bar, bar over bar, line by line, line over line, melody chord system, open score, outline, paragraph, section by section, short form scoring, single line,* or *vertical score.*

For layout of tactile text, record one or more of the following terms: *single sided, double sided,* or *double-line spacing.*

RDA 3.12 Book Format

Book format results from *folding a printed sheet to form a gathering of leaves.* For book format record one of the following terms: *folio, 4to, 8vo, 12mo, 16mo, 24mo, 32mo, 48mo,* or *64mo.* The new MARC tag for book format is field 340 subfield $m.

> 340 $m 24mo

RDA 3.13 Font Size

Font size is defined as *the size of the type used to represent the characters and symbols in a resource*. For font size, record *giant print*, *large print*, or some other concise term. Optionally, add the dimensions of the type in parentheses (e.g., *giant print (36 point)*). The new MARC tag for font size is field 340 subfield $n.

340      $n large print

RDA 3.14 Polarity

Polarity is defined as *the relationship of the colours and tones in an image to the colours and tones of the object reproduced*. For polarity, record *negative, positive,* or *mixed polarity*. For motion picture films, the details involve the form of print, such as *negative, positive, reversal, reversal internegative, internegative, interpositive, colour separation, duplicate, fine grain duplicating positive,* and *fine grain duplicating negative*. The new MARC tag for polarity is field 340 subfield $o.

340      $o positive

RDA 3.15 Reduction Ratio

Reduction ratio is defined as *the size of a micro-image in relation to the original from which it was produced*. The new MARC tag for reduction ratio is field 340 subfield $f.

340      $f low reduction *(for ratios of less than 16x)*
340      $f normal reduction *(for ratios between 16x and 30x)*
340      $f high reduction *(for ratios between 31x and 60x)*
340      $f very high reduction *(for ratios between 61x and 90x)*
340      $f ultra high reduction (150x) *(for ratios over 90x)*

RDA 3.16 Sound Characteristic

Sound characteristic is defined as *a technical specification relating to the encoding of sound in a resource*. The new MARC field for sound characteristic is field 344.

For *type of recording*, record *analog, digital,* or some other concise term in MARC field 344 subfield $a.

344      $a digital

For *recording medium*, record *magnetic, magneto-optical, optical,* or some other concise term in MARC field 344 subfield $b.

344      $b optical

Playing speed is recorded in MARC field 344 subfield $c. Record the playing speed of an analog disc in rpm. Record the playing speed of a digital disc in m/s. Record the playing speed of an analog tape in cm/s or in inches per second (ips). Record the playing speed of a sound-track film in frames per second (fps).

> 344 $c 78 rpm

Groove characteristic is recorded in MARC field 344 subfield $d. For groove width of an analog disc, record *coarse groove, microgroove,* or some other concise term. For groove pitch of an analog cylinder, record *fine, standard,* or some other concise term.

> 344 $c coarse groove

For *track configuration* record either *center track* or *edge track* in MARC field 344 subfield $e.

> 344 $e edge track

Record *tape configuration* in MARC field 344 subfield $f.

> 344 $f 12 track

For *configuration of playback channels,* record *mono, stereo, quadraphonic, surround,* or some other concise term in MARC field 344 subfield $g.

> 344 $g stereo

For *special playback characteristic,* record one or more terms like *CCIR standard, Dolby, Dolby-A encoded,* or some other concise term in MARC field 344 subfield $h.

> 344 $h Dolby

RDA 3.17 Projection Characteristic of Motion Picture Film

Projection characteristic of motion picture film is defined as a *technical specification relating to the projection of a motion picture film* and is recorded in the new MARC field 345.

For *presentation format,* record one or more terms such as *Cinerama, IMAX, Panavision, 3D,* or some other concise term in MARC field 345 subfield $a.

> 345 $a 3D

Record *projection speed* in frames per second (fps) in MARC field 345 subfield $b.

> 345 $b 20 fps

RDA 3.18 Video Characteristic

Video characteristic is defined as *a technical specification relating to the encoding of video images in a resource* and is recorded in the new MARC field 346.

For *video format* record a term such as *Beta, 8mm, Laser optical, U-matic, VHS*, or some other concise term in MARC field 346 subfield $a.

> 346 $a VHS

For *broadcast standard*, record *HDTV, NTSC, PAL, SECAM*, or some other concise term in MARC field 346 subfield $b.

> 346 $a PAL

RDA 3.19 Digital File Characteristic

Digital file characteristic is defined as *a technical specification relating to the digital encoding of text, image, audio, video, and other types of data in a resource.* It is recorded in the new MARC field 347.

For *file type* record one or more terms like *audio file, data file, image file, program file, text file, video file*, or some other concise term in MARC field 347 subfield $a.

> 347 $a audio file

For *encoding format* record one or more terms like *CD audio, MP3, Excel, XML, JPEG, CAD, HTML, PDF, RealVideo*, or some other concise term in MARC field 347 subfield $b.

> 347 $b PDF

Record *file size* in terms of kilobytes (KB), megabytes (MB), or gigabytes (GB) in MARC field 347 subfield $c.

> 347 $c 270 KB

Record *resolution* in terms of pixels in MARC field 347 subfield $d.

> 347 $d 2 megapixels

Record *regional encoding* in MARC field 347 subfield $e.

> 347 $e region 3

Record *transmission speed* in terms of kilobytes per second (kbs) in MARC field 347 subfield $f.

347        $f 32 kbs

For digital representation of cartographic content record the data type (i.e., *raster*, *vector*, or *point*), the object type (e.g., *point*, *line*, *polygon*, or *pixel*), or the number of objects used to represent spatial information.

RDA 3.20 Equipment or System Requirement

Equipment or system requirement is defined as *the equipment or system required for use, playback, etc., of an analog, digital, etc., resource.* It is recorded in MARC field 340 subfield $i or in MARC field 538.

340        $i Ibord Model 74 tape reader
538        $a System requirements: IBM PC; 64K; color card; 2 disk drives.

RDA 3.21 Item-Specific Carrier Characteristic

Item-specific carrier characteristic is defined as *a characteristic that applies to the carrier or carriers of the specific item being described and is assumed not to apply to other items exemplifying the same manifestation.* It is recorded in a MARC note field.

500        $a Library's copy missing page 45. $5 [code identifying the
           library]

RDA 3.22 Note

Note is defined as *an annotation providing additional information relating to data recorded in another element* and is usually recorded in MARC field 500.

500        $a Stuffed animals made to look like microbes, magnified
           1 million times, with eyes added.
500        $a Pages also numbered 348–580.
500        $a Opposite pages bear duplicate numbering.
500        $a Printed area measures 25 × 14 cm.

RDA CHAPTER 4: PROVIDING ACQUISITION
AND ACCESS INFORMATION

RDA Chapter 4 provides guidelines on how to record elements that mainly help users obtain resources. The chapter's contents include its purpose and scope, general guidelines on providing acquisition and access information, and detailed guidelines for the five elements contained in the chapter. For all elements in Chapter 4, the source of information is any source.

RDA 4.2 Terms of Availability

Terms of availability is defined as *the conditions under which the publisher, distributor, etc., will normally supply a resource or the price of a resource.* It includes the price for resources that are for sale and other terms for resources that are not for sale.

020     $a 0893331163: $c18.00 ($15.00 to members)
024   2_ $a M571100511: $c $20.00
037     $b Sheldon Museum of Art, P.O. Box 880300, Lincoln, NE 68588–0300 $c $4.95 (single issue) $c (free with museum membership)
500     $a "Not for sale. This CD is free to all 2010–2011 ITG members"—Container.

RDA 4.3 Contact Information

Contact information is defined as *information relating to an organization, etc., from which a resource may be obtained.* It usually includes the name and address of the publisher, distributor, or archival repository holding the resource. Record contact information if considered important for access.

037     $b Globe Pequot Press, PO Box 480, Guilford, CT 06437
037     $b University of Washington Libraries, Box 352900, Seattle, WA 98195–2900 $c open access

RDA 4.4 Restrictions on Access

Restrictions on access is defined as *limitations placed on access to a resource.*

506     $a Access restricted to subscribing institutions.

RDA 4.5 Restrictions on Use

Restrictions on use is defined as *limitations placed on uses such as reproduction, publication, exhibition, etc.*

540     $a Restricted: reproduction or resale prohibited without written permission, Smithsonian Institution.

RDA 4.6 Uniform Resource Locator

Uniform resource locator, or URL, is defined as *the address of a remote access resource.*

856   40 $u http://frontera.library.ucla.edu/

CONCLUSION

This chapter provided detailed coverage of the bibliographic elements used for help-ing users identify, select, and obtain manifestations and items. It outlined the general guidelines for transcription and provided the scope notes and sources of information for many of the elements. It showed examples of how many of the elements are transcribed and recorded in the MARC bibliographic record, illustrating the relevant ISBD punctuation and the appropriate MARC field, subfields, and indicators.

The RDA elements described in this chapter constitute a substantial portion of the description of a resource, encoded in the MARC bibliographic record in fields 2XX–5XX. Some of the elements chapter 5 of this book also cover descriptive infor-mation. However, other elements address access and authority data. Chapter 5 makes the distinction between elements meant to be recorded in the bibliographic record and those meant exclusively for the authority record. Throughout the process, the reader will slowly uncover the various data elements available to the cataloger that can collectively provide rich data to optimize the functionality of both bibliographic and authority data.

5

Attributes of Works and Expressions

The second section of RDA contains three chapters (Chapters 5–7) that provide instructions for recording attributes of works and expressions. Specifically:

- RDA Chapter 5, "General Guidelines on Recording Attributes of Works and Expressions," offers general guidelines that provide the context for the concepts covered in RDA Chapters 6 and 7. It also provides instructions for recording authority data in support of the FRAD user tasks "contextualizing" and "justifying."
- RDA Chapter 6, "Identifying Works and Expressions," provides instructions on recording attributes that support the "identify" user task.
- RDA Chapter 7, "Describing Content," provides instructions on recording attributes that mainly support the "select" user task.

This chapter begins with a focus on RDA Chapter 5 guidelines that provide information on the level of establishment for an access point, guidance for documenting the sources used to justify data in the access points and variable fields of authority records, and instructions on recording notes for contextualizing authority data. It then details the data elements covered in RDA Chapters 6 and 7, noting if the element is core and providing the relevant MARC fields for many of the elements. Because RDA makes no explicit distinction between bibliographic and authority records, this chapter explains when an element or group of elements should be recorded in either or both types of record. As with many RDA elements, information for most RDA Section 2 elements can be taken from any source. Therefore, the source of information is mentioned in this chapter only for those elements that stray from this pattern.

RDA CHAPTER 5: GENERAL GUIDELINES ON RECORDING ATTRIBUTES OF WORKS AND EXPRESSIONS

RDA Chapter 5 provides general guidelines on recording work and expression attributes and on constructing authorized and variant access points for works and expressions. It gives an explanation of the terminology used throughout RDA Section 2; outlines the functional objectives and principles addressed by Section 2 elements; lists the RDA Chapter 6 and 7 elements that are core; and explains how to address language and script for transcription of certain elements. It also has three elements—*status of identification, source consulted,* and *cataloguer's note*—which provide instructions for catalogers working with authority data. The following discussion focuses on those three elements.

RDA 5.7 Status of Identification

Status of identification is defined as *an indication of the level of authentication of the data identifying a work or expression.* It maps to MARC authority control field 008, byte 33 for "Level of establishment." If there are enough data to fully establish an authorized access point for a work or expression, code the byte with "a" for *fully established.* If there are not enough data to satisfactorily establish an authorized access point for a work or expression, code the byte with "c" for *provisional.* If the data are taken from a record without the resource in hand, code the byte with "d" for *preliminary.*

RDA 5.8 Source Consulted

Source consulted is defined as *a resource used in determining the title or other identifying attributes of a work or expression.* For citing the sources used for determining the preferred title, variant title, and other identifying attributes, provide the data in MARC authority field 670. For citing sources that provided no information, use field 675. RDA 5.8.1.3 instructs the cataloger to add the statement "(No information found)" to the citation of a source that provided no information, but in the MARC environment, encoding such a source in the MARC 675 field (which is itself defined as "Source Data Not Found") is a substitute for the explicit statement.

> 670 $a Pacheco, Cristina. La luz de México, 1988 $b series title page (Autores de Guanajuato) title page verso (Colección Autores de Guanajuato)
> 675 $a Grove music online, searched December 8, 2007

RDA 5.9 Cataloguer's Note

Cataloguer's note is defined as *an annotation that might be helpful to those using or revising the authorized access point representing a work or expression, or creating an au-*

thorized access point representing a related work or expression. It can be used for citing the RDA instructions used for constructing access points, justifying information, for explaining the limitations on access point usage, and differentiating works with similar titles. It can also be used to for providing information that may assist other catalogers in revising the data. It maps to MARC authority field 667.

> 667 $a Preferred title chosen as Don Giovanni per 6.14.2.3, better known title in the same language
> 667 $a Not the same as FAO animal production and health paper

RDA CHAPTER 6: IDENTIFYING WORKS AND EXPRESSIONS

RDA Chapter 6 provides guidelines on recording attributes that help users identify works and expressions. The instructions detail how to construct authorized access points for works and expressions used in bibliographic and authority records. They also cover the various elements that can be added to an access point to differentiate works and expressions with similar titles. The guidelines also explain when and how to construct variant access points for use in authority records. Finally, they provide guidance on recording data, mainly in the variable fields of authority records.

Many of the elements in Chapter 6 map to MARC fields that were created in both the bibliographic and authority format. This includes authorized access points as well as variable fields. Although authorized access points are routinely used in both bibliographic and authority records, the variable fields for Chapter 6 elements—with the exception of *content type*—are, in practice, recorded only in authority records. This is explained for each of those elements as they are covered. Also note that although authorized access points for works and expressions can appear in bibliographic records, for the sake of simplicity the examples used in this chapter will show them only in the form in which they would appear if in an authority record.

Chapter 6 covers five types of works: general works, musical works, religious works, legal works, and official communications. It begins with works in general and provides instructions on the preferred title for the work, the variant title for the work, other work-related attributes, and then expression-level attributes. It follows this same pattern for musical works, religious works, legal works, and official communications. The chapter ends with guidelines on how to construct access points for each type of resource.

Conventions for Preferred Titles

Many of the conventions outlined in RDA 1.7 apply to titles of all types of works. Preferred titles are capitalized according to RDA Appendix A. Numbers are recorded as numerals or as words, depending on how they appear on the source. Diacritical marks are recorded as they appear on the source and can optionally be added if absent, following the standard usage for the language. Acronyms and initials are recorded without spaces. Only abbreviations that appear on the source should be recorded. In addition to these conventions, Chapter 6 provides guidelines on titles with initial articles. The default instruction says to retain the initial article, but catalogers may optionally omit it unless it is integral to the title (e.g., *Los Angeles times*).

Generalities for Variant Titles

Many of the same guidelines for variant titles apply to all types of works. Variant titles can include titles cited in reference sources, titles resulting from different transliterations, and titles of manifestations that differ significantly from the preferred title and that would reasonably be searched. If the preferred title of a work has one or more alternative linguistic forms—such as different spellings, different translations, different transliterations, or different scripts—these forms can be recorded as variant titles.

> Preferred title: *Aesop's fables*
> Variant title: *Aisōpou mythoi*

Variant titles can also be titles that differ from the preferred title other than having alternative linguistic forms.

> Preferred title: *Two towers*
> Variant title: *2 towers*
> Variant title: *Lord of the rings. Two towers*

RDA 6.2 Title of the Work

Title of the work is defined as *a word, character, or group of words and/or characters by which a work is known.* It has two subelements: *preferred title for the work* and *variant title for the work.*

Preferred Title for the Work

Preferred title for the work is a core element. It is defined as *the title or form of title chosen to identify the work.* For sources of information for the preferred titles of works created after 1500, use resources embodying the works or reference sources. For works created before 1501, use (in order of preference) modern reference sources, modern editions, early editions, or manuscript copies.

Determining the preferred title for general works. For works created after 1500, base the preferred title on the title in the original language in which it is most commonly known. Otherwise, use the title appearing on the original edition or (if the work is simultaneously published with different titles under the same language) on the first resource received.

First published under the title: The tragicall historie of Hamlet,
Prince of Denmarke
Most commonly known title: Hamlet
Preferred title: *Hamlet*

For works created before 1501, base the preferred title on the title in the original language in which it is identified in reference works. Otherwise, use the title most frequently found (in order of preference) in modern editions, in early editions, or in manuscript copies.

Preferred title: *Beowulf*

For certain Greek and Byzantine works, base the preferred title on (in order of preference) a well-established title in the preferred language of the cataloging agency, the Latin title (if applicable), or the Greek title. For anonymous works written neither in Greek nor in a preferred script of the agency, choose a well-established title in the cataloging agency's preferred language.

Parts of general works. Record the distinctive title of a part as the preferred title.

Preferred title: *Two towers* (**not** *Lord of the Rings. Two towers*)

However, record single parts with indistinctive titles and consecutively numbered parts with nondistinctive titles as subdivisions of the preferred title for the work.

Preferred title: *Iliad. Book 1*
Preferred title: *Iliad. Book 1–6*

Record groups of nonconsecutively numbered parts with nondistinctive titles under the preferred titles for each part or alternatively designate them collectively as *Selections* of the main work.

Preferred title: *Iliad. Book 2*   &   Preferred title: *Illiad. Book 4*

OR

Preferred title: *Iliad. Selections*

Compilations. Record *Works* for complete works of various forms. Record the appropriate term for works in a single form. For incomplete works, add the term *Selections* as appropriate.

Preferred title: *Works*
Preferred title: *Novels*
Preferred title: *Works. Selections.*
Preferred title: *Speeches. Selections.*

Variant Title for the Work

    Variant title for the work is defined as *a title or form of title by which a work is known that differs from the title or form of title chosen as the preferred title for the work.*

        Preferred title: *Plays. Selections*
        Variant title: *Selected plays of Lady Gregory*

RDA 6.3 Form of Work

    Form of work is a core element when needed to distinguish one work from other similarly named works, persons, families, or corporate bodies. It is defined as *a class or genre to which a work belongs.* Form of work can be recorded as a separate element, as part of an access point, or both. When recorded as a separate element, the form of work is recorded in MARC authority field 380 subfield $a. The form of work may also be recorded in the same field and subfield in a bibliographic record.

        130   _0 $a Charlemagne (**Play**)
        380      $a Play

RDA 6.4 Date of Work

    Date of work is a core element when needed to distinguish a work from other similarly named works, persons, families, or corporate bodies. *Date of work* is defined as *the earliest date associated with a work*, which can be the date it was created or the date it was first published or released. For treaties record the year, month, and date. For other works, just record the year (or years). Date of work can be recorded as a separate element, as part of an access point, or both. When recorded as a separate element, the date of work is recorded in MARC authority field 046 subfields $k and $l.

        046      $k 1965
        130   _0 $a Dublin magazine (**1965**)
        046      $k 1987 $l 1989
        130   _0 $a Paris is burning (**1987–1989**)

RDA 6.5 Place of Origin of the Work

    Place of origin of the work is a core element when needed to distinguish a work from other similarly named works, persons, families, or corporate bodies. It is defined as *the country or other territorial jurisdiction from which a work originated.* Place of origin of the work can be recorded as a separate element, as part of an access point, or both. Regardless of where it is recorded, formulate the place of origin the way it would appear in the qualifier of an access point. When recording the place as a separate element, record it in MARC authority field 370 subfield $g.

```
130   _0 $a Science and society (New York, N.Y.)
370      $g New York, N.Y.
```

RDA 6.6 Other Distinguishing Characteristic of the Work

Other distinguishing characteristic of the work is a core element when needed to distinguish a work from other similarly named works, persons, families, or corporate bodies. It is defined as *a characteristic other than form of work, date of work, or place of origin of the work.* Other distinguishing characteristic of the work can be recorded as a separate element, as part of an access point, or both. When recorded as a separate element, the other distinguishing characteristic is recorded in MARC authority field 381 subfield $a. Other distinguishing characteristic may also be recorded in the same field and subfield in a bibliographic record.

```
130   _0 $a Genesis (Old Saxon poem)
381      $a Old Saxon poem
```

RDA 6.7 History of the Work

History of the work is defined as *information about the history of a work.* This element is never recorded as part of an access point. It is recorded as a separate element, and it maps to MARC authority field 678 subfield $a.

```
678      $a Originally written as a serial and published in 19 issues over
         20 months from March 1836 to October 1837. There was no issue
         in May 1837 as Dickens was in mourning for his sister-in- law.
```

RDA 6.8 Identifier for the Work

Identifier for the work is a core element. It is defined as *a character string uniquely associated with a work, or with a surrogate for a work (e.g., an authority record).* Its purpose is to differentiate a work from other works. RDA instructs the cataloger to precede the identifier with the name of the agency assigning it. In the MARC environment, this number is generally assigned by the system, and the MARC field number usually conveys information about the cataloging agency associated with the identifier.

```
010   $a no2010196005          Library of Congress Control Number
016   $a 0010C0008    Library and Archives Canada Control Number
035   $a (OCoLC)oca08704072        OCLC System Control Number
```

RDA 6.9 Content Type

Content type is a core element. It is the first expression-level attribute covered by Chapter 6. *Content type* is defined as *a categorization reflecting the fundamental form of communication in which the content is expressed and the human sense through which it is intended to be perceived.* The content type can also reflect the number of spatial dimensions (e.g., cartographic three-dimensional form) and the presence or absence of movement (e.g., three-dimensional moving image). For content type, record one or more terms listed in RDA 6.1, such as *cartographic image, notated movement, performed music, spoken word, still image, text, three-dimensional form, two-dimensional moving image,* or some other term from the closed list. If none of the terms applies, record *other.* If the content type cannot be determined, record *unspecified.*

The content type can be recorded as a separate element, as part of an access point, or both. When recorded as a separate element of an authority record, the content type is recorded in MARC authority field 336 subfield $a. The same field exists in the bibliographic format where the content type is always recorded. When the content type forms part of an access point, pure application of MARC 21 coding calls for it to be placed in $h; however, the current policy for those who use the Library of Congress Name Authority File is to place it in $s and to capitalize the term. The following example follows pure MARC 21 coding.

> 100   1_ $a Bradley, C. Alan, $d 1938– $t Flavia de Luce mystery.
> **$h spoken word**
> 336 $a spoken word

RDA 6.10 Date of Expression

Date of expression is a core element when needed to differentiate expressions of the same work. It is defined as *the earliest date associated with an expression.* If the date of expression cannot be determined, use the date of the earliest published manifestation. The date of expression can be recorded as a separate element, as part of an access point, or both. When recorded as a separate element, the date of expression is recorded in MARC authority field 046 subfields $k and $l.

> 046 $k 2000
> 100   0_ $a Aeschines. $t Works. $l English. $f **2000**

RDA 6.11 Language of Expression

Language of expression is a core element. It is defined as *a language in which a work is expressed.* Record the language using a term preferred by the cataloging agency. Language of expression can be recorded as a separate element, as part of an access point, or both. When recorded as a separate element, the language will be recorded in MARC authority field 377. Language may also be recorded in the same field in a bibliographic record.

> 100   1_ $a Shakespeare, William, $d 1564–1616. $t Romeo and Juliet.
> **$l Spanish**
> 377 $a spa

In MARC, language terms are recorded in the three-digit code listed in the *MARC Code List for Languages* and are recorded in the subfield $a. If the language term does not appear on the list, then the term is spelled out and recorded in the subfield $l, while the code for the general language under which the more specific language falls is recorded in the subfield $a.

> 377 $a bnt $l Lenje

RDA 6.12 Other Distinguishing Characteristic of the Expression

Other distinguishing characteristic of the expression is a core element when needed to differentiate expressions of the same work. It is defined as *a characteristic other than content type, language of expression, or date of expression.* When recorded as a separate element, the other distinguishing characteristic is recorded in MARC authority field 381. Other distinguishing characteristic may also be recorded in the same field in a bibliographic record.

> 130   _0 $a Gesar (**Buriat version**)
> 381 $a Buriat version

RDA 6.13 Identifier for the Expression

Identifier for the expression is a core element. It is defined as *a character string uniquely associated with an expression, or with a surrogate for an expression (e.g., an authority record).* Its purpose is to differentiate an expression from other expressions. As with the identifier for the work, RDA instructs the cataloger to precede the identifier for the expression with name of the agency assigning it, this number is generally assigned by the system, and the agency associated with the identifier can be gleaned from the MARC field number.

> 010 $a n 82100264 *Library of Congress Control Number*

RDA 6.14 Title of a Musical Work

Title of a musical work is defined as *a word, character, or group of words and/or characters by which a musical work is known.* It has two subelements: *preferred title for a musical work* and *variant title for a musical work.*

Preferred Title for a Musical Work

Preferred title for a musical work is a core element. It is defined as *the title or form of title chosen to identify the musical work.* As with general works, the preferred titles for musical works created after 1500 can be determined from resources embodying the works or from reference sources. For works created before 1501, use (in order of preference) modern reference sources, modern editions, early editions, or manuscript copies.

Generally base the preferred title on the composer's original title in the language in which the musical work was presented.

> Resource described: The golden cockerel
> Preferred title: *Zolotoĭ petushok*

Exceptions include works that are more commonly known by other titles in the original language, titles that are lengthy, and titles that involve the same type of composition and numbered sequence.

Omissions. When recording the preferred title for a musical work, omit medium of performance, key, numbers (such as serial numbers, opus numbers, thematic index numbers, and other numbers not integral to the title), date of composition, and adjectives and epithets not part of the original title.

> ~~String~~ quartet
> Concerto ~~in A minor, op. 54~~
> Symphonie ~~no. 40~~
> ~~Five~~ little pieces ~~for piano~~
> ~~Mozart's favorite~~ minuet

Titles comprising solely the name of one type of composition. Record the preferred title for musical works comprising solely the name of one type of composition, if applicable. Generally record it in the plural.

> Resource described: Quintetto VI in sol maggiore
> Preferred title: *Quintets*

For concert performances, record *Étude*, *Fantasia*, or *Sinfonia concertante* (or their cognates) where applicable. Record *Duets*, where applicable.

Parts of musical works. Record parts of musical works as appropriate.

> Preferred title: *Ungarische Tänze. Nr. 1* (numbered part)
> Preferred title: *Ungarische Tänze. Nr. 5–6* (consecutively numbered parts)
> Preferred title: *Aïda. Celeste Aïda* (named part, unnumbered)
> Preferred title: *Così fan tutte. Come scoglio* (individual name for each numbered part)
> Preferred title: *Estro armonico. N. 8* (same name for all numbered parts)
> Preferred title: *Messiah. Pifa* (part of a larger part)

Compilations. Record the preferred titles for compilations of musical works as appropriate.

> Preferred title: *Works* (complete works of various types and media)
> Preferred title: *Chamber music* (complete works in one broad medium)
> Preferred title: *Piano music* (complete works in one specific medium)
> Preferred title: *Orchestra music. Selections* (incomplete works)

Variant Title for a Musical Work

Variant title for a musical work is defined as *a title or form of title by which a musical work is known that differs from the title or form of title chosen as the preferred title for the work.* It can be taken from resources embodying the work or from reference sources.

> Preferred title: *O Tannenbaum*
> Variant title: *O Christmas tree*

RDA 6.15 Medium of Performance

Medium of performance is a core element when needed to distinguish a work from another work or identify a work with an indistinct title. It is defined as *the instrument, instruments, voice, voices, etc., for which a musical work was originally conceived.* Record medium of performance elements in the following order: voices, keyboard instrument (if there is more than one non-keyboard instrument), other instruments in score order, and continuo.

Medium of performance can be recorded as a separate element, as part of an access point, or both. When recorded as a separate element, medium of performance is recorded in MARC authority field 382 subfield $a. Medium of performance may also be recorded in the same field in a bibliographic record.

> 100   1_ $a Widor, Charles Marie, $d 1844–1937. $t Symphonies, $m **organ**
> 382 $a organ

Standard combinations of instruments. RDA provides a table (table 6.2) for standard combinations of instruments played by three to five musicians. If the preferred title conveys the number of players (e.g., trio, quintets), omit that designation from the medium of performance.

> Preferred title: *Quintets*
> 382 $a piano

If the preferred title lacks such a term, and the instruments match the standard combination listed in RDA table 6.2, include the term for the number of players in the medium of performance.

> Preferred title: *Air and jig*
> 382 $a piano trio

If the preferred title lacks a term conveying the number of players and the instruments differ from those listed as the standard combination, record each instrument.

> Preferred title: Blues
> 382 $a piano $a tubas (2) $a strings

Individual instruments. Record individual instruments using a term in the language preferred by the cataloging agency. RDA provides guidelines for common terms.

    382      $a cello
    382      $a harpsichord
    382      $a pianos (2), 4 hands

Accompanying ensembles. Record accompanying ensembles with one performer to a part when applicable.

    382      $a percussion ensemble

For instrumental music intended for orchestra, record *orchestra*, *string orchestra*, or *band*.

    382      $a band

Voices with or without accompaniment. Record solo voices where applicable.

    382      $a mezzo-soprano
    382      $a mixed solo voices
    382      $a men's solo voices

Record choral ensembles where applicable.

    382      $a unison voices
    382      $a women's voices

Record the accompaniment for songs, lieder, and melodies where applicable.

    382      $a guitar accompaniment

Generally specified and unspecified medium of performance. Record a collective term or general family of instruments where applicable.

    382      $a plucked instrument
    382      $a chordal instrument

Record the range or general type of instrument or voice where applicable.

    382      $a low instrument
    382      $a male voice

Indicate when some instruments are unspecified.

    382      $a unspecified instrument $a piano

Indicate if the medium of performance is not specified and cannot be ascertained.

    382      $a unspecified

RDA 6.16 Numeric Designation of a Musical Work

Numeric designation of a musical work is a core element when needed to distinguish a work from another work or identify a work with an indistinct title. It is defined as *a serial number, opus number, or thematic index number assigned to a musical work by a composer, publisher, or a musicologist.* The numeric designation can be recorded as a separate element, as part of an access point, or both. When recorded as a separate element, the numeric designation is recorded in MARC authority field 383. Numeric designation may also be recorded in the same field in a bibliographic record.

> 100 1_ $a Peeters, Flor, $d 1903–1986. $t Chorale preludes, $n **op. 69**
> 383 $a op. 69

When recording the numeric designation in MARC field 383, use subfield $a for the serial number, subfield $b for the opus number, and subfield $c for the thematic index number.

> 383 $a no. 5
> 383 $a 2nd book
> 383 $b op. 2, no. 2
> 383 $c BWV 232

RDA 6.17 Key

Key is a core element when needed to distinguish a work from another work or identify a work with an indistinct title. It is defined as *the set of pitch relationships that establishes the tonal center, or principal tonal center, of a musical work. Key is indicated by its pitch name and its mode, when it is major or minor.* Record the key if it is commonly identified in reference sources, if it appears in the composer's original title or the title of the first manifestation, or if it is apparent from the resource being cataloged (and it was not transposed). The key can be recorded as a separate element, as part of an access point, or both. When recorded as a separate element, the key is recorded in MARC authority field 384. The key may also be recorded in the same field in a bibliographic record. The first indicator of field 384 is coded "0" for the original key and "1" for a transposed key.

> 100 1_ $a Poulenc, Francis, $d 1899–1963. $t Mass, $r **G major**
> 384 0_ $a G major

RDA 6.18 Other Distinguishing Characteristic of the Expression of a Musical Work

Other distinguishing characteristic of the expression of a musical work is a core element when needed to distinguish a work from another work. It is defined as *a characteristic that serves to differentiate an expression of a musical work from another expression of the same work (e.g., an arrangement, sketches, vocal score).*

Other distinguishing characteristic can be recorded as a separate element, as part of an access point, or both. When recorded as a separate element, the other distinguishing characteristic is recorded in MARC authority field 381. Other distinguishing characteristic may also be recorded in the same field in a bibliographic record.

> 100   1_ $a John, Elton. $t Candle in the wind; $o **arranged**
> **381 $a arranged**

> 100   1_ $a Gillis, Don, $d 1912–1978. $t Quartets, $m strings, $n no. 6.
> $p Passacaglia (**Sketches**)
> 381 $a Sketches

> 100   1_ $a Sullivan, Arthur, $d 1842–1900. $t Mikado. $s **Chorus score**
> 381 $a Chorus score

RDA 6.19 Title of a Legal Work

Title of a legal work is defined as *a word, character, or group of words and/or characters by which a legal work is known.* It has two subelements: *preferred title for a legal work* and *variant title for a legal work.*

Preferred Title for a Legal Work

Preferred title for a legal work is a core element. It is defined as *the title or form of title chosen to identify the work.* As with general works and musical works, the preferred titles of legal works created after 1500 can be determined from resources embodying the works or from reference sources. For works created before 1501, use (in order of preference) modern reference sources, modern editions, early editions, or manuscript copies.

Compilations of legislative enactments. For partial or complete compilations of legislative enactments of a jurisdiction *not* on a particular subject, record *Laws, etc.* as the preferred title.

> Preferred title: *Laws, etc.*

For compilations of legislative enactments of a jurisdiction on a particular subject that has a citation title, record the citation title as the preferred title.

> Preferred title: *Labor Code*

For compilations on a particular subject that lacks a citation code, follow the guidelines for recording preferred titles for general works.

Single legislative enactment. For a single legislative enactment, record (in order of preference) the official short title or citation title, an unofficial short title or citation title used in legal literature, the official title of the enactment, or any other official designation (such as the number or date).

Preferred title: *Corporations Act*
Preferred title: *Copyright Act of 1994*

Ancient laws, certain medieval laws, and customary laws. For works created after 1500, base the preferred title for ancient laws, certain medieval laws, and customary laws on the title in the original language in which it is most commonly known. Otherwise, use the title appearing on the original edition or (if the work is simultaneously published with different titles under the same language) on the first resource received. For works created before 1501, base the preferred title on the title in the original language in which it is identified in reference works. Otherwise, use the title most frequently found (in order of preference) in modern editions, in early editions, or in manuscript copies.

Resource described: The oldest code of laws in the world: the code of laws promulgated by Hammurabi, King of Babylon
Preferred title: *Code of Hammurabi*

Treaties and other agreements. Record *Treaties, etc.* for a treaty or some other agreement between two or more national governments, international intergovernmental bodies, the Holy See, and jurisdictions below the national level with treaty-making powers.

Preferred title: *Treaties, etc.*

However, if the treaty is multilateral and the name of the first signatory is unknown, record as the preferred title the name by which the treaty is known.

Preferred title: *Agreement Establishing the World Trade Organization*

For compilations of treaties and agreements between a party on one side and one or more parties on the other, record *Treaties, etc.* However, for a compilation identified by a collective name, record the collective name as the preferred title.

Preferred title: *Treaty of Utrecht*

Variant Title for a Legal Work

Variant title for a legal work is defined as *a title or form of title by which a legal work is known that differs from the title or form of title chosen as the preferred title for the work.* It can be taken from resources embodying the work or from reference sources.

Preferred title: *Treaty of Utrecht*
Variant title: *Freden i Utrecht*

Preferred title: *Matrimonial Affairs Act 1953*
Variant title: *Act No. 37 of 1953*

RDA 6.20 Date of a Legal Work

Date of a legal work is defined as *the earliest date associated with a legal work.* It has two subelements: *date of promulgation of a law, etc.* and *date of signing of a treaty, etc.*

Date of Promulgation of a Law, Etc.

Date of promulgation of a law, etc. is a core element when needed to distinguish a legal work from other works, persons, families, or corporate bodies. It is defined as *the year a law, etc., was promulgated or brought into force.* Record it as a year.

```
046     $k 1998
110   1_ $a Madagascar. $t Code pénal (1998)
```

Date of Signing of a Treaty, Etc.

Date of signing of a treaty, etc. is a core element. It is defined as *the date a treaty, etc., or a protocol to a treaty, etc., was formally signed.* Record it in the access point as *year, name of month, number of day.* In MARC, the date of signing of a treaty is recorded in the 046 field and must follow ISO standard 8601, which prescribes the pattern *yyyymmdd.*

```
046     $k 19881201
110   1_ $a Spain. $t Treaties, etc. $g United States, $d 1988 December 1
```

RDA 6.21 Other Distinguishing Characteristic of a Legal Work

Other distinguishing characteristic of a legal work is a core element when needed to distinguish a legal work from other works, persons, families, or corporate bodies. It is defined as *a characteristic other than form of work, date of work, or place of origin of the work.* Record *Protocols, etc.* for separately cataloged protocols, extensions, amendments, and other pacts ancillary to a treaty or other agreement. The other distinguishing characteristic of a legal work can be recorded as a separate element, as part of an access point, or both. When recorded as a separate element, the other distinguishing characteristic is recorded in MARC authority field 381. Other distinguishing characteristic may also be recorded in the same field in a bibliographic record.

```
110   1_ $a Mali. $t Treaties, etc. $g United States, $d 1997 September 19.
          $k Protocols, etc., $d 2012 August 15
381       $a Protocols, etc.
```

RDA 6.22 Signatory to a Treaty, Etc.

Signatory to a treaty, etc. is a core element when needed to distinguish one legal work from another. It is defined as *a government or other party that has formally signed a treaty, etc., as an adherent to its terms and conditions.* The signatory to a treaty can be recorded as a separate element, as part of an access point, or both. When recorded as a separate element, the signatory to a treaty is recorded in MARC authority field 381. Signatory to a treaty may also be recorded in the same field in a bibliographic record.

110   1_ $a Mali. $t Treaties, etc. $g **United States**, $d 1997 November 19
381       $a Mali $a United States

RDA 6.23 Title of a Religious Work

Title of a religious work is defined as *a word, character, or group of words and/or characters by which a religious work is known.* It has two subelements: *preferred title for a religious work* and *variant title for a religious work.*

Preferred Title for a Religious Work

Preferred title for a religious work is a core element. It is defined as *the title or form of title chosen to identify the work.* For determining the preferred title for a sacred scripture, use a title from a reference source that covers the religious group to which the scripture belongs. Otherwise, use general reference sources. For apocryphal books, use a title frequently found in sources. For theological creeds and confessions of faith, use (in order of preference) a well-established title or the title in the original language. For liturgical works, generally use a well-established title written in the cataloging agency's preferred language. However, if the language of the corporate body sanctioning the liturgy differs from the preferred language, use a brief title in the language of the liturgy.

For parts of scriptures, generally record subdivisions under the main work. Record further subdivisions where applicable.

   Parts of the Bible
     Preferred title: *Bible. Old Testament*
     Preferred title: *Bible. Jeremiah*
     Preferred title: *Bible. Apocrypha. Esdras, 1st*
   Parts of Jewish scriptures
     Preferred title: *Talmud. Ḥagigah*
     Preferred title: *Mishnah. Avot*
     Preferred title: *Midrash ha-gadol. Numbers*
   Parts of Buddhist scriptures
     Preferred title: *Tipiṭaka. Abhidhammapiṭaka*
     Preferred title: *Tripiṭaka. Sūtrapiṭaka. Tantra*
   Parts of the Vedas
     Preferred title: *Vedas. Sāmaveda*
   Parts of the Aranyakas, Brahmanas, and Upanishads
     Preferred title: *Upanishads. Chāndogyopaniṣad*

Parts of the Jaina Āgama
   Preferred title: *Jaina Āgama. Aṅga*
Parts of the Avesta
   Preferred title: *Avesta. Yasna*
Parts of the Qur'an
   Preferred title: *Qur'an. Sūrat al-Baqarah*
   Preferred title: *Qur'an. Juz' 'Amma*
Parts of other sacred scriptures
   Preferred title: *Book of Mormon. Jacob*
   Preferred title: *Daswen Pādshāh kā Granth. Caubīsa avatāra. Kṛṣhṇāvatāra*

For a part of scripture more commonly known by its own title than by its designation as part of a larger work, record that title directly.

   Preferred title: *Lord's prayer*

For parts of liturgical works, record a well-established title.

   Preferred title: *Liturgy of St. John Chrysostom*
   Preferred title: *Mass, Sainte Thérèse*

Variant Title for a Religious Work

Variant title for a religious work is defined as *a title or form of title by which a religious work is known that differs from the title or form of title chosen as the preferred title for the work*. It can be taken from resources embodying the work or from reference sources.

   Preferred title: *Talmud Yerushalmi*
   Variant title: *Jerusalem Talmud*
   Preferred title: *Bible. Old Testament*
   Variant title: *Old Testament*

RDA 6.24 Date of Expression of a Religious Work

Date of expression of a religious work is a core element when needed to distinguish religious expressions of the same work. It is defined as *the earliest date associated with an expression of a religious work*, which may be the earliest manifestation embodying the expression. The date of expression of a religious work can be recorded as a separate element, as part of an access point, or both. When recorded as a separate element, the date is recorded in MARC authority field 046 subfield $k.

   046      $k 1923
   130   _0 $a Bible. $p Old Testament. $l Ethiopic. $f **1923**

RDA 6.25 Other Distinguishing Characteristic of the Expression of a Religious Work

Other distinguishing characteristic of the expression of a religious work is a core element when needed to distinguish religious expressions of the same work. It is defined as *a characteristic other than content type, language of expression, or date of expression*. It is used for recording version or translator. The other distinguishing characteristic can be recorded as a separate element, as part of an access point, or both. When recorded as a separate element, the other distinguishing characteristic is recorded in MARC authority field 381. Other distinguishing characteristic may also be recorded in the same field in a bibliographic record.

> 130 _0 $a Bible. $l English. $s **Authorized**. $f 2004
> 381 $a Authorized
>
> 130 _0 $a Bible. $l English. $s **Phillips**
> 381 $a Phillips

RDA 6.26 Title of an Official Communication

Title of an official communication is defined as *a word, character, or group of words and/or characters by which an official communication is known*. It has two subelements: *preferred title for an official communication* and *variant title for an official communication*.

Preferred Title for an Official Communication

Preferred title for an official communication is a core element. It is defined as *the title or form of title chosen to identify the work*. If the creator of an individual communication is the pope, use as the preferred title a short title by which the work is commonly known in the original language (generally Latin).

> Preferred title: *Populorum progressio*

If the communication from the Roman Curia is known by a brief title, choose it as the preferred title.

> Preferred title: *Communionis notio*

For other communications, follow the guidelines for general works.

Variant Title for an Official Communication

Variant title for an official communication is defined as *a title or form of title by which an official communication is known that differs from the title or form of title chosen as the preferred title for the work.* It can be taken from resources embodying the work or from reference sources.

> Preferred title: *In God's image*
> Variant title: *A imagen y semejanza de Dios*

RDA 6.27 Constructing Access Points to Represent Works and Expressions

RDA 6.27.1 Authorized Access Point Representing a Work

The preferred title for the work serves as the basis for the authorized access point representing that work. Sometimes the authorized access point for a work comprises solely the preferred title. This includes works with no known creator; works that are compilations by different creators; and works that are motion pictures, videos, or video games.

> **preferred title for work**
> 130　_0 $a Mysterious bottle of old hock
> 130　_0 $a Anthologie de la poésie baroque française
> 130　_0 $a Gunner palace

Sometimes the authorized access point for a work will comprise the preferred title for the work preceded by the authorized access point for the creator. This applies to a single work or a specifically titled compilation of works written by one creator.

> authorized access point for creator + **preferred title for work**
> 100　1_ $a Cassatt, Mary, $d 1844–1926. $t Children playing on the beach
> 100　1_ $a Whitman, Walt, $d 1819–1892. $t Leaves of grass
> 100　3_ $a Barner (Family). $t Barner family newsletter
> 111　2_ $a Capo Boi Conference on Neuroscience. $t Receptors as supramolecular entities

If a work has more than one creator, precede the preferred title with the authorized access point for the principal or first-named creator. However, if the collaborators responsible for creating a work include one or more corporate bodies, precede the preferred title with the authorized access point for the first-named body, regardless of whether it is preceded by names of persons or families in the source's layout.

> 110　2_ $a California Academy of Sciences. $t Catalog of the asteroid type-specimens and Fisher voucher specimens at the California Academy of Sciences

If a work has been adapted or revised with added commentary, annotations, illustrations, or other content to such an extent that it changes the nature of the work and it is presented as the work of the person, family, or corporate body who made the changes, construct the access point using the name of the adapter or reviser and the preferred title.

> 100 1_ $a Gray, Patsey. $t J.R.R. Tolkien's The hobbit
> 100 1_ $a Akram, Malik M. $t Comprehensive and exhaustive commentary on the Transfer of Property Act, 1882

Otherwise, if the work is presented as an edition or revision of a previously existing work, treat it as an expression of that work.

Sometimes one or more additions are needed to differentiate similarly named works, persons, families, corporate bodies, and places. These additions can be taken from other attributes, including form of work, date of the work, place of origin of the work, and other distinguishing characteristic of the work.

> {authorized access point for creator} + **preferred title for work** + *addition(s)*
> 130 _0 $a Scottish History Society (**Series**) *form of work added*
> 130 _0 $a Dublin magazine (**1965**) *date of the work added*
> 130 _0 $a Science and society (**New York, N.Y.**) *place of origin added*
> 100 1_ $a Eyck, Jan van, 1390–1440. $t Saint Francis receiving the stigmata (**Philadelphia Museum of Art**) *other distinguishing characteristic added*
> 130 _0 $a Harlow (**Motion picture: 1965: Segal**) *form of work, date of work, and other distinguishing characteristic added*

RDA 6.27.2 Authorized Access Point Representing a Part or Parts of a Work

Construct the authorized access point for one or more parts with distinctive and nondistinctive titles according to the conventions in the following examples:

> 100 1_ $a Tolkien, J. R. R. $q (John Ronald Reuel), $d 1892–1973. $t Two towers
> 100 0_ $a Homer. $t Iliad. $n Book 1
> 130 _0 $a Annual report on carcinogens. $p Executive summary
> 130 _0 $a Emergency health series. $n F
> 130 _0 $a Simpsons (Television program). $p King of the hill
> 100 _0 $a Homer. $t Iliad. $n Book 1–6
> 130 _0 $a Simpsons (Television program). $k Selections

RDA 6.27.3 Authorized Access Point Representing an Expression

To construct an access point for an expression, first start with the authorized access point for the work and add one or more expression-level attributes.

> **authorized access point for work** + *expression-level attribute(s)*

Add content type where applicable. (Note: When the content type forms part of an access point, pure application of MARC 21 coding calls for it to be placed in $h; however, the current policy at the time of this writing for those who use the Library of Congress Name Authority File is to place it in $s and to capitalize the term. The following example follows pure MARC 21 coding.)

> 100   1_ $a Bradley, C. Alan, $d 1938– $t Flavia de Luce mystery.
> $h **spoken word**

Add date of the expression where applicable.

> 100   1_ $a Catullus, Gaius Valerius. $t Works. $l Spanish. $f **2005**

Add language of the expression where applicable.

> 100   1_ $a Shakespeare, William, $d 1564–1616. $t Romeo and Juliet.
> $l **Czech**

Add another distinguishing characteristic of the expression where applicable.

> 100   1_ $a Langland, William, $d 1330?–1400? $t Piers Plowman (**A-text**)

Or add any combination of the above, such as language and another distinguishing characteristic (e.g., the name of the translator).

> 100   1_ $a Pushkin, Aleksandr Sergeevich, $d 1799–1837. $t Evgeniĭ
> Onegin. $l **English $s (Beck)**

RDA 6.27.4 Variant Access Point Representing a Work or Expression

When constructing variant access points representing works and expressions, use the variant title for the work as the basis.

variant title

If the authorized access point for the work was constructed using the name of the creator and the preferred title for the work, use the same structure for the variant access point.

> authorized access point for creator + **variant title**
> 400   1_ $a Dickens, Charles, $d 1812–1870. $t Posthumous papers of
> the Pickwick Club

When creating such an access point, also create a separate access point comprising solely the variant title.

> 430   _0 $a Posthumous papers of the Pickwick Club

Make additions to variant access points if considered necessary for identification.

> **variant title +** *additions*
> 430   _0 $a Science series (Cypress, Calif.)

Construct additional variant access points if considered important for access.

> 130   _0 $a Labor bulletin (Boston, Mass.)
> 410   1_ $a Massachusetts. $b Bureau of Statistics of Labor. $t Labor bulletin
> 410   1_ $a Massachusetts. $b Bureau of Statistics of Labor. $t Labor bulletin
> 410   1_ $a Massachusetts. $b Department of Labor and Industries. $b Division of Statistics. $t Labor bulletin

RDA 6.28 Constructing Access Points to Represent Musical Works and Expressions

RDA 6.28.1 Authorized Access Point Representing a Musical Work

For compilations of previously existing compositions for pasticcios and ballad operas by various composers, and for compilations of excerpts from a pasticcio or ballad opera, construct the access point using the preferred title for the work alone.

> **preferred title for musical work**
> 130   _0 $a Beggar's wedding

For musical works with lyrics, libretto, or text, original compositions for pasticcios and ballad operas, single excerpts from a pasticcio or ballad opera, musical works composed for choreographic movement, adaptations, cadenzas, and incidental music for dramatic works, construct the access point by preceding the preferred title for the work with the authorized access point for the composer or adapter.

> authorized access point for composer/adapter + **preferred title for musical work**
> 100   1_ $a Viardot-García, Pauline, $d 1821–1910. $t Filles de Cadix
> 100   1_ $a Marshall, Wayne. $t Organ improvisations
> 100   1_ $a Schumann, Clara, 1819–1896. $t Cadenzen zu Beethoven's Clavier-Concerten

Additions to Access Points Representing Musical Works

Make additions to access points for musical works following this basic structure:

> authorized access point for composer + **preferred title for musical work** + *additions*

For works with nondistinctive titles (e.g., "Sonatas"), add one or more of the following: medium of performance, numeric designation, or key.

100   1_ $a Enesco, Georges, $d 1881–1955. $t Sonatas, $m **violin, piano, $n no. 2, op. 6, $r F minor**

Add other information such as year of completion of the composition, year of original publication, place of composition, or name of first publisher if the medium of performance, key, or numeric designation does not provide sufficient distinction.

100   1_ $a Delius, Frederick, $d 1862–1934. $t Pieces, $m piano $n **(1890)**
100   1_ $a Philidor, Pierre Danican, 1681–1731. $t Suites, $n op. 1 **(Foucault)**

For works with distinctive titles that still need further distinction, add either the medium of performance or another distinguishing characteristic of the work.

100   1_ $a Debussy, Claude, $d 1862–1918. $t Images, $m **piano**

If even further distinction is needed, add one or more of the following: a numeric designation, the key, the year of completion of composition, the year of original publication, or any other identifying element, such as the place of composition or the name of the first publisher.

100   1_ $a Bach, Johann Sebastian, $d 1685–1750. $t Was Gott tut, das ist wohlgetan (Cantata), $n **BWV 98**
100   1_ $a Bach, Johann Sebastian, $d 1685–1750. $t Was Gott tut, das ist wohlgetan (Cantata), $n **BWV 99**

RDA 6.28.2 Authorized Access Point Representing a Part or Parts of a Musical Work

Construct the authorized access point for one or more parts according to the conventions in the following examples:

100   1_ $a Brahms, Johannes, $d 1833–1897. $t Ungarische Tänze. Nr. 5
100   1_ $a Larson, Jonathan. $t Rent. $p Seasons of love
100   1_ $a Rodgers, Richard, $d 1902–1979. $t King and I. $k Selections

RDA 6.28.3 Authorized Access Point Representing a Musical Expression

Construct access points for musical expressions using the following structure:

authorized access point for musical work + *expression-level attribute(s)*

For arrangements and transcriptions, add the term *arranged*.

100   1_ $a Townshend, Pete. $t Songs. $k Selections; $o **arranged**

For a composer's sketches, add the term *Sketches*.

> 100 1_ $a Szymanowski, Karol, $d 1882–1937. $t Harnasie (**Sketches**)

For a vocal or chorus score, add the appropriate term in the singular or plural.

> 100 1_ $a Wagner, Richard, $d 1813–1883. $t Operas. $s **Vocal scores**

For translations, add the language.

> 100 1_ $a Bizet, Georges, $d 1838–1875. $t Carmen. $l **German**

RDA 6.28.4 *Variant Access Point Representing a Musical Work or Expression*

Create variant access points if considered necessary for access.

> 100 1_ $a Bach, Johann Sebastian, $d 1685–1750. $t Works. $k Selections
> 400 1_ $a Bach, Johann Sebastian, $d 1685–1750. $t Best of Bach
>
> 100 1_ $a Lœillet, Jacques, $d 1685–1748. $t Sonatas, $m recorders (2), flutes (2), continuo, $r B minor
> 400 1_ $a Lœillet, Jacques, $d 1685–1748. $t Quintet, $m recorders, flutes, continuo, $r B minor

RDA 6.29 Constructing Access Points to Represent Legal Works and Expressions

RDA 6.29.1 *Authorized Access Point Representing a Legal Work*

For some legal works, the access point is constructed using the preferred title of the work alone. These include laws governing more than one jurisdiction; ancient laws, certain medieval laws, and customary laws; treaties with unknown signatories; compilations of court rules; compilations of treaties; and compilations of official proceedings or records of trials.

> **preferred title for legal work**
> 130 _0 $a Narcotic laws of Mexico and the United States of America
> 130 _0 $a Lex Salica
> 130 _0 $a West's California rules of court, 1975, state and federal
> 130 _0 $a Agreement Establishing the World Trade Organization
> 130 _0 $a Treaties and alliances of the world

For some legal works, the access point is constructed by preceding the preferred title for the legal work with the authorized access point for the jurisdiction governed by the law. These include laws governing one jurisdiction, compilations of rules governing more than one court of a single jurisdiction, treaties between national governments, and agreements contracted by international intergovernmental bodies.

> authorized access point for jurisdiction + **preferred title for legal work**
> 110   1_ $a Alaska. $t Constitution of the State of Alaska
> 110   1_ $a Australia. $t Laws, etc.
> 110   1_ $a Peru. $t Reglamentos de tribunales, de jueces de paz y comercio
> 110   1_ $a United States. $t Treaties, etc.

For bills and drafts of legislation, the access point is constructed by preceding the preferred title for the legal work with the authorized access point for the legislative body.

> authorized access point for legislative body + **preferred title for legal work**
> 110   1_ $a United States. $b Congress $n (70th, 1st session: $d 1927–1928). $b Senate. $t Bill to designate a building site for the National Conservatory of Music of America, and for other purposes

For some legal works, the access point is constructed by preceding the preferred title for the legal work with the authorized access point for the court. These include rules governing a single court, court reports not ascribed to one or more reporters by name, charges to juries, and judicial decisions.

> authorized access point for court + **preferred title for legal work**
> 110   1_ $a Ontario. $b Superior Court of Justice. $t Ontario Superior Court practice
> 110   1_ $a Canada. $b Federal Court. $t Canada Federal Court reports
> 110   1_ $a United States. $b Circuit Court (Middle Circuit). $t Charge of Judge Paterson to the jury in the case of Vanhorne's lessee against Dorrance

For some legal works, the access point is constructed by preceding the preferred title for the legal work with the authorized access point for a corporate body. These include administrative regulations that are not laws, constitutions and charters of international intergovernmental bodies, agreements contracted by international intergovernmental bodies, agreements contracted by the Holy See, criminal proceedings and appeals where a corporate body is being prosecuted, civil and other noncriminal proceedings and appeals where the corporate body initiates the action, and briefs and pleas involving corporate bodies.

> authorized access point for corporate body + **preferred title for legal work**
> 110   1_ $a Illinois. $b Department of Public Health. $t Rules and regulations for recreational areas
> 110   2_ $a United Nations. $t Charter of the United Nations
> 110   2_ $a Asian Development Bank. $t Treaties, etc.

110   2_ $a Catholic Church. $t Treaties, etc.
110   2_ $a Goodwin Film and Camera Company. $t Goodwin Film and
      Camera Company, complainant-appellee, vs. Eastman Kodak Com-
      pany, defendant-appellant

For some legal works, the access point is constructed by preceding the preferred title for the legal work with the authorized access point for the name of a person. These include reports ascribed to one or more reporters by name; citations, digests, and indexes of court reports with responsibility ascribed to a prominently named person; criminal proceedings and appeals where the person is being prosecuted; civil and other noncriminal proceedings and appeals where the person initiates the action; judicial opinions of a judge; briefs and pleas involving a person; and courtroom arguments by lawyers.

authorized access point for person + **preferred title for legal work**
100   1_ $a Manning, James, $d 1781–1866. $t Common bench reports
100   1_ $a Phillips, Richard H. $q (Richard Henry), $d 1890–1971.
      $t Connecticut digest, 1785 to date
100   1_ $a Riel, Louis, $d 1844–1885. $t Queen vs. Louis Riel
100   1_ $a Sutliff, Milton, $d 1806–1879. $t Dissenting opinion of Hon.
      Milton Sutliff, one of the judges
100   1_ $a Gowen, Franklin B. $q (Franklin Benjamin), $d 1836–1889.
      $t Argument of Franklin B. Gowen, Esq., of counsel for the Com-
      monwealth, in the case of the Commonwealth vs. Thomas Munley

Additions to Access Points Representing Legal Works

Some additions to the access points for legal works are necessary, while others are only required to differentiate similarly named legal works.

{person, corporate body, jurisdiction} + **preferred title for legal work** +
additions
Add the year of promulgation to distinguish between similarly named laws.
110   1_ $a Zimbabwe. $t Constitution of Zimbabwe (**1994**)
110   1_ $a Zimbabwe. $t Constitution of Zimbabwe (**2007**)

Add the preferred name for the second signatory to a treaty when only two parties are involved. Also add the earliest date of signing.

110   2_ $a Catholic Church. $t Treaties, etc. $g **Slovakia**, $d **2000
      November 24**

If there are more than two signatories, only add the date of signing.

110   1_ $a United States. $t Treaties, etc. $d **1952 May 9**

Add the date of the work to treaties identified by their own name.

> 130   _0 $a Agreement Establishing the World Trade Organization $d
>   (**1994 April 15**)

For protocols, amendments, extensions, or other agreements ancillary to a treaty, add the term *Protocols, etc.* and the date (or range of dates) of their signing.

> 110   2_ $a European Economic Community. $t Treaties, etc. $g Morocco, $d 1976 April 27. $k **Protocols, etc.,** $d **1982 March 11–1991 June 26**

Make other additions to legal works as necessary.

> 130   _0 $a Judicial Council of California criminal jury instructions (**West (Firm)**)

RDA 6.29.2 Authorized Access Point Representing an Expression of a Legal Work

Construct the access point for an expression of a legal work by combining the authorized access point representing a legal work and adding one or more expression-level attributes.

> **authorized access point for legal work** + *expression-level attribute(s)*
> 110   1_ $a Kosovo (Republic). $t Kushtetuta e Republikës së Kosovës.
> $l **English**

RDA 6.29.3 Variant Access Point Representing a Legal Work or Expression

Create variant access points if considered necessary for access.

> 130   _0 $a Lex agraria
> 410   1_ $a Rome. $t Lex agrarian

> 110   1_ $a Ireland. $t Treaties, etc. $g Portugal, $d 1993 June 1.
> $k Protocols, etc., $d 2005 November 11
> 410   1_ $a Portugal. $t Treaties, etc. $g Ireland, $d 1993 June 1.
> $k Protocols, etc., $d 2005 November 11

> 110   1_ $a Kosovo (Republic). $t Kushtetuta e Republikës së Kosovës. $l English
> 410   1_ $a Kosovo (Republic). $t Constitution of the Republic of Kosovo

RDA 6.30 Constructing Access Points to Represent Religious Works and Expressions

RDA 6.30.1 Authorized Access Point Representing a Religious Work

For most sacred scriptures, theological creeds and confessions of faith, and Jewish liturgical works, construct the access point using the preferred title alone.

preferred title for religious work

130 _0 $a Qur'an

130 _0 $a Nicene Creed

130 _0 $a Augsburg Confession

130 _0 $a Haggadah

For a sacred scripture for which responsibility is attributed to a person by reference sources for the religious group emanating that scripture, construct the access point using the preferred title preceded by the authorized access point for the person.

authorized access point for person + **preferred title for religious work**

100 0_ $a Bahá'u'lláh, $d 1817–1892. $t Kitāb al-aqdas

For most liturgical works, construct the access point using the preferred title preceded by the authorized access point for the church.

authorized access point for religious body + **preferred title for religious work**

110 2_ $a Catholic Church. $t Missale Romanum

110 2_ $a Orthodox Eastern Church. $t Horologion

RDA 6.30.2 Authorized Access Point Representing a Part or Parts of a Religious Work

Generally, construct the access points for parts of scripture and liturgical works according to the conventions in the following examples:

130 _0 $a Bible. $p New Testament

130 _0 $a Talmud. $p Minor tractates

130 _0 $a Bible. $p Psalms, XLII

130 _0 $a Qur'an. $k Selections

110 _2 $a Catholic Church. $t Rite of election

RDA 6.30.3 Authorized Access Point Representing an Expression of a Religious Work

Construct the access point for an expression of a religious work by combining the authorized access point representing a religious work and adding one or more expression-level attributes.

authorized access point for religious work + *expression-level attribute(s)*

For the Bible, add one or more of the following (in this order): language of the expression, other distinguishing characteristic of the expression, or date of the expression.

130 _0 $a Bible. $l **English**

130 _0 $a Bible. $p Gospels. $l **English**. $s **Revised Standard**. $f **1975**

For the Talmud, Mishnah and Tosefta, or Midrashim, add the name of the language.

130 _0 $a Tosefta. $p Beẓah. $l **German**

For the Vedas, add the name of the version in parentheses.

> 130   _0 $a Vedas. $p Sāmaveda (**Kauthumasaṃhitā**)

For variants or special texts of liturgical works, add one of the following terms (in order of preference): the name of a special rite, the name of the place or institution in which the variant is authorized or traditional, or the name of the religious order for which the variant is authorized or traditional.

> 130   _0 $a Haggadah (**Sephardic**)
> 110   2_ $a Catholic Church. $t Officia propria (**Spain**)
> 110   2_ $a Catholic Church. $t Missal (**Dominican**)

RDA 6.30.5 Variant Access Point Representing a Religious Work or Expression

Create variant access points if considered necessary for access.

> 110   2_ $a Catholic Church. $t Missale Romanum (1970)
> 410   2_ $a Catholic Church. $t Sacramentary (1970)

> 130   _0 $a Bible. $l English. $s Authorized
> 430   _0 $a Bible. $l English. $s King James Version

> 100   0_ $a Bahá'u'lláh, $d 1817–1892. $t Kitāb al-aqdas. $l Albanian
> 400   0_ $a Bahá'u'lláh, $d 1817–1892. $t Qitapi akdas

RDA 6.31 Constructing Access Points to Represent Official Communications

RDA 6.31.1 Authorized Access Point Representing an Official Communication

For compilations of official communications and other works, construct the authorized access point using the preferred title alone.

> preferred title for official communication
> 130   _0 $a Papal documents on figured music from the 14th to the 20th
> century and examples for demonstration

For communications of a single official, construct the access point by preceding the preferred title for the communication with the authorized access point for the name of the official.

> authorized access point for official **+ preferred title for official communication**
> 110   1_ $a Louisiana. $b Governor (1988–1992 : Roemer). $t Governor's
> action agenda for fighting crime in Orleans Parish
> 110   2_ $a Catholic Church. $b Pope (1978–2005 : John Paul II).
> $t Familiaris consortio.

For communications that accompany and transmit a document and for compilations of communications from multiple holders of the same office, construct the access point by preceding the preferred title for the communication with the authorized access point for the corporate body responsible for the communication.

> authorized access point for body + **preferred title for official communication**
>
> 110 1_ $a United States. $b War Department. $t Message from the President of the United States, transmitting a report of the Secretary of War, relative to murders committed by the Indians in the state of Tennessee
>
> 110 2_ $a Catholic Church. $b Pope. $t Encyclicals

RDA 6.31.2 Authorized Access Point Representing an Expression of an Official Communication

Construct the access point for an expression of an official communication by combining the authorized access point representing the work with one or more expression-level attributes.

> **authorized access point for official communication** + *expression-level attribute(s)*
>
> 110 2_ $a Catholic Church. $b Pope (1978–2005 : John Paul II). $t Sollicitudo rei socialis. $l **Spanish**

RDA 6.31.3 Variant Access Point Representing an Official Communication

Create variant access points if considered necessary for access.

> 110 2_ $a Catholic Church. $b Pope (1963–1978 : Paul VI). $t Humanae vitae
>
> 430 _0 $a Humanae vitae
>
> 110 1_ $a United States. $b President (1861–1865 : Lincoln). $t Speeches. $l Japanese
>
> 410 1_ $a United States. President (1861–1865 : Lincoln). $t Rinkān enzetsushu

RDA CHAPTER 7: DESCRIBING CONTENT

RDA Chapter 7 provides guidelines on how to record elements that help users select works and expressions. The elements in Chapter 7 differ from those in Chapter 6 in that they are recorded in the descriptive fields of bibliographic records; they are never recorded in access points and seldom in authority records. Chapter 7 includes general guidelines on describing content and detailed guidelines on the twenty-eight major content elements.

RDA 7.2 Nature of the Content

Nature of the content is defined as *the specific character of the primary content of a resource (e.g., legal articles, interim report).* This element maps to several MARC fields. It maps to field 245 subfield $k for form, field 513 subfield $a for type of report, field 516 for type of computer file or data note, and field 500 for other nature of content.

> 513 $a **Interim report**; $b January-July 1977.
> 500 $a Combined time series analysis and graph plotting system.

RDA 7.3 Coverage of the Content

Coverage of the content is defined as *the chronological or geographic coverage of the content of a resource.* As with nature of the content, coverage of content also maps to several MARC fields. It maps to field 513 subfield $b for period covered, field 522 subfield $a for geographic coverage, and field 500 for other coverage of content.

> 513 $a Interim report; $b **January–July 1977**.
> 522   _8 $a County-level data from four Northwestern states (Idaho, Montana, Oregon, Washington).
> 500 $a Based on 1981 statistics.

RDA 7.4 Coordinates of Cartographic Content

Coordinates of cartographic content is defined as *a mathematical system for identifying the area covered by the cartographic content of a resource.* It has three subelements: *longitude and latitude, strings of coordinate pairs,* and *right ascension and declination.* The first two are for terrestrial content, and the third is for celestial content. Information for all three subelements can be taken from any source within the resource. Otherwise, it can be taken from any source.

Longitude and Latitude

Longitude and latitude is defined as *a system for identifying the area covered by the cartographic content of a resource using longitude of the westernmost and easternmost boundaries and latitude of the northernmost and southernmost boundaries.* The longitude and latitude element maps to MARC field 255 subfield $c. Longitude and latitude are also recorded in normalized form in the MARC 034 field, subfields $d through $g.

> 255 $a Scale 1:1,750,000 $c **(W 75°—W 66° /S 38°—S 56°)**.
> 255 $a Scale approximately 1:10,000 $c **(W 9°13′52″— W 9°04′47″/N 38°48′35″—N 38°41′29″)**.

Strings of Coordinate Pairs

Strings of coordinate pairs is defined as *a system for identifying the precise area covered by the cartographic content of a resource using coordinates for each vertex of a polygon.* When more precise geographic coverage is desired, describe the polygon area by recording a string of coordinate pairs in MARC field 255 subfield $f. For situations in which a section of the area is excluded, list the coordinate pairs for the excluded area in MARC field 255 subfield $g.

Right Ascension and Declination

Right ascension and declination is defined as *a system for identifying the location of a celestial object in the sky covered by the cartographic content of a resource using the angles of right ascension and declination.* Record right ascension and declination in MARC field 255 subfield $d. Declination and right ascension are also recorded in normalized form in the MARC 034 field, subfields $j-$k and $m-$n.

> 255 $a Scale not given $d (**Right ascension 0 hr. to 24 hr./ Declination +90° to -90**; $e 1980).

RDA 7.5 Equinox

Equinox is defined as *one of two points of intersection of the ecliptic and the celestial equator, occupied by the sun when its declination is 0°.* It can be taken from any source within the resource. Record it if coordinates for celestial cartographic content are also recorded. Equinox maps to MARC field 255 subfield $e. Equinox is also recorded in normalized form in the MARC 034 field, subfield $p.

> 255 $a Scales vary $d (Zones +90° to +81° to 63°, -81° to 98°; $e **1950**).

RDA 7.6 Epoch

Epoch is defined as *an arbitrary moment in time to which measurements of position for a body or orientation for an orbit are referred.* As with equinox, epoch maps to MARC field 255 subfield $e, and it is recorded in addition to the equinox if they differ.

> 255 $a Scales vary $d (Right ascension 16 hr. 30 min. to 19 hr. 30 min./Declination -16° to -49°; $e 1950, **1948.5**).

RDA 7.7 Intended Audience

Intended audience is defined as *the class of user for which the content of a resource is intended, or for whom the content is considered suitable, as defined by age group (e.g., children, young adults, adults), educational level (e.g., primary, secondary), type of disability, or other categorization.* Record this information in MARC field 521.

> 521 $a For children ages 8–13.

RDA 7.8 System of Organization

System of organization is defined as *a system of arranging materials in an archival resource or a collection*. It maps to MARC field 351.

> 351 $a Organized by type of material; $b **Arranged chronologically**.

RDA 7.9 Dissertation or Thesis Information

Dissertation or thesis information is defined as *information relating to a work presented as part of the formal requirements for an academic degree*. It has three subelements: *academic degree, granting institution or faculty,* and *year degree granted*. Dissertation or thesis maps to MARC field 502.

Academic Degree

Academic degree is defined as *a rank conferred as a guarantee of academic proficiency*. It maps to subfield $b of field 502.

> 502 $b **M.A.** $c Brown University $d 2000

Granting Institution or Faculty

Granting institution or faculty is defined as *an institution or faculty conferring an academic degree on a candidate*. It maps to subfield $c of field 502.

> 502 $b Ph. D. $c **Iowa State University** $d 2003

Year Degree Granted

Year degree granted is defined as *the calendar year in which a granting institution or faculty conferred an academic degree on a candidate*. It maps to subfield $d of field 502.

> 502 $b M.S. $c University of California, Los Angeles $d **2012**

RDA 7.10 Summarization of the Content

Chapter 7 attributes covered thus far have been work-level attributes. *Summarization of the content* is the first expression-level attribute. It is defined as *an abstract, summary, synopsis, etc., of the content of a resource*. It maps to MARC field 520.

> 520 $a Describes associations made between different animal species for temporary gain or convenience as well as more permanent alliances formed for mutual survival.

RDA 7.11 Place and Date of Capture

Place and date of capture is defined as *the place and date associated with the capture (i.e., recording, filming, etc.) of the content of a resource.* It has two subelements: *place of capture* and *date of capture.*

Place of Capture

Place of capture is defined as *the place associated with the capture (i.e., recording, filming, etc.) of the content of a resource.* It maps to MARC field 033 subfield $p or 518 subfield $a or $p. Give the name of the institution along with the city, if applicable.

> 518 $a Recorded at Mountainside Audio Labs, Nashville, Tennessee.
> 518 $d 2002 September 13 $p **Coolidge Auditorium, Library of Congress, Washington, D.C.**

Date of Capture

Date of capture is defined as *a date or range of dates associated with the capture (i.e., recording, filming, etc.) of the content of a resource.* It maps to MARC field 033 subfield $a or field 518 subfield $a or $d. Give the year, month, day, and time, if applicable.

> 518 $a Recorded between 1916 and 1955.
> 518 $d **1997 April 22–23** $p Paradise Studios, Sydney.

RDA 7.12 Language of the Content

Language of the content is defined as *a language used to express the content of a resource.* It maps to MARC field 546 subfield $a.

> 546 $a Text in German, Dutch, and English.
> 546 $a Welsh with English marginalia.

RDA 7.13 Form of Notation

Form of notation is defined as *a set of characters and/or symbols used to express the content of a resource.* It has four subelements: *script, form of musical notation, form of tactile notation,* and *form of notated movement.*

Script

Script is defined as *a set of characters and/or symbols used to express the written language content of a resource.* It maps to MARC field 546 subfield $b. Use one or more terms listed in ISO 15924[1] or, if those terms are insufficient, record the details of the script, as appropriate.

> 546 $a In Azerbaijani $b **Roman**.
> 546 $a Sanskrit (Latin and Devanagari) and English.

Form of Musical Notation

Form of musical notation is defined as *a set of characters and/or symbols used to express the musical content of a resource.* It maps to MARC field 546 subfield $b. For form of musical notation, record one of the following: *graphic notation, letter notation, mensural notation, neumatic notation, number notation, solmization, staff notation, tablature,* or *tonic sol-fa.* If none of those terms is sufficient, record the details of the form of musical notation, as appropriate.

> 546 $b staff notation.

Form of Tactile Notation

Form of tactile notation is defined as *a set of characters and/or symbols used to express the content of a resource in a form that can be perceived through touch.* For form of tactile notation, code the 007 field for tactile material with tags analogous to one or more of the following: *braille code, computing braille code, mathematics braille code, Moon code, music braille code, tactile graphic,* or *tactile musical notation.* If none of those terms is sufficient, record the details of the form of tactile notation, as appropriate.

> 500 $a Contains print, braille, and tactile images.

Form of Notated Movement

Form of notated movement is defined as *a set of characters and/or symbols used to express the movement content of a resource.* For form of notated movement, code the 007 field for musical notation with tags analogous to one or more of the following: *action stroke dance notation, Beauchamp-Feuillet notation, Benesh movement notation, Dance Writing, Eshkol-Wachman movement notation, game play notation, Kinetography Laban, Labanotation,* and *Stepanov dance notation.* If none of those terms is sufficient, record the details of the form of notated movement, as appropriate.

> 500 $a Partly reconstructed from a video of the first performance.

---

1. http://www.unicode.org/iso15924/codelists.html.

RDA 7.14 Accessibility Content

Accessibility content is defined as *content that assists those with a sensory impairment in the greater understanding of content which their impairment prevents them fully seeing or hearing.* It maps to MARC field 546 subfield $a or the general field 500.

>   546 $a Closed captioning in English.

RDA 7.15 Illustrative Content

Illustrative content is defined as *content designed to illustrate the primary content of a resource.* If a resource has illustrative content, record *illustration* or *illustrations* in MARC field 300 subfield $b.

>   300 $a 34 pages : $b **illustrations** ; $c 24 cm

As an alternative, record the type of illustration instead of or in addition to the general term, using one or more of the following terms: *charts, coats of arms, facsimiles, forms, genealogical tables, graphs, illuminations, maps, music, photographs, plans, portraits,* and *samples.*

>   300 $a 34 pages : $b **charts, graphs** ; $c 24 cm

If none of those terms is sufficient, record the details of the illustrative content, as appropriate.

>   500 $a Map on lining papers.

Optionally, add the number of illustrations.

>   300 $a v, 281 pages : $b **25 illustrations** ; $c 26 cm

RDA 7.16 Supplementary Content

Supplementary content is defined as *content (e.g., an index, a bibliography, an appendix) designed to supplement the primary content of a resource.* Supplementary content comprising solely one or more indexes maps to MARC field 500.

>   500 $a Includes indexes.

Supplementary content comprising one or more bibliographies (with or without indexes) maps to MARC field 504.

>   504 $a Includes bibliographical references.
>   504 $a Includes bibliographical references and index.

RDA 7.17 Colour Content

Colour content is defined as *the presence of colour, tone, etc., in the content of a resource*. It has four subelements: *colour of still image, colour of moving image, colour of three-dimensional form*, and *colour content of resource designed for persons with visual impairments*. For each subelement, information on color content can be determined from evidence presented by the resource itself (or on accompanying matter). If desired, additional evidence can be taken from any source. The color content element maps to MARC field 300 subfield $b. For resources other than still images, moving images, and three-dimensional forms, if the content is in colors other than black and white or shades of gray, record the presence of color. (Both "color" and "colour" are allowable spellings.)

    300     $a iii, 187 pages : $b **color** illustrations ; $c 31 cm
    300     $a 1 online resource (93 pages) : $b maps (**some color**)

Colour of Still Image

Colour of still image is defined as *the presence of colour, tone, etc., in a still image or images contained in a resource*. Record one of the following as appropriate: *black and white, sepia*, or *color*.

    300     $a 1 poster : $b **color** ; $c 54 x 72 cm

For black and white images, record *tinted, toned*, or *tinted and toned*, in parentheses following the designation *black and white*, if applicable.

    300     $a 1 photograph : $b **black and white (tinted)** ; $c 16 x 22 cm

If an image is in one or two colors, specify the color or colors.

Colour of Moving Image

Colour of moving image is defined as *the presence of colour, tone, etc., in a moving image or images contained in a resource*. Record one of the following as appropriate: *black and white, color*, or *sepia*. For black and white content, record *tinted, toned*, or *tinted and toned*, in parentheses following the designation *black and white*, if applicable. For color content, record *some color* or *chiefly color*, if applicable. Record any combinations of color and black and white content as succinctly as possible.

    300     $a 1 filmstrip (54 frames) : $b **color** ; $c 35 mm
    300     $a 2 videocassettes (48 min.) : $b sound, **black and white with
            color introductory sequence ;** $c 1/2 in.

Colour of Three-Dimensional Form

Colour of three-dimensional form is defined as *the presence of colour, tone, etc., in a three-dimensional form or forms contained in a resource.* If the three-dimensional form is in black and white, record *black and white.* If it is in one or two colors, specify the color or colors. If it is in three or more colors, record *color.* Record *some color* or *chiefly color,* if applicable.

> 300 $a 1 stuffed toy : $b **color** ; $c 24 x 38 x 10 cm

Colour Content of Resource Designed for Persons with Visual Impairments

Colour content of resource designed for persons with visual impairments is defined as *the presence of colour, tone, etc., in a resource designed for persons with visual impairments.* Record the colors of the text and background if they are anything other than black on white.

> 300 $a 50 pages : $b blue text on yellow background ; $ 22 cm

RDA 7.18 Sound Content

Sound content is defined as *the presence of sound in a resource other than one that consists primarily of recorded sound.* Information on sound content can be determined from evidence presented by the resource itself (or on accompanying matter). If desired, additional evidence can be taken from any source. Sound content maps to MARC field 300 subfield $b. For resources other than moving images, record *sound* to indicate the presence of sound, unless the resource consists primarily of recorded sound. For moving image resources, record *sound* or *silent,* as appropriate.

> 300 $a 1 CD-ROM : $b **sound**, color ; $c 4 3/4 in.
> 300 $a 2 film reels (3 min., 6 sec.) : $b **silent**, color

RDA 7.19 Aspect Ratio

Aspect ratio is defined as *the ratio of the width to the height of a moving image.* Information on aspect ratio can be determined from evidence presented by the resource itself (or on accompanying matter). If desired, additional evidence can be taken from any source. Aspect ratio maps to the general MARC field 500. Record *full screen* for ratios less than 1.5:1, *wide screen* for ratios greater than 1.5:1, and *mixed* for resources that have multiple aspect ratios. Record the details of the aspect ratio, as appropriate.

> 500 $a Wide screen 1.77:1.
> 500 $a Anamorphic widescreen.

RDA 7.20 Format of Notated Music

Format of notated music is defined as *the musical or physical layout of the content of a resource that is presented in the form of musical notation*. It can be taken from any source within the resource. Format of notated music serves as the basis for determining the subunit to be recorded in MARC field 300 subfield $a. It can also be recorded in a 500 field. Record one or more of the following terms: *score, condensed score, study score, piano conductor part, violin conductor part, vocal score, piano score, chorus score, part, choir book*, and *table book*. If none of those terms is sufficient, record the details of the format of music, as appropriate.

      300     $a 1 **study score** (25 pages) ; **$c** 31 cm

RDA 7.21 Medium of Performance of Musical Content

Medium of performance of musical content is defined as *the instrument, instruments, voice, voices, etc., used (or intended to be used) for performance of musical content*. It can be taken from any source within the resource. It maps to the general MARC field 500. Abbreviate voices according to Appendix B.

      500     $a Reduction for clarinet and piano.

RDA 7.22 Duration

Duration is defined as *the playing time, running time, etc., of the content of a resource*. Record the duration as it is stated on the resource in MARC field 300 $a or field 500. The information can also be recorded in the machine-actionable field 306. Abbreviate according to Appendix B. Precede estimated times with the word "approximately," follow the time recorded for multiple units with the same duration with the word "each." Correct duration times as applicable.

      300     $a 5 sound discs (**approximately 40 min. each**) ; $c 12 in.
      300     $a 1 DVD (**1:30:00, that is, 1:33:00**) : $b sound, color ; $c 1/2 in.

Record duration for notated music and notated movement as it is stated on the resource.

      500     $a Duration: about 2 hr., 40 min.

When preparing comprehensive descriptions, record multiple durations for individual parts.

      500     $a Durations: 31:00; 18:39.

RDA 7.23 Performer, Narrator, and/or Presenter

Performer, narrator, and/or presenter is defined as a *person, family, or corporate body responsible for performing, narrating, and/or presenting a work*. Record this information in MARC field 511. For musical performers, also record the medium in which they perform.

> 511 1_ $a Kimberly Williams-Paisley, Tammy Blanchard, Matt Letscher.
> 511 0_ $a Alessio Bidoli, violin; Stefania Mormone, piano.
> 511 0_ $a Narrator: Sam Otage.
> 511 0_ $a Presenter: Daniel Giancaterino.

RDA 7.24 Artistic and/or Technical Credit

Artistic and/or technical credit is defined as *a listing of persons, families, or corporate bodies making contributions to the artistic and/or technical production of a resource*. Provide a statement of function with each name. Artistic and/or technical credit maps to MARC field 508.

> 508 $a Executive producers, Debra and Paul Johnson; cinematography & editing, Vladislav Ponomarov; original music, Steve Haun.

RDA 7.25 Scale

Scale is defined as *the ratio of the dimensions of an image or three-dimensional form contained or embodied in a resource to the dimensions of the entity it represents*. It has four subelements: *scale of still image or three-dimensional form, horizontal scale of cartographic content, vertical scale of cartographic content*, and *additional scale information*.

Record scale as a representative fraction expressed as a ratio. Alternatively, for noncartographic content, record *full size* or *life size*, as appropriate. Record the scale, even if it appears in the title proper. If the resource does not show the scale expressed as a representative fraction, convert it. For example, if the scale statement reads "7.5 miles to 1 inch," record *1:475,000*. Precede estimated scales with "approximately." Record *Scale not given, Not drawn to scale*, or *Scale varies*, where applicable.

Scale of Still Image or Three-Dimensional Form

Scale of still image or three-dimensional form is defined as *the ratio of the dimensions of a still image or three-dimensional form contained or embodied in a resource to the dimensions of the entity it represents*. It maps to MARC field 507. Note that in pre-AACR2 bibliographic records, the MARC 507 field was used for scale statements for maps.

> 507 $a Scale 1:500,000.

Horizontal Scale of Cartographic Content

Horizontal scale of cartographic content is a core element. It is defined as *the ratio of horizontal distances in the cartographic content of a resource to the actual distances they represent.* It can be taken from any source within the resource. Otherwise, it can be taken from outside the resource. It maps to MARC field 255 subfield $a. Horizontal scale of cartographic content is also recorded in normalized form in the MARC 034 field, subfield $b.

> 255 $a Scale 1:30,000,000.
> 255 $a Scale approximately 1:40,000.

Vertical Scale of Cartographic Content

Vertical scale of cartographic content is a core element. It is defined as *the scale of elevation or vertical dimension of the cartographic content of a resource.* It can be taken from any source within the resource, and it maps to MARC field 255 $a. For relief models, three-dimensional cartographic materials, and two-dimensional representations of three-dimensional cartographic forms, record the vertical scale in addition to the horizontal scale. Vertical scale of cartographic content is also recorded in normalized form in the MARC 034 field, subfield $c.

> 255 $a Scale 1:900,000. **Vertical scale 1:200,000**.

Additional Scale Information

Additional scale information is defined as *supplemental information pertaining to scale such as a statement of comparative measures or limitation of the scale to particular parts of the content of a resource.* It can be taken from any source within the resource, and it maps to MARC field 255 subfield $a. Capitalize terms according to Appendix A and abbreviate terms according to appendix B.

> 255 $a Scale 1:6,000,000. **1 cm. = 60 km.**

RDA 7.26 Projection of Cartographic Content

Projection of cartographic content is defined as *the method or system used to represent the surface of the earth or of a celestial sphere on a plane.* It can be taken from any source within the resource, and it maps to MARC field 255 subfield $b.

> 255 $a Scale 1:135,000,000; $b **Miller cylindrical projection**.

RDA 7.27 Other Details of Cartographic Content

Other details of cartographic content include *mathematical data and other features of the cartographic content of a resource not recorded in statements of scale, projection, and coordinates*. It maps to MARC field 342 for geospatial reference data, field 343 for planar coordinate data, and the general field 500 for other details.

```
342   02 $a North American Datum of 1927 $q Clarke 1866 $r
      6378206.4 $s 294.98
500      $a Relief shown by satellite imagery.
```

RDA 7.28 Award

An award is defined as *a formal recognition of excellence, etc., for the content of a resource given by an award- or prize-granting body*. It maps to MARC field 586.

```
586      $a Academy Award for Best Picture, 1987.
```

RDA 7.29 Note on Expression

Note on expression is defined as *an annotation providing additional information relating to content recorded as an expression attribute*. Information for note on expression can be determined from evidence presented by the resource itself (or on accompanying matter). If desired, additional evidence can be taken from any source. It has one subelement: *note on changes in content characteristics*.

Note on Changes in Content Characteristics

Note on changes in content characteristics is defined as *a note providing information on changes in content characteristics that occur in subsequent issues or parts of a resource issued in successive parts or between iterations of an integrating resource*. It maps to the general MARC field 500.

```
500      $a Volumes 1–3 in French, volumes 4–7 in German.
500      $a Volumes 3–5 lack illustrations.
500      $a Volumes 3, 10–11 lack indexes.
```

CONCLUSION

This chapter provided detailed coverage of the bibliographic and authority elements used to identify and select works and expressions. It also covered the three RDA Chapter 5 elements that help users (including other catalogers) contextualize and justify authority data. RDA Chapter 7 elements, combined with elements in RDA Chapters 2–4, make up most of the elements in the descriptive portion of the bibliographic record. Elements in RDA Chapters 5 and 6 introduce the cataloger to elements that populate authority records for the relevant Group 1 entities: *works* and *expressions*. Sections 3 and 4 of RDA are covered in the next chapter, which addresses the elements used to populate authority records for Group 2 entities and the one Group 3 entity that was carried over from AACR2: *places*. The next chapter of this book completes the coverage of attributes and is followed by chapters that address the recording of relationships using RDA.

6

Attributes of Persons, Families, Corporate Bodies, and Places

The third section of RDA contains four chapters (8–11) that provide instructions on recording attributes of persons, families, and corporate bodies. The fourth section contains only one partially developed chapter (16), which provides instructions on recording attributes of places. Specifically:

- RDA Chapter 8, "General Guidelines on Recording Attributes of Persons, Families, and Corporate Bodies," offers general guidelines that provide the context for the concepts covered in RDA Chapters 9–11. It also provides instructions for recording information beneficial to users of authority data in support of the FRAD user tasks "contextualizing" and "justifying."
- RDA Chapter 9, "Identifying Persons," provides instructions on recording attributes of persons.
- RDA Chapter 10, "Identifying Families," provides instructions on recording attributes of families.
- RDA Chapter 11, "Identifying Corporate Bodies," provides instructions on recording attributes of corporate bodies.
- RDA Chapter 16, "Identifying Places," provides instructions on recording attributes of places.
- RDA Chapters 9, 10, 11, and 16 all provide instructions that support the "identify" user task.

This chapter of this book begins with a focus on RDA Chapter 8, which provides general guidelines on recording names and specific instructions for recording authority data. It then details the data elements covered in RDA Chapters 9, 10, 11, and 16, noting if an element is core and providing the relevant MARC fields for many of the elements. As in previous chapters, information for most elements in RDA

Sections 3 and 4 can be taken from any source. Therefore, the source of information is only mentioned in this chapter for those elements that stray from this pattern.

RDA CHAPTER 8: GENERAL GUIDELINES ON RECORDING ATTRIBUTES OF PERSONS, FAMILIES, AND CORPORATE BODIES

RDA Chapter 8 provides general guidelines on recording the attributes of Group 2 entities (i.e., persons, families, and corporate bodies) and on constructing authorized access points and variant access points for those entities. It gives an explanation of the terminology used throughout RDA Section 3; outlines the functional objectives and principles addressed by Section 3 elements; lists the RDA Chapters 9, 10, and 11 elements that are core; explains how to address language and script for transcription of certain elements; and provides general guidelines on recording names. It also has six elements—*scope of usage, date of usage, status of identification, undifferentiated name indicator, source consulted,* and *cataloguer's note*—which provide instructions for catalogers working in the authority environment. The following discussion covers the general guidelines on recording names and then details the six elements.

General Guidelines on Recording Names

As with works and expressions, many of the conventions outlined in RDA 1.7 apply to the names of persons, families, and corporate bodies. Names are capitalized according to Appendix A. Numbers are recorded as numerals or as words, depending on how they appear on the source. Diacritical marks are recorded as they appear on the source and can optionally be added if absent, following the standard usage for the language.

Some conventions are unique to certain types of names. Acronyms and initials are generally recorded with spaces for names of persons and families and without spaces for names of corporate bodies. Abbreviation conventions should follow Appendix B, where applicable. Hyphens should be retained if they are used by the bearer of the name or if they are prescribed by a transliteration system.

RDA 8.8 Scope of Usage

Scope of usage is defined as *the type or form of work associated with the name designated as the preferred name for a person, family, or corporate body.* It maps to MARC authority field 667 subfield $a.

> 667 $a Name used in detective novels

RDA 8.9 Date of Usage

Date of usage is defined as *a date or range of dates associated with the use of the name designated as the preferred name for a person.* It maps to MARC authority field 667 subfield $a.

RDA 8.10 Status of Identification

Status of identification is defined as *an indication of the level of authentication of the data identifying a person, family, or corporate body.* It maps to MARC authority control field 008, byte 33 for "Level of establishment." If there are enough data to fully establish an authorized access point for a person, family, or corporate body, code the byte with "a" for *fully established.* If there are not enough data to satisfactorily establish the authorized access point, code the byte with "c" for *provisional.* If the data are taken from a record without the resource in hand, code the byte with "d" for *preliminary.*

RDA 8.11 Undifferentiated Name Indicator

Undifferentiated name indicator is defined as *a categorization indicating that the core elements recorded are insufficient to differentiate between two or more persons with the same name.* It maps to MARC authority control field 008, byte 32 for "Undifferentiated personal name." If two or persons have the same name and neither can be differentiated with any other element, code the byte with "b" for *undifferentiated.* Otherwise, code the byte with "a," which in MARC stands for "differentiated personal name" or with "n" for entities that are not persons.

RDA 8.12 Source Consulted

Source consulted is defined as *a resource used in determining the name or other identifying attributes of a person, family, or corporate body.* For citing the sources used for determining the preferred name, variant name, and other identifying attributes, provide the data in MARC authority field 670. For citing sources that provided no information, use field 675. RDA 5.8.1.3 instructs the cataloger to add the statement "(No information found)" to the citation of a source that provided no information, but in the MARC environment encoding such a source in the MARC 675 field (which is itself defined as "Source Data Not Found") is a substitute for the explicit statement.

> 670 $a Rodgers, Sam. Opinions of military personnel on sexual minor-ities in the military, ©2006: $b PDF title page (Michael D. Palm Center)
>
> 675 $a Who's who in France, 2006/07

RDA 8.13 Cataloguer's Note

Cataloguer's note is defined as *an annotation that might be helpful to those using or revising the authorized access point representing a person, family, or corporate body, or creating an authorized access point representing a related person, family, or corporate body.* It can be used for citing the RDA instructions used for constructing access points; justifying information; explaining the limitations on access point usage; or differentiating persons, families, and corporate bodies with similar names. It can also be used to provide information that may assist other catalogers in revising the data. It maps to MARC authority field 667.

> 667 $a Not the same as: Imray, James (nr 93026430)
> 667 $a Coded "provisional" because Uzbek form of name unavailable

RDA CHAPTER 9: IDENTIFYING PERSONS

RDA Chapter 9 provides guidelines on recording attributes that help users identify persons. The instructions detail how to construct authorized access points for persons used in bibliographic and authority records. They also cover the various elements that can be added to an access point to differentiate persons with similar names. The guidelines also explain when and how to construct variant access points for use in authority records. Finally, they provide guidance on recording data in the variable fields of authority records.

RDA 9.2 Name of the Person

Name of the person is defined as *a word, character, or group of words and/or characters by which a person is known*. It has two subelements: *preferred name for the person* and *variant name for the person*.

Preferred Name for the Person

Preferred name for the person is a core element. It is defined as *the name or form of name chosen to identify the person*. The source for determining the preferred name for a person can be (in order of preference) preferred sources of information in resources associated with the person, other formal statements in resources associated with the person, or other sources (such as reference sources).

Generally base the preferred name for the person on the most commonly found form, be it a real name, a nickname, a pseudonym, one or more initials, or a title of nobility. Record the name as it would appear in authoritative alphabetical listings in that person's associated country or language (e.g. *Surname, First Name* in American alphabetical listings), unless the person prefers a different form.

Different forms of the same name. If the person's name varies in fullness, choose (in this order of preference) the predominant form, the latest form, or the fullest form. If the person's name appears in different languages on the resources, generally choose the form associated with the most predominant language in which the resources are written. If the person's name has different spellings that are not the result of different transliterations, choose the form in the first resource received.

Different names for the same person. If a person is known by more than one name, generally choose the most commonly found form. If the person changed his or her name, use the most recent form. If the person has created or contributed to resources under multiple identities, choose separate preferred names for each identity. For example, choose *Charles L. Dodgson* for some works and *Lewis Carroll* for others. However, if the person creates or contributes to resources under only one identity, choose the name associated with that identity. For example, choose *George Orwell* for all works and never *Eric Arthur Blair*.

General guidelines for names containing a surname. Record the surname as the preferred name if that is the only element.

> Mantovani (surname: Mantovani)
> Preferred name: *Mantovani*

If there are other elements, record them after the surname and separate them from the surname with a comma.

> A. S. Byatt (surname: Byatt)
> Preferred name: *Byatt, A. S.*
> Chiang Kai-shek (surname: Chiang)
> Preferred name: *Chiang, Kai-shek*

Do this for name parts that function as a surname and for surnames that are represented by initials.

> Malcolm X (name part that functions as a surname: X)
> Preferred name: *X, Malcolm*
> Michael G. (surname represented by initial: G.)
> Preferred name: *G., Michael*

Also do this for persons known only by their surname.

> Dr. Seuss (surname: Seuss)
> Preferred name: *Seuss, Dr.*

Familial relationships and preferred names. If a married person is known only by a partner's name, record the appropriate term of address as the last element.

> Preferred name: *Davis, Maxwell,* **Mrs.**

For Portuguese names, record the relationship terms *Filho, Junior, Neto, Netto,* and *Sobrinho* as part of the surname.

> Preferred name: *Castro* **Sobrinho**, *Antonio Ribeiro de*

For other languages, record such a term as the last element.

> Preferred name: *Saur, Karl-Otto,* **Jr.**

Compound surnames. When recording compound names, record the first element in compliance with the person's preference or with the way he or she is listed in reference sources in his or her associated language or country. If this cannot be determined, consult *Names of Persons: National Usages for Entry in Catalogues* for guidance on usage in the person's country of residence. If the country is not listed, record the first part of the compound name as the first element. For compound surnames containing articles or prepositions, record the part most commonly found as the first element. Consult RDA Appendix F or reference sources in that person's associated language or country for additional guidance. For compound surnames containing other prefixes, record the first part as the first element.

> Preferred name: *Fitz Gerald, Gregory*
> Preferred name: *Mac Murchaidh, Ciarán*

Former members of royal houses and titles of nobility. For members of royal houses who are no longer identified as royalty, apply the general guidelines for surnames. If there is no surname, record the first element in compliance with the way the person is listed in resources or reference sources. For names containing titles of nobility, titles in the United Kingdom peerage that include territorial designation, and judges of the Scottish court, use the following construction:

> *proper name or title, personal name (in direct order), term of rank*
> Preferred name: *Cumberland, William Augustus, Duke of*
> Preferred name: *Moore of Drogheda, Alice Moore, Viscountess*
> Preferred name: *Kames, Henry Home, Lord*

Persons with neither surnames nor titles of nobility and persons of royalty. In general, record the first element in compliance with the way the person is listed in reference sources. In case of doubt, record the last part of the name as the first element.

Record the name of a person lacking both a surname and a title of nobility according to common usage.

> Preferred name: *Nelly*

Include a place of origin or domicile, an occupation, or any another characteristic commonly associated with the person, and record it as the last element.

> Preferred name: *Paul, the Deacon*
> Preferred name: *Alexander, of Aphrodisias*

Treat roman numerals commonly associated with the person as integral to the name.

> Preferred name: *John Paul II*
> Preferred name: *Gregory II, of Cyprus*

For royalty, include royal house, dynasty, territorial designation, surname, or any other designation commonly associated with the person. Record the name in direct order (even if a surname is involved).

> Preferred name: *John II Comnenus*
> Preferred name: *Eleanor, of Aquitaine*

Names with initials, separate letters, or numerals. Record names containing only initials, letters, or numerals in direct order. Include any commonly associated words or phrases.

> Preferred name: *H. D.*
> Preferred name: *DJ 20/20*
> Preferred name: *D. S., Master*

Names consisting of a phrase. In general, record phrases with or without given names in direct order.

> Preferred name: *Poor Old No. 3*
> Preferred name: *Miss Piggy*
> Preferred name: *Little Richard*

Also record in direct order phrases containing the name of another person, characterizing words or phrases, and phrases naming another work by the person. In the latter case, catalogers can optionally omit the initial article.

> Preferred name: *Mother of Mary Lundie Duncan*
> Preferred name: *A Physician*
> Preferred name: *The Author of Honesty the best policy*

OR

> Preferred name: *Author of Honesty the best policy*

An exception to recording phrases in direct order is instances in which the phrase appears to have a given name (or initials) and a surname. In such cases, apply the general guidelines for surnames and record the part functioning as the surname as the first element.

> Preferred name: *Peeved, I. M.*

Another exception is phrases with a term of address preceding a given name. In such cases, record the given name as the first element followed by the term of address

> Preferred name: *Jemima, Aunt*
> Preferred name: *Robert, Chef*

Variant Name for the Person

Variant name for the person is defined as *a name or form of name by which a person is known that differs from the name or form of name chosen as the preferred name*. It can be taken from resources associated with the person and/or from reference sources. Following are a few examples of variant names that can be added if considered important for access:

> Preferred name: *Eliot, George*
> Variant name: *Cross, Marian Evans* (real name)
>
> Preferred name: *Teresa, Mother*
> Variant name: *Bojaxhiu, Agnes Gonxha* (secular name)
>
> Preferred name: *Clinton, Hillary Rodham*
> Variant name: *Rodham, Hillary Diane* (earlier name)
>
> Preferred name: *Joan, of Arc*
> Variant name: *Jeanne, d'Arc* (alternative linguistic form)
>
> Preferred name: *Charles XIV John*
> Variant name: *Bernadotte, Jean-Baptiste-Jules*
>
> Preferred name: *Day-Lewis, Daniel*
> Variant name: *Lewis, Daniel Day-*
>
> Preferred name: *De Polnay, Peter*
> Variant name: *Polnay, Peter de*
>
> Preferred name: *H. D.*
> Variant name: *D., H.*
>
> Preferred name: *Peeved, I. M.*
> Variant name: *I. M. Peeved*
>
> Preferred name: *Little Richard*
> Variant name: *Richard, Little*

RDA 9.3 Date Associated with the Person

Date associated with the person is defined as *a significant date associated with a person (e.g., date of birth, date of death)*. It has three subelements: *date of birth, date of death,* and *period of activity of the person*. The date can be recorded as a separate element, as part of an access point, or both. When recorded as a separate element, the date is recorded in MARC authority field 046 subfields $f, $g, $s, or $t.

When the date is given in an access point, indicate the probable date by following the year with a question mark, indicate uncertainty by putting the word "or" between two consecutive years, and indicate estimation by preceding the date with the word "approximately."

    100   1_ $a Garrett, Elizabeth, $d 1885?-1947
    100   1_ $a Jones, Rosalind, $d 1945 or 1946–
    100   1_ $a Argyros, Isaac, $d approximately 1305–approximately 1375

When recorded as a separate element, the date is usually recorded following ISO standard 8601, which prescribes the form *yyyymmdd*, *yyyy-mm*, or *yyyy*.

    046      $g 1947
    046      $s 1983–04

Centuries are recorded in the form *yy*, B.C. dates are preceded by a negative sign, and both centuries and B.C. dates are recorded by subtracting "1" from the absolute value (e.g., "19" for twentieth century and "-361" for 362 B.C.). Probable, uncertain, and estimated dates are recorded following the EDTF date scheme.

    046      $f 1885? $2 edtf
    046      $f [1945,1946] $2 edtf
    046      $f 1305~ $2 edtf

Date of Birth

Date of birth is a core element. It is defined as *the year a person was born. Date of birth may also include the month and day of the person's birth*. When recorded as a separate element, the date of birth is recorded in MARC field 046 subfield $f.

    046      $f 1968

When used in an access point, RDA prescribes no specific way of recording date of birth. In some examples, it is followed by a hyphen; in others it is preceded by the word "born." The cataloging agency is left to decide its preferred convention.

    100   1_ $a Brulin, Éric, $d born 1968

OR

    100   1_ $a Brulin, Éric, $d 1968–

However, the standard convention for libraries contributing to the U.S. national authority file (hereafter LCNAF) is to follow the date with a hyphen.

If the person has the same name and year of birth as another person, distinguish that person by adding the month and day, if known.

> 100   1_ $a Brulin, Éric, $d 1968 February 7–

Date of Death

  Date of death is a core element. It is defined as *the year a person died. Date of death may also include the month and day of the person's death.* When recorded as a separate element, the date of death is recorded in MARC field 046 subfield $g.

> 046 $g 2012

As with date of birth, RDA does not explicitly prescribe a specific way to record the date of death when used in an access point. However, all of the examples show it preceded by the word "died."

> 100   1_ $a Basketts, Anne, $d died 2012

Still, the standard convention for libraries contributing to the LCNAF is to precede the date with a hyphen.

> 100   1_ $a Basketts, Anne, $d -2012

Period of Activity of the Person

  Period of activity of the person is a core element when needed to distinguish a person from similarly named persons. It is defined as *a date or range of dates indicative of the period in which a person was active in his or her primary field of endeavour.* Record this information if both the date of birth and the date of death are unknown. When recorded as a separate element, the period of activity is recorded in MARC field 046 subfields $s and $t.

> 046 $s 1916 $t 1943
> 046 $s -03

When it is used in an access point, RDA prescribes no specific way of recording period of activity. It is preceded by the word "flourished" in some examples and the word "active" in other examples. The cataloging agency is left to decide which form it wants to use.

> 100   1_ $a Barrett, William J., $d flourished 1916–1943

OR

> 100   1_ $a Barrett, William J., $d active 1916–1943

However, the standard convention for libraries contributing to the LCNAF is to use the word "active."

Centuries can be recorded if the specific years of activity cannot be determined.

```
100    0_ $a Aeneas, $c Tacticus, $d active 4th century B.C.
100    0_ $a Renaud, $c de Beaujeu, $d active 12th century-13th century
```

RDA 9.4 Title of the Person

Title of the person is a core element when it is *a word or phrase indicative of royalty, nobility, or ecclesiastical rank or office, or a term of address for a person of religious vocation.* Title of the person may also be *another term indicative of rank, honour, or office.* The title of the person can be recorded as a separate element, as part of an access point, or both. When recorded as a separate element, the title is recorded in MARC authority field 368 subfield $d.

```
100    0_ $a Benedict $b XVI, $c Pope, $d 1927–
368       $d Pope
```

Record titles for persons with the highest royal status within a state; consorts (or "spouses") of royal persons; children and grandchildren of royal persons; persons of nobility whose title has not been recorded as the first element in the preferred name; popes; bishops, cardinals, abbots, and other ecclesiastical officials; and other persons of religious vocation. For royal persons and ecclesiastical officials, add the territories over which they preside, where applicable.

```
100    0_ $a Elizabeth $b II, $c Queen of Great Britain, $d 1926–
100    0_ $a Philip, $c Prince, consort of Elizabeth II, Queen of Great
          Britain, $d 1921–
100    1_ $a Malaspina di Sannazaro, Luigi, $c marchese, $d 1754–1835
100    0_ $a Adam $b II, $c Abbot of Dore, $d active 1216–1226
100    1_ $a Deutsch, Abraham, $c Rabbi, $d 1902–1992
```

RDA 9.5 Fuller Form of Name

Fuller form of name is a core element when needed to distinguish one person from similarly named persons. It is defined as *the full form of a part of a name represented only by an initial or abbreviation in the form chosen as the preferred name or [the full form of] a part of the name not included in the form chosen as the preferred name.* Record this information if fuller forms are not included in the preferred name. The fuller form of name can be recorded as a separate element, as part of an access point, or both. When recorded as a separate element, it is recorded in MARC authority field 378 subfield $q.

```
100    1_ $a Johnson, Carol S. $q (Carol Sue)
378       $q Carol Sue
```

```
100  1_ $a Johnson, Carol S. $q (Carol Stephanie)
378     $q Carol Stephanie
```

RDA 9.6 Other Designation Associated with the Person

Other designation associated with the person is a core element for a Christian saint or a spirit. As of this writing it is unclear whether it is also a core element for the additional categories of term identified in RDA 9.19.1.2. *Other designation associated with the person* is defined as *a term other than a title that is associated with a person's name.* It can be recorded as a separate element, as part of an access point, or both. When recording the other designation as a separate element, use MARC authority field 368 subfield $c.

```
100  0_ $a Sava, $c Saint, $d 1169–1237
368     $c Saint

100  1_ $a Garland, Judy $c (Spirit)
368     $c Spirit
```

RDA 9.7 Gender

Gender is defined as *the gender with which a person identifies.* Record *female, male, not known,* or some other concise term or phrase as a separate element in MARC authority field 375 subfield $a.

```
375     $a male
375     $a transsexual woman
```

RDA 9.8 Place of Birth

Place of birth is defined as *the town, city, province, state, and/or country in which a person was born.* Record the place in MARC authority field 370 $a and in the form in which it would appear if it were in the qualifier of an access point.

```
370     $a Mesa, Ariz.
```

RDA 9.9 Place of Death

Place of death is defined as *the town, city, province, state, and/or country in which a person died.* Record the place in MARC authority field 370 $b and in the form in which it would appear if it were in the qualifier of an access point.

```
370     $b Berlin, Germany
```

RDA 9.10 Country Associated with the Person

Country associated with the person is defined as *a country with which a person is identified*. Record the country in MARC authority field 370 $c and in the form in which it would appear if it were in the qualifier of an access point.

370      $c U.S.

RDA 9.11 Place of Residence, Etc.

Place of residence, etc. is defined as *a town, city, province, state, and/or country in which a person resides or has resided, or another significant place associated with the person other than place of birth, place of death*. Record the place in MARC authority field 370 $e and in the form in which it would appear if it were in the qualifier of an access point.

370      $e Ill.

RDA 9.12 Address of the Person

Address of the person is defined as *the address of a person's place of residence, business, or employer and/or an e-mail or Internet address*. Record the address in MARC authority field 371. Generally record it as it appears on the source. In the interests of privacy, it may be preferable to record only an e-mail address for a living person.

371      $a BOX 1234 $b Los Angeles $c CA $e 90001
371      $m jdoe@university.edu

RDA 9.13 Affiliation

Affiliation is defined as *a group with which a person is affiliated or has been affiliated through employment, membership, cultural identity, etc.* Record the person's affiliation in MARC authority 373 subfield $a.

373      $a American Baptist Board of International Ministries
373      $a University of Michigan. Department of Near Eastern Studies

RDA 9.14 Language of the Person

Language of the person is defined as *a language a person uses when writing for publication, broadcasting, etc.* It is recorded in MARC authority field 377. Record the language in the three-digit code listed in the *MARC Code List for Languages* in the subfield $a. Terms absent from the list are spelled out and recorded in the subfield $l.

377      $a eng

RDA 9.15 Field of Activity of the Person

Field of activity of the person is defined as *a field of endeavour, area of expertise, etc., in which a person is engaged or was engaged.* Record it in MARC authority field 372 subfield $a.

> 372 $a Carpentry

RDA 9.16 Profession or Occupation

Profession or occupation is a core element when the preferred name does not convey the idea of a person. It is also core when needed to distinguish a person from other similarly named persons. It is defined as *a person's vocation or avocation.* The profession or occupation can be recorded as a separate element, as part of an access point, or both. When recorded as a separate element, it maps to MARC authority field 374 subfield $a.

> 100   1_ $a 250 lbs. of Blue $c (**Musician**)
> 374 $a Musician

RDA 9.17 Biographical Information

Biographical information is defined as *information about the life or history of a person.* Record it in MARC authority field 678 subfield $a.

> 678 $a Timothy D. Cook was born on November 1, 1960 in Robertsdale, Alabama. He earned his B.S. in industrial engineering in 1982 from Auburn University and his M.B.A. in 1988 from Duke University. He joined Apple Inc. in 1998 and became CEO on August 24, 2011.

RDA 9.18 Identifier for the Person

Identifier for the person is a core element. It is defined as *a character string uniquely associated with a person, or with a surrogate for a person (e.g., an authority record).* Its purpose is to differentiate one person from other persons. In the MARC environment, there is no need to precede the identifier with name of the assigning agency as RDA instructs, because this information is conveyed by the MARC field number.

> 010 $a no2006032721

RDA 9.19 Constructing Access Points to Represent Persons

RDA 9.19.1 Authorized Access Point Representing a Person

The preferred name for the person serves as the basis for the authorized access point representing that person. Sometimes the authorized access point for the person comprises solely the preferred name. This occurs when the name is unique, conveys the idea of a person, and does not require obligatory additions such as titles or other designations.

> *preferred name for the person*
> 100   1_ $a Holdeman, Nicky R.
> 100   1_ $a Davis, Maxwell, $c Mrs.
> 100   1_ $a Pompadou, Luke, $c III

In some cases, additions to the preferred name are required, whether or not the name is distinctive. The following are required additions, if applicable, and should be added in this preferred order if there are more than one: a title of royalty or nobility, the term *Saint*, a title of religious rank, the term "Spirit," or a term of profession or occupation (when the name does not convey the idea of a person). In the 2013 revision of RDA, three additional categories were added to this list, but at the time of this writing it is unclear whether these three categories are required additions: a term indicating a person named in a sacred scripture or an apocryphal book; the term *Fictitious character, Legendary character*, etc.; a term indicating type, species, or breed.

> preferred name for the person + *required additions*
> 100   0_ $a Amenhotep $b III, $c **King of Egypt**
> 100   0_ $a Gregory, $c of Nazianzus, **Saint**
> 100   0_ $a Anacletus, $c **Pope**
> 100   1_ $a Garland, Judy $c (**Spirit**)
> 100   0_ $a Stone Mountain $c (**Writer**)

In other cases, additions are required only if needed to distinguish one person from similarly named persons. These include (in order of preference): date of birth and/or death, fuller form of name, period of activity of the person, profession or occupation, and other term of rank, honor, or office. For each element, except *profession or occupation*, catalogers have the option of making the addition, even when not needed to distinguish between names. (The standard convention for libraries contributing to the LCNAF is to apply this option only for birth and death dates.) If needed, more than one type of element can be added to the same access point (usually a date of birth and/or death with a fuller form of name).

> preferred name for the person + *additions for differentiation*
> 100   1_ $a Ravel, Maurice, $d **1875–1937**
> 100   1_ $a González E., José I. $q (**José Ignacio González Escobar**)
> 100   0_ $a Albertus, $c de Parma, $d **active 13th century**
> 100   1_ $a Barratt, David $c (**Engineer**)
> 100   1_ $a Allen, John C., $c Jr. $q (**John Crile**), $d **1970–**

Many access points in the LCNAF may have both a required addition and the type of addition used for differentiation, particularly since in cataloging practice dates are added (if available), regardless of conflict.

preferred name for the person + *required additions* + *additions for differentiation*
100   0_ $a Anne, $c **Queen of Great Britain, $d 1665–1714**
100   0_ $a Hallvard, $c **Saint, $d approximately 1020–1043**
100   0_ $a Pius $b II, $c **Pope, $d 1405–1464**

If no additions can be found to differentiate one or more names, then an undifferentiated authority record can be created for the name. However, this may be less preferable in the increasing linked data environment, and catalogers contributing to the
LCNAF may eventually use data such as unique identifiers to differentiate persons.

RDA 9.19.2 Variant Access Point Representing a Person

Use the variant name for the person as the basis for the variant access point. If
appending additions, follow the same guidelines for making additions to authorized
access points for persons.

variant name for the person + *{additions}*
100   1_ $a McWilliams, A. L. $q (Audra LaVaun)
400   1_ $a McWilliams, Audra LaVaun

100   0_ $a Teresa, $c Mother, $d 1910–1997
400   1_ $a Bojaxhiu, Agnes Gonxha, $d 1910–1997

100   0_ $a Napoleon $b I, $c Emperor of the French, $d 1769–1821
400   1_ $a Bonaparte, Napoleon, $d 1769–1821

100   0_ $a Boy George, $d 1961–
400   0_ $a George, $c Boy, $d 1961–

RDA CHAPTER 10: IDENTIFYING FAMILIES

RDA Chapter 10 provides guidelines on recording attributes that help users identify
families. The instructions detail how to construct authorized access points for families used in bibliographic and authority records. They also cover the various elements
that can be added to an access point to differentiate families with similar names. The
guidelines also explain when and how to construct variant access points for use in
authority records. Finally, they provide guidance on recording data in the variable
fields of authority records.

RDA 10.2 Name of the Family

Name of the family is defined as *a word, character, or group of words and/or characters
by which a family is known*. It has two subelements: *preferred name for the family* and
variant name for the family.

Preferred Name for the Family

Preferred name for the family is a core element. It is defined as *the name or form of name chosen to identify the family.* The sources for determining the preferred name for a family can be (in order of preference) preferred sources of information in resources associated with the family, other formal statements in resources associated with the family, or other sources (such as reference sources).

Base the preferred name for the family on the form by which it is most commonly known. If the family's name varies in fullness, choose (in this order of preference) the predominant form, the latest form, or the fullest form. If the family's name appears in different languages on the resources, generally choose the form associated with the most predominant language in which the resources are written. If the family's name has different spellings that are not the result of different transliterations, choose the form in the first resource received. If a family is known by more than one name, generally choose the most commonly found form. If a family's name has changed, use the earlier name for resources associated with the earlier form and use the later name for resources associated with the later form. For family names consisting of surnames, apply the same instructions for persons with surnames, including compound surnames, hyphenated surnames, and surnames with prefixes.

Variant Name for the Family

Variant name for the family is defined as *a name or form of name by which a family is known that differs from the name or form of name chosen as the preferred name.* It can be taken from resources associated with the family and/or from reference sources. Record as variant names any alternative linguistic forms that differ from the preferred name, names with hereditary titles, and other variant forms.

> Preferred name: *Romanov*
> Variant name: *Romanoff*
> Preferred name: *Chandos*
> Variant name: *Chandos, Dukes of*
> Preferred name: *De Broglie*
> Variant name: *Broglie*

RDA 10.3 Type of Family

Type of family is a core element. It is *a categorization or generic descriptor for the type of family.* The type of family can simply be described as "Family," or it could have a more specific term, like "Clan," "Dynasty," or "Royal House." It can be recorded as a separate element, as part of an access point, or both. When recorded as a separate element, it is recorded in MARC authority field 376 subfield $a.

> 100   3_ $a Tāmhanakara (**Family**)
> 376 $a Family

RDA 10.4 Date Associated with the Family

Date associated with the family is a core element. It is defined as *a significant date associated with a family.* The date can be recorded as a separate element, as part of an access point, or both. When recorded as a separate element, it is recorded in MARC authority field 046 subfields $s and $t.

> 046 $s 1613 $t 1917
> 100   3_ $a Romanov (Dynasty : $d **1613–1917**)

RDA 10.5 Place Associated with the Family

Place associated with the family is a core element when needed to distinguish a family from similarly named families. It is defined as *a place where a family resides or has resided or has some connection.* The place can be recorded as a separate element, as part of an access point, or both. Regardless of where it is recorded, formulate the place as it would appear in the qualifier of an access point. When recording the place as a separate element, record it in MARC authority field 370 subfield $e.

> 100   3_ $a Chatman (Family : $c **S.C.**)
> 370 $e S.C.

RDA 10.6 Prominent Member of the Family

Prominent member of the family is a core element when needed to distinguish one family from similarly named families. It is defined as *a well-known individual who is a member of a family.* The prominent member can be recorded as a separate element, as part of an access point, or both. Regardless of where it is recorded, formulate it by following the guidelines for constructing access points for persons. When recorded as a separate element, the prominent member maps to MARC authority field 376 subfield $b.

> 100   3_ $a Chambers (Family : $g **Chambers, Joseph, 1843–1927**)
> 376 $a Family $b **Chambers, Joseph, 1843–1927**

RDA 10.7 Hereditary Title

Hereditary title is defined as a *title of nobility, etc., associated with a family.* The hereditary title can be recorded as a separate element, as a variant name, or both. When recorded as a separate element, the hereditary title maps to MARC authority field 376 subfield $c and is recorded in direct order. When recorded as a variant name, it is inverted. Regardless of where it is recorded, it is always in the plural form.

> 376 $c Dukes of Chandos
> 400   3_ $a Chandos, Dukes of

RDA 10.8 Family History

Family history is defined as *biographical information about the family and its members*. It is recorded in MARC authority field 678 subfield $a.

> 678 $a Italian rulers, bankers, merchants, collectors, and patrons of the arts, active in Florence particularly from 15th through mid-18th centuries.

RDA 10.9 Identifier for the Family

Identifier for the family is defined as *a character string uniquely associated with a family, or with a surrogate for a family (e.g., an authority record)*. Its purpose is to differentiate one family from other families. As with identifiers for works, expressions, and persons, when working in the MARC environment, the identifier for the family will typically not need to be preceded by the name of the assigning agency, because the MARC field conveys this information.

> 010 $a 2010189088

RDA 10.10 Constructing Access Points to Represent Families

RDA 10.10.1 Authorized Access Point Representing a Family

The preferred name for the family is used as the basis for the authorized access point for that family.

> *preferred name for the family*

One or more of the following elements can or should be added to the preferred name (in this order): *type of family, date associated with the family, place associated with the family,* and *prominent member of the family*.

The preferred name for the family will never appear without additions in an authorized access point. The access point must always include at least a term for the type of family so that the name can be identified as a family. If there is a date associated with the family, it is also added regardless of whether the family needs to be differentiated.

> preferred name for the family + *required additions*
> 100   3_ $a Chichibu no Miya (**Royal house**)
> 100   3_ $a Romanov (**Dynasty** : $d **1613–1917**)

Other elements can be added if needed to differentiate the family.

> preferred name for the family + *required additions* + *additions for differentiation*
> 100   3_ $a Hammons (Family : $c W. Va.)
> *(type of family and place associated with the family added)*

```
100   3_ $a Leyen (Family : $d 1241–1500 : $c Germany)
```
(type of family, date associated with family, and place associated with the family added)
```
100   3_ $a Carroll (Family : $g Carroll, Charles N. (Charles Negus),
        1817–1902)
```
(type of family and prominent member of the family added)

RDA 10.10.2 Variant Access Point Representing a Family

Use the variant name for the family as the basis for the variant access point. When appending additions, follow the same guidelines for making additions to authorized access points for families.

variant name for the family + *required additions +{additions for differentiation}*
```
100   3_ $a Romanov (Dynasty)
400   3_ $a Romanof (Dynasty)
```

RDA CHAPTER 11: IDENTIFYING CORPORATE BODIES

RDA Chapter 11 provides guidelines on recording attributes that help users identify corporate bodies. The instructions detail how to construct authorized access points for corporate bodies used in bibliographic and authority records. They also cover the various elements that can be added to an access point to differentiate corporate bodies with similar names. The guidelines also explain when and how to construct variant access points for use in authority records. Finally, they provide guidance on recording data in the variable fields of authority records.

RDA 11.2 Name of the Corporate Body

Name of the corporate body is defined as *a word, character, or group of words and/or characters by which a corporate body is known.* It has two subelements: *preferred name for the corporate body* and *variant name for the corporate body.*

Preferred Name for the Corporate Body

Preferred name for the corporate body is defined as *the name or form of name chosen to identify the corporate body.* The sources for determining the preferred name can be (in order of preference) preferred sources of information in resources associated with the corporate body, other formal statements in resources associated with the corporate body, or other sources (such as reference sources).

The preferred name is based on the most commonly found form. If there is no such form, choose a brief form (such as an initialism or acronym) that sufficiently differentiates it from other corporate bodies.

> Preferred name: *AFL-CIO* **not** *American Federation of Labor and Congress of Industrial Organizations*

If no brief form sufficiently differentiates the body, use the form found in reference sources rather than the official form.

> Preferred name: *Metropolitan Applied Research Center* **not** *MARC*, which is the name of another corporate body

If variant spellings appear in resources associated with the corporate body, choose the form found in the first resource received. If the name appears in different languages, generally choose the form in the official language of the corporate body. RDA outlines specific situations in which to deviate from this and to instead choose the form preferred by the cataloging agency, the predominant form, or the form found in the first resource received. Finally, if the name of an international body appears in multiple languages and one of them is the cataloging agency's preferred language, choose that form as the preferred name.

Conventional name and exceptions. If a body is more commonly known by its conventional name than by its official name in reference sources written in its language, generally choose the conventional name as the preferred name.

> Preferred name: *Museo del Prado* **not** *Museo Nacional de Pintura y Escultura*

However, there are exceptions.

For ancient and international bodies, base the preferred name on a well-established form in the cataloging agency's preferred language.

> Preferred name: *Benedictines*

For autocephalous patriarchates and archdioceses of the Eastern Church, record the name of the place by which it is identified followed by the type of ecclesiastical jurisdiction.

> Preferred name: *Cyprus (Archdiocese)*

For religious orders and societies, generally choose the best-known form in the cataloging agency's preferred language. If this cannot be determined, choose (in order of preference) the conventional name in the cataloging agency's preferred language, the form used by units of the order or society located in countries where the cataloging agency's preferred language is spoken, or the form in the language of the country of its origin.

> Preferred name: *Franciscans* **not** *Ordo Fratrum Minorum*
> Preferred name: *Jesuits* **not** *Compañía de Jesús*
> Preferred name: *Ordo Templi Orientis* **not** *Order of Oriental Templars*

For governments, generally use the conventional name, unless the official name is in common use.

Preferred name: *France* **not** *République française*

BUT

Preferred name: *Greater Anchorage Area Borough (Alaska)*

For conferences, congresses, and meetings, if different forms of the name appear on the preferred source, choose the form that includes the name of the associated body.

Preferred name: *FAO Technical Meeting on Coffee Production and Protection*

If a conference has its own specific name as well as a general name that is part of a series of conferences, choose the specific name as the preferred name.

Preferred name: *Symposium on Protein Metabolism,* which is the specific name of conference held in 1953 and is part of a general conference series called "Nutrition Symposium"
Preferred name: *Symposium on Endocrines and Nutrition,* which is the specific name of conference held in 1956 and is part of a general conference series called "Nutrition Symposium"

For local places of worship, if different forms of the name appear on the preferred source, generally choose the most predominant form. If this cannot be determined, choose a name that contains (in this order of preference) the name of a person, object, place, or event after which the place of worship is named; a word or phrase descriptive of the type of place of worship; the name of the place in which it is located.

Preferred name: *St. Paul's Cathedral*
Preferred name: *Unitarian Universalist Church*
Preferred name: *Oak Park Temple*

Change of name. If the corporate body changes its name, choose the earlier form as the preferred name for resources associated with the earlier name and the later form as the preferred name for resources associated with the later name.

Recording the preferred name. If the name has initials, include or omit full stops and other punctuation marks, according to the usage found. In case of doubt, omit the stops.

Preferred name: *L.I.F.E. Choir*
Preferred name: *USDLA*

Include initial articles when recording the preferred name. Alternatively, omit the initial article, unless it is integral to the name of the corporate body.

> Preferred name: *The Library Association*
> Alternate preferred name: *Library Association*

BUT

> Preferred name: *Las Vegas Art Museum*

Omit terms of incorporation unless they are integral to the name or are needed to make it clear that it is a corporate body.

> Preferred name: *American Cancer Society* **not** *American Cancer Society, Inc.*

BUT

> Preferred name: *Nature Photographers Ltd.*

Omit abbreviations that precede the name of a ship.

> Preferred name: *Arizona* **not** *U.S.S. Arizona*

Omit from the name of a conference, congress, meeting, exhibition, fair, or festival, the number and year of convocation.

> Preferred name: *Biennial Symposium on Active Control of Vibration and Noise* **not** *Sixth Biennial Symposium on Active Control of Vibration and Noise*
> Preferred name: *Symposium on Some Mathematical Questions in Biology* **not** *1992 Symposium on Some Mathematical Questions in Biology*

If the name is written in a nonpreferred script, generally transliterate it according to the scheme chosen by the cataloging agency.

> Preferred name: *Zhongguo wen zi gai ge wei yuan hui*

RDA offers the alternative to use whatever transliteration is found on the source. However, if there is more than one transliteration, and one of them matches the agency's preferred scheme, choose that as the preferred form.

Subordinate bodies. Generally, record the name of a subordinate body directly under its own name, unless it falls under one of eighteen types. Until mid-2013, RDA replicated the AACR2 division of rules for subordinate bodies entered subordinately into two basic groups: nongovernmental bodies and governmental bodies.

This division led to some duplication of instructions between the two groups and was abandoned in mid-2013. The instructions for subordinate bodies entered subordinately are now integrated into a single sequence in RDA 11.2.2.14.

> Preferred name: *Association for Collections & Technical Services* **not** *American Library Association. Association for Collections & Technical Services*

> Preferred name: *Committee on Foreign Investment in the United States* **not** *United States. Committee on Foreign Investment in the United States*

If a subordinate body falls under one of the eighteen types listed in RDA 11.2.2.14, record it as a subdivision of the higher body.

RDA 11.2.2.14.1: A name with a term that indicates it is part of another, such as *Division, Department, Branch*, or *Section*.

> Name as it appears on the source: Finance Division
> Preferred name: *British Broadcasting Corporation. Finance Division*

> Name as it appears on the source: Medical Records Unit
> Preferred name: *Rarotonga Hospital. Medical Records Unit*

> Name as it appears on the source: Department of Immigration and Citizenship
> Preferred name: *Australia. Department of Immigration and Citizenship*

RDA 11.2.2.14.2: A name with a term that indicates subordination (such as *Committee* or *Commission*) and that requires the name of the higher body for identification.

> Name as it appears on the source: Statistical Committee
> Preferred name: *Edison Electric Institute. Statistical Committee*

BUT

> Name as it appears on the source: UW-Madison Campus Planning Committee
> Preferred name: *UW-Madison Campus Planning Committee*

> Name as it appears on the source: Federal Trade Commission
> Preferred name: *United States. Federal Trade Commission*

BUT

> Name as it appears on the source: Alaska Commission on Aging
> Preferred name: *Alaska Commission on Aging*

RDA 11.2.2.14.3: A name that is general or simply connotes a chronological, geographic, lettered, or numbered subdivision of a higher body.

>   Name as it appears on the source: Technical Reference Library
>   Preferred name: *St. Bride Foundation Institute. Technical Reference Library*

>   Name as it appears on the source: Class of 1957
>   Preferred name: *Dartmouth College. Class of 1957*

>   Name as it appears on the source: Northeast Region
>   Preferred name: *United States. National Park Service. Northeast Region*

In case of doubt, record the name directly.

>   Preferred name: *National Institutes of Health (U.S.)*

RDA 11.2.2.14.4: A subordinate body with a name that does not convey the idea of a corporate body and does not contain the name of the higher body.

>   Name as it appears on the source: Economics and Research
>   Preferred name: *CBS Inc. Economics and Research*

>   Name as it appears on the source: *Research & Analysis*
>   Preferred name: *Illinois. Bureau of Employment Security. Research & Analysis*

BUT

>   Name as it appears on the source: *California Records & Information Management*
>   Preferred name: *California Records & Information Management* **not** *California. Records & Information Management*

RDA 11.2.2.14.5: A name of a university school, college, faculty, laboratory, or institute that indicates a field of endeavor.

>   Name as it appears on the source: College of Medicine
>   Preferred name: *Syracuse University. College of Medicine*

BUT

>   Name as it appears on the source: John F. Kennedy School of Government
>   Preferred name: *John F. Kennedy School of Government* **not** *Harvard University. John F. Kennedy School of Government*

RDA 11.2.2.14.6: A nongovernmental body whose name contains the entire name of the parent body.

Name as it appears on the source: University of Vermont Choral Union
Preferred name: *University of Vermont. Choral Union*

Name as it appears on the source: Annual Meeting of the International
    Whaling Commission
Preferred name: *International Whaling Commission. Annual Meeting*

RDA 11.2.2.14.7: A ministry or major executive agency.

Name as it appears on the source: National Aeronautics and Space Administration
Preferred name: *United States. National Aeronautics and Space Administration*

Name as it appears on the source: Ministry of Health
Preferred name: *Bahamas. Ministry of Health*

RDA 11.2.2.14.8: A government official or a religious official.

Preferred name: *United States. President*
Preferred name: *United Hebrew Congregations of the Commonwealth.
    Chief Rabbi*

RDA 11.2.2.14.9: A legislative body.

Preferred name: *United States. Congress*

RDA 11.2.2.10: A constitutional convention.

Preferred name: *Portugal. Assembleia Constituinte (1975)*

RDA 11.2.2.14.11: A court.

Preferred name: *United States. Supreme Court*

RDA 11.2.2.14.12: A principal service of a government's armed forces.

Preferred name: *United States. Navy*

RDA 11.2.2.13: An embassy, consulate, etc.

Preferred name: *Canada. Embassy (U.S.)*
Preferred name: *United States. Consulate (Asunción, Paraguay)*

RDA 11.2.2.14: A delegation to an international or intergovernmental body.

> Preferred name: *Canada. Delegation to the General Assembly of the United Nations*

RDA 11.2.2.15: A council, etc., of a single religious body

> Preferred name: *Mennonite Church. Lancaster Conference*

RDA 11.2.2.16: A religious province, diocese, synod, etc.

> Preferred name: *Church of England. Diocese of Ely*

RDA 11.2.2.17: A central administrative organ of the Catholic Church.

> Preferred name: *Catholic Church. Signatura Gratiae*

RDA 11.2.2.18: A papal diplomatic mission, etc.

> Preferred name: *Catholic Church. Apostolic Nunciature (Ethiopia)*

Direct and indirect subdivision. If a subordinate body is within a hierarchy, record it as a subdivision of the lowest organizational unit that is recorded directly under its own name.

> Hierarchy: American Library Association—Association of College and Research Libraries—Bibliographic Instruction Section
> Lowest organizational unit recorded directly under its own name: Association of College and Research Libraries
> Preferred name: *Association of College and Research Libraries. Bibliographic Instruction Section.*

> Hierarchy: United States—Department of Health and Human Services—Office of Human Development Services
> Preferred name: *United States. Office of Human Development Services* **not** *United States. Department of Health and Human Services. Office of Human Development Services*

BUT

> Preferred name: *California. Air Resources Board. Research Division*
> Preferred name: *California. Department of Corrections. Research Division*

Omit intervening units in the hierarchy, unless it is likely that another body with the same name would be subordinate to a different unit within the larger organization.

If including an intervening unit, use the lowest unit within the hierarchy that will distinguish the bodies.

> Preferred name: *Association of College and Research Libraries. Clearing-house Committee* **not** *Association of College and Research Libraries. Bibliographic Instruction Section. Clearinghouse Committee*

BUT

> Preferred name: *Association of College and Research Libraries. Bibliographic Instruction Section. Continuing Education Committee*
> Preferred name: *Association of College and Research Libraries. College Libraries Section. Continuing Education Committee*

Joint committees and commissions. Record the name of a joint committee or commission under its own name, omitting the parent bodies if they occur at the beginning or end of the name or if their omission still renders a distinctive name.

> Name as it appears on the source: Joint Committee on Insulator Standards of the Edison Electric Institute and the National Electrical Manufacturers Association
> Preferred name: *Joint Committee on Insulator Standards*

BUT

> Name as it appears on the source: Joint Committee of the American Library Association and the Rural Sociological Society
> Preferred name: *Joint Committee of the American Library Association and the Rural Sociological Society*

If the parent bodies are subdivisions of a larger body, record the joint committee or commission as a subdivision of that larger body.

> Preferred name: *American Library Association. Joint Committee to Compile a List of International Subscription Agents* (a joint committee of the Acquisitions Section and the Serials Section of the American Library Association's Resources and Technical Services Division)

Conventionalized names for state and local units of U.S political parties. Record the name of a local or state unit of a U.S. political party as a subdivision of the party and omit the name of the state and party from the subdivision.

> Name as it appears on the source: California Democratic State Central Committee
> Preferred name: *Democratic Party (Calif.). State Central Committee*

Heads of state and heads of government. Record the title of a chief government executive as a subdivision of the jurisdiction. Record it in the cataloging agency's preferred language, unless there is no equivalent term in that language.

> Preferred name : *Indonesia. President*

For specific incumbents, add the relevant range of years and a brief name.

> Preferred name : *United States. President (1801–1809 : Jefferson)*

If the executive title varies with gender (e.g., "King" vs. "Queen"), use a general term, such as *Sovereign*.

> Preferred name : *Scotland. Sovereign (1649–1685 : Charles II)*

Ruling executive bodies. Record the title of a ruling executive body as a subdivision of the jurisdiction. Record it in the official language of the jurisdiction.

> Preferred name : *Argentina. Junta Militar*

Add the relevant years, if necessary for distinction.

> Preferred name : *Chile. Junta de Gobierno (1973–1990)*

Heads of international intergovernmental bodies. Record the title of a head of an international or intergovernmental organization as a subdivision of the organization, in the official language of the preferred name for the organization.

> Preferred name : *Asociación Latinoamericana de Integración. Secretaría General*

For specific incumbents, add the relevant range of years and a brief name.

> Preferred name : *United Nations. Secretary-General (1997–2006 : Annan)*

Governors of dependent or occupied territories. Record the title of a governor of a dependent or occupied territory as a subdivision of the territory, in the language of the governing power.

> Preferred name : *French Polynesia. Gouverneur*

For specific incumbents, add the relevant range of years and a brief name.

> Preferred name : *Macau. Governador (1951–1956 : Esparteiro)*

Other officials. For other officials, use the preferred name for the ministry or agency that the official represents, if applicable. Otherwise, record the official's title as a subdivision of the jurisdiction.

> Preferred name : *Northern Ireland. Audit Office*
> Preferred name : *North Carolina. State Geologist*

Legislatures. Record the names of legislatures as subdivisions of the jurisdiction. Record legislative chambers as subdivisions of the legislature and legislative committees and other subordinate units as subdivisions of the chamber.

> Preferred name : *Australia. Parliament*
> Preferred name : *Australia. Parliament. Senate*
> Preferred name : *Australia. Parliament. Senate. Legal and Constitutional References Committee*

Record legislative subcommittees of the U.S. Congress as subdivisions of the committees to which they are subordinate.

> Preferred name : *United States. Congress. Senate. Committee on Foreign Relations. Subcommittee on African Affairs*

Record successive legislatures and numbered sessions with the relevant ordinal numbers and years.

> Preferred name : *United States. Congress (107th : 2001–2002)*
> Preferred name : *United States. Congress (107th : 2001–2002). Senate*
> Preferred name : *United States. Congress (107th, 1st session : 2001)*
> Preferred name : *United States. Congress (107th, 1st session : 2001). Senate*

Record the name of a constitutional convention as a subdivision of the jurisdiction, adding the relevant years. If there are different forms of names for the constitutional convention, and English is the jurisdiction's official language, record *Constitutional Convention*.

> Preferred name : *Germany. Nationalversammlung (1919–1920)*
> Preferred name : *New Hampshire. Constitutional Convention (1984)* **not** *New Hampshire. Convention to Revise the Constitution (1984)*

Courts. Record the name of civil and criminal courts as subdivisions of the jurisdiction. Add a conventional name in parentheses, if necessary for distinction.

> Preferred name : *Brazil. Supremo Tribunal de Justiça*
> Preferred name : *United States. Court of Appeals (2nd Circuit)*
> Preferred name : *United States. Court of Appeals (District of Columbia Circuit)*

Armed forces. Record principal services of the armed forces at or below the national level as subdivisions of the jurisdiction. Add further subdivisions for branches and smaller military units. If component branches are identified by a number, follow the style that appears on the source.

> Preferred name: *United States. Army*
> Preferred name: *New York (State). Militia*
> Preferred name: *United States. Army. Special Forces*
> Preferred name: *United States. Army. Infantry Division, 27th*
> Preferred name: *New York (State). Militia. Regiment, 71st*

Embassies, consulates, and delegations. Record the name of an embassy, consulate, or legation as a subdivision of the country represented, in the language of that country. For embassies and legations, add the name of the country to which it is accredited. For consulates and other local offices, add the name of the city. In both cases, record the place-name as it would appear in the qualifier of an access point.

> Preferred name: *Canada. Embassy (Belgium)*
> Preferred name: *United States. Legation (Sweden)*
> Preferred name: *France. Consulat (Buenos Aires, Argentina)*

Record the name of a delegation or commission representing a country in an international or intergovernmental undertaking as a subdivision of the country represented. Add the name of the international or intergovernmental undertaking in parentheses if needed for distinction.

> Preferred name: *India. Delegation (International Labour Conference)*

Councils of a single religious body. Record the name of a council of the clergy or membership of a single religious body as a subdivision of the religious body. If the form of name appears in more than one language, use the form found on the first resource received. Record the name of a council subordinate to a particular district of a religious body as a subdivision of that district in the official language of the district.

> Preferred name: *Catholic Church. Bishops' Conference of Bangladesh*
> Preferred name: *Catholic Church. Concilium Plenarium Americae Latinae*
> Preferred name: *Catholic Church. Province of Mexico City. Concilio Provincial*

Religious officials and popes. Record the title of a religious official, such as a bishop, abbot, rabbi, or mullah, as a subdivision of the religious jurisdiction. For specific incumbents, add the relevant range of years and a brief name.

> Preferred name: *United Hebrew Congregations of the Commonwealth. Chief Rabbi*

Preferred name : *Catholic Church. Archdiocese of St. Paul and Minneapolis. Archbishop (1995–2008 : Flynn)*

Record the title of a pope as a subdivision of the Catholic Church. For specific incumbents, add the relevant range of years and the pontifical name.

Preferred name : *Catholic Church. Pope*
Preferred name : *Catholic Church. Pope (1978–2005 : John Paul II)*

Subordinate religious bodies. Record the name of a subordinate unit of a religious body presiding over a geographical jurisdiction as a subdivision of the religious body.

Preferred name : *Church of England. Diocese of Ely*
Preferred name : *Lutheran Church in America. Florida Synod*

Record the name of a Catholic diocese, province, or patriarchate as a subdivision of the Catholic Church.

Preferred name : *Catholic Church. Province of Nicaragua*

Record the name of a central administrative organ of the Catholic Church as a subdivision of the Catholic Church. Record the subdivision in Latin.

Preferred name : *Catholic Church. Congregatio Sacrorum Rituum*

Record papal diplomatic and nondiplomatic apostolic missions as subdivisions of the Catholic Church. Use the term *Apostolic Nunciature, Apostolic Internunciature,* or *Apostolic Delegation,* as appropriate, and add the place-name in parentheses for the government to which the mission is accredited.

Preferred name : *Catholic Church. Apostolic Nunciature (Ethiopia)*

Variant Name for the Corporate Body

Variant name for the corporate body is defined as *a name or form of name by which a corporate body is known that differs from the name or form of name chosen as the preferred name.* It can be taken from resources associated with the corporate body and/ or from reference sources.

Following are examples of variant names that can be recorded for corporate bodies if it is thought that the name would be searched under that form.

Preferred name: *AFL-CIO*
Variant name: *American Federation of Labor and Congress of Industrial Organizations* (expanded form of name)

Preferred name: *European Economic Community*
Variant name: *EEC* (initialism or acronym)

Preferred name: *Unesco*
Variant name: *U.N.E.S.C.O.* (name recorded with full stops)

Preferred name: *United Nations*
Variant name: *Naciones Unidas* (different linguistic form)

Preferred name: *International Colour Vision Society*
Variant name: *International Color Vision Society* (different spelling)

Preferred name: *Franciscans*
Variant name: *Ordo Fratrum Minorum* (alternate name)

Preferred name: *Symposium on Protein Metabolism*
Variant name: *Nutrition Symposium* (generic name of conference)

Preferred name: *Association for Collections & Technical Services*
Variant name: *American Library Association. Association for Collections & Technical Services* (subdivision of the parent body)

Preferred name: *Association of College and Research Libraries. Clearing-house Committee*
Variant name: *Association of College and Research Libraries. Bibliographic Instruction Section. Clearinghouse Committee* (indirect subdivision)

Preferred name: *Lesotho. Parliament. National Assembly*
Variant name: *Lesotho. National Assembly* (direct subdivision)

RDA 11.3 Place Associated with the Corporate Body

Place associated with the corporate body is defined as *a significant location associated with a corporate body (e.g., location of a conference, etc., location of the headquarters of an organization).* It has two subelements: *location of conference, etc.* and *location of headquarters.*

The place associated with the corporate body can be recorded as a separate element, as part of an access point, or both. Regardless of where it is recorded, formulate the place as it would appear in the qualifier of an access point. When recording the place as a separate element, use MARC authority field 370 subfield $e.

Location of Conference, Etc.

Location of conference, etc. is a core element. It is defined as *a local place in which a conference, congress, meeting, exhibition, fair, festival, etc., was held.*

111   2_ $a Clambake Conference on the Nature and Source of Human Error $c (**Columbia Falls, Me.**)
370      $e Columbia Falls, Me.

Record as many places as applicable. Record *Online* for conferences held online. As an alternative to the location of a conference, record the associated institution if it would provide better identification or if the location of the conference cannot be determined.

Location of Headquarters

Location of headquarters is a core element if needed to distinguish a corporate body from similarly named corporate bodies. It is defined as a *country, state, province, etc., or local place in which an organization has its headquarters*. It can also refer to the *geographic area (state, province, city, etc.) in which a corporate body carries out its activities*.

110   2_ $a Republican Party (**Ill.**)
370      $e Ill.

110   2_ $a St. John's Church (**Lafayette Square, Washington, D.C.**)
370      $e Lafayette Square, Washington, D.C.

RDA 11.4 Date Associated with the Corporate Body

Date associated with the corporate body is a core element for conferences and when needed to distinguish one corporate body from another with the same name. It is defined as *a date significant in its history, such as date of establishment or date of termination. For a conference, it is the date or range of dates on which a conference, etc., was held. Date associated with the corporate body* has three subelements: *date of conference, date of establishment*, and *date of termination*. The date can be recorded as a separate element, as part of an access point, or both. When recording the date as a separate element, use MARC authority field 046 subfields $s and $t.

Date of Conference, Etc.

Date of conference, etc. is a core element. It is defined as *the date or range of dates on which a conference, congress, meeting, exhibition, fair, festival, etc., was held*. Record the year or range of years, as applicable.

046      $s 1995
111   2_ $a International Conference on Georgian Psalmody $n (1st : $d **1995** : $c Colchester Institute)

046      $s 1911 $t 1912
111   2_ $a Deutsche Antarktische Expedition $d (**1911–1912**)

Record specific dates if needed to distinguish between two similarly named conferences held in the same year.

> 046 $s 19780213 $t 19780215
> 111   2_ $a Federal-Provincial Conference of First Ministers $d (**1978 February 13–15**)

> 046 $s 19781127 $t 19781129
> 111   2_ $a Federal-Provincial Conference of First Ministers $d (**1978 November 27–29**)

Date of Establishment

Date of establishment is a core element. It is defined as *the date on which a corporate body was established or founded.* Record the date of establishment in MARC authority field 046 subfield $s.

> 046 $s 1977
> 110   2_ $a Double Image (**1977**)

Date of Termination

Date of termination is a core element. It is defined as *the date on which a corporate body was terminated or dissolved.* Record the date of termination in MARC authority field 046 subfield $t.

> 046 $t 1906
> 110   2_ $a Gesellschaft für Musikforschung (1906)

RDA 11.5 Associated Institution

Associated institution is a core element if it is needed for differentiation, if it provides better identification than a local place, or if the local place cannot be determined. It is defined as *an institution commonly associated with a corporate body.* The associated institution can be recorded as a separate element, as part of an access point, or both. When recording it as a separate element, use MARC authority field 373 subfield $a. For corporate bodies other than conferences, record the associated institution in the preferred form of name for the institution.

> 110   2_ $a Center for Biodiversity and Conservation (**American Museum of Natural History**)
> 373 $a American Museum of Natural History

> 111   2_ $a International Conference on Georgian Psalmody $n (1st : $d 1995 : $c **Colchester Institute**)

RDA 11.6 Number of a Conference, Etc.

Number of a conference, etc. is a core element. It is defined as *a designation of the sequencing of a conference, etc., within a series of conferences, etc.* The number of a conference can be recorded as a separate element, as part of an access point, or both.

> 111   2_ $a International Conference on Georgian Psalmody $n (**1st** : $d 1995 : $c Colchester Institute)

RDA 11.7 Other Designation Associated with the Corporate Body

Other designation associated with the corporate body is a core element when the name does not convey the idea of a corporate body. It is also a core element when needed to distinguish a corporate body from other similarly named corporate bodies. It is defined as *a word, phrase, or abbreviation that indicates incorporation or legal status of a corporate body* or *any term that differentiates the body from other corporate bodies, persons, etc.* The other distinguishing characteristic can be recorded as a separate element, as part of an access point, or both. When recording it as a separate element, use MARC authority field 368 $a.

Record another distinguishing characteristic for names that do not convey the idea of a corporate body.

> 110   2_ $a Red Hot Chili Peppers (**Musical group**)
> 368 $a Musical group

> 110   2_ $a St. Mary (**Church**)
> 368 $a Church

For a government other than a city or town, record the type of jurisdiction if needed for distinction.

> 151 $a New York (**State**)
> 368 $b State

Record the term in the cataloging agency's preferred language. Otherwise, use the official language of the jurisdiction.

> 151 $a Darmstadt (Germany : Landkreis)

Record another suitable term if the place, date, associated institution, or type of jurisdiction is insufficient for distinguishing similarly named corporate bodies.

> 110   2_ $a World Cup (**Cricket**)
> 368 $c Cricket

> 110   2_ $a World Cup (**Soccer**)
> 368 $c Soccer

RDA 11.8 Language of the Corporate Body

Language of the corporate body is defined as *a language a corporate body uses in its communications.* The language is recorded in MARC authority field 377. Record the language in the three-digit code listed in the *MARC Code List for Languages* in the subfield $a. Terms absent from the list are spelled out and recorded in the subfield $l.

> 377 $a spa $a fre

RDA 11.9 Address of the Corporate Body

Address of the corporate body is defined as *the address of a corporate body's headquarters or offices, or an e-mail or Internet address for the body.* Record the address in MARC authority field 371, usually in the form found on the source.

> 371 $a BOX 99 $b Los Angeles $c CA $e 90001 $m office@firm.com

RDA 11.10 Field of Activity of the Corporate Body

Field of activity of the corporate body is defined as *a field of business in which a corporate body is engaged and/or the body's area of competence, responsibility, jurisdiction, etc.* Record the field of activity in MARC authority field 372 subfield $a.

> 372 $a Medicine

RDA 11.11 Corporate History

Corporate history is defined as *historical information about the corporate body.* Record it in MARC authority field 678 $a.

> 678 $a The Salem Female Academy was originally founded in 1772
> and chartered as Salem Female Academy and College in 1866. In
> 1907 name was changed to Salem Academy and College, and in
> 1912, the institution was separated into Salem College and Salem
> Academy.

RDA 11.12 Identifier for the Corporate Body

Identifier for the corporate body is a core element. It is defined as *a character string uniquely associated with a corporate body, or with a surrogate for a corporate body (e.g., an authority record).* Its purpose is to differentiate one corporate body from other corporate bodies. As with identifiers for works, expressions, persons, and families, when working in the MARC environment, the identifier for the corporate body will usually not need to be preceded by the name of the assigning agency, because the MARC field conveys this information (e.g., MARC 010 field = Library of Congress Control Number).

> 010 $a no 88000581

RDA 11.13 Constructing Access Points to Represent Corporate Bodies

RDA 11.13.1 Authorized Access Point Representing a Corporate Body

The preferred name for the corporate body is used as the basis for constructing the authorized access point for that corporate body. Sometimes the authorized access point representing the corporate body comprises the preferred name alone.

> preferred name for the corporate body
> 110   2_ $a Museum of American Folk Art
> 110   2_ $a University of Vermont. $b Choral Union

Other corporate bodies need one or more additions appended to the preferred name.

> preferred name for the corporate body + *additions*

Sometimes an addition is needed for a name that does not convey the idea of a corporate body.

> 110   2_ $a Health of the Public (Program)

Sometimes the place associated with the corporate body is needed to distinguish two or more similarly named bodies.

> 110   2_ $a National Measurement Laboratory (Australia)
> 110   2_ $a National Measurement Laboratory (U.S.)

For local places of worship, such as churches, temples, and mosques, the local place or the local ecclesiastical jurisdiction is added, unless it is already part of the name.

> 110   2_ $a Beth Tikvah Synagogue (Toronto, Ont.)

BUT

> 110   2_ $a Grande synagogue de Bruxelles

For television and radio stations, the local place is added, unless it is already part of the name.

> 110   2_ $a Rádio Moçambique (Maputo, Mozambique)

BUT

> 110   2_ $a KBS Kyōto (Radio station)
> 110   2_ $a TV Tacoma

Sometimes an associated institution is needed to distinguish two or more similarly named bodies or to provide better identification, particularly if the institution's name is commonly associated with the name of the corporate body.

> 110   2_ $a B'nai B'rith Hillel Federation Jewish Student Center (University of Cincinnati)

Sometimes a date is needed to distinguish two or more similarly named corporate bodies if neither the place associated with the body nor the associated institution is available.

> 110   1_ $a South Dakota. Department of Public Safety (1973–1984)
> 110   1_ $a South Dakota. Department of Public Safety (2003–)

Sometimes the type of jurisdiction is added to a government (other than a city or town) to distinguish two or more similarly named bodies.

> 151 $a New York (N.Y.) *the city*
> 151 $a New York (**State**)
> 151 $a Guadalajara (Spain) *the city*
> 151 $a Guadalajara (Spain : **Province**)

Sometimes another distinguishing characteristic is added to differentiate similarly named government bodies.

> 151 $a Korea (North)
> 151 $a Korea (South)

Sometimes the number, date, and location of a conference are added to the name of an individual instance of a conference, if readily available. In the case of a conference held online, the word *Online* is recorded as the location. In some cases, the associated institution may be recorded in lieu of the location.

> 110   2_ $a Australian Bioethics Association. $b National Conference $n (6th : $d 1998 : $c Hobart, Tas.)
> 111   2_ $a Electronic Conference on Land Use and Land Cover Change in Europe $d (1997 : $c Online)
> 111   2_ $a Marine Awareness Workshop for Beqa Lagoon $d (1996 : $c Pacific Harbour International Hotel)

If the access point is for an ongoing conference, the date, number, and location are omitted.

> 111   2_ $a Annual Symposium on Sea Turtle Biology and Conservation

Sometimes more than one addition may be needed. In cases such as television and radio stations, where the name consists mainly of call letters, another distinguishing characteristic is added along with the local place.

>   110   2_ $a KUON (Television station : Lincoln, Neb.)

In other cases, one or more terms may be used to distinguish similarly named corporate bodies, often in concert with other obligatory additions (such as conference number, location, and date). If two or more additions are appended to a name, record them in this order: *addition to a name not conveying the idea of a corporate body; place associated with the body; associated institution; date associated with the body; type of jurisdiction; other designation associated with the body;* and *number, date, and location of a conference, etc.*

>   110   2_ $a Mary (Sloop : 1752)
>   110   2_ $a Indiana (Battleship : BB-58)
>   110   2_ $a All Hallows (Church : London, England : Bread Street)
>   111   2_ $a Governor's Conference on Aging (Fla.) $n (3rd : $d 1992 :
> $c Tallahassee, Fla.)
>   111   2_ $a U.S. Open (Golf tournament) $d (1989 : $c Oak Hill Country
>   Club)

RDA 11.13.2 Variant Access Point Representing a Corporate Body

Use the variant name for the corporate body as the basis for constructing the variant access point. If appending additions, follow the same guidelines for making additions to authorized access points for corporate bodies.

>   variant name for the corporate body + *{additions}*
>   110   2_ $a Group of Seventy-seven
>   410   2_ $a Group of 77
>
>   110   2_ $a Arizona (Battleship)
>   410   2_ $a U.S.S. Arizona
>
>   110   2_ $a Koryŏ Taehakkyo. $b Pŏmnyul Hakhoe
>   410   2_ $a Legal Association of Korea University
>
>   111   2_ $a International Conference of Soil Mechanics $d (1982 : $c
>   Mexico City, Mexico)
>   411   2_ $a Conférence internationale de mécanique des sols $d (1982 :
> $c Mexico City, Mexico)
>
>   110   2_ $a AMNH Digital Library Project
>   410   2_ $a Digital Library Project (American Museum of Natural History)

RDA CHAPTER 16: IDENTIFYING PLACES

The current text of Chapter 16 of RDA was derived from Chapter 23 of AACR2. Although the ultimate intent of Chapter 16 is to provide guidelines for recording all the relevant attributes that help users identify places, the current guidelines focus on preferred and variant names for places, and the guidelines for recording other attributes will be developed in future releases of RDA.

The main purpose of Chapter 16 as currently written is to provide guidance on formulating the name of a place that is used as the conventional name for a government. It also provides instructions on how to record the name of a place in the qualifier of an access point or in the variable field of another entity's authority record. "Identifying Places" is the chapter to consult for formulating the place-name for the following elements: *place of origin of a work, place associated with a person, place associated with a family, place associated with a corporate body, location of a conference, etc.,* and *location of the headquarters of a corporate body.*

RDA 16.2 Name of the Place

Name of the place is defined as *a word, character, or group of words and/or characters by which a place is known.* It has two subelements: *preferred name for the place* and *variant name for the place.*

Preferred Name for the Place

Preferred name for the place is defined as *the name or form of name chosen to represent a place when a place name is used as the conventional name of a government, etc., or as an addition to the name of a family, a corporate body, a conference, etc., or a work, or when recording a place associated with a person, family, or corporate body.*

The sources for determining the preferred name include gazetteers and other reference sources written in the cataloging agency's preferred language. Otherwise, use gazetteers and other reference sources issued in the jurisdiction in which the place is located and written in that jurisdiction's official language. Choose a form of name that is written in the cataloging agency's preferred language. Otherwise, use a form that is written in the official language of the jurisdiction in which the place is located.

Recording the preferred name. A place-name can be recorded as the conventionalized name of a government, in the qualifier of an access point, or in a variable field of another entity's authority record. When a place-name is recorded in a qualifier or in a variable field, follow the abbreviation conventions in RDA Appendix B, as applicable.

In some cases, a place-name is recorded alone. This generally occurs when the place is at the national level or higher.

151	$a United States
370	$c U.S.

In some limited cases (which are described later), a place below the national level can be recorded alone.

     151      $a California
     370      $e Calif.

In all other cases, the place-name is followed by the name of the larger jurisdiction. If the place-name is being used as the conventional name of a government, the larger jurisdiction is recorded in parentheses.

     151      $a Florence **(Italy)**

If the name is recorded in the qualifier of an access point or in a variable field of another entity's authority record, the larger jurisdiction is preceded by a comma.

     110 2_ $a Grand Hotel (Florence, **Italy**)
     370      $e Florence**, Italy**

If the name is written in a nonpreferred script, generally transliterate it according to the scheme chosen by the cataloging agency.

> Preferred name: ʿAqabah (transliteration of an Arabic script using the ALA-LC Romanization Tables)

RDA offers the alternative to use whatever transliteration is found on the source. However, if there is more than one transliteration, and one of them matches the agency's preferred scheme, then that form should be chosen.

Different language forms. Choose the form in the cataloging agency's preferred language, as determined from gazetteers and other reference sources written in that language.

> Example: *Austria* **not** *Österreich*

If there is no form in the agency's preferred language that is in general use, use the form that is in the official language of the jurisdiction in which the place is located.

> Example: *Buenos Aires*

If there is more than one official language, choose the most common form found in sources written in the agency's preferred language.

> Example: *Helsinki* **not** *Helsingfors*

Place names with terms indicating type of jurisdiction. RDA provides instructions in Chapter 11 for adding a term indicating the type of jurisdiction to differentiate similarly named places. In some cases, the term appears on the source in conjunction with the name of the place or is integral to the name. If the term appears in conjunction with the name, but is typically omitted in published listings, omit the term from the name.

> Preferred name: *Kerry (Ireland)* **not** *County Kerry (Ireland)*

Otherwise, retain the term.

> Preferred name: *Mexico City (Mexico)*
> Preferred name: *Distrito Federal (Brazil)*

Places in Australia, Canada, the United States, the former U.S.S.R., or the former Yugoslavia. For states, provinces, and territories in Australia, Canada, the United States, the former U.S.S.R., and the former Yugoslavia, omit the larger jurisdiction from the preferred name. (Note that until July 2013, Malaysia was included in this list of jurisdictions.)

> Preferred name: *Wisconsin* **not** *Wisconsin (U.S.)*
> Preferred name: *Ontario* **not** *Ontario (Canada)*

For places within the states, provinces, or territories of Australia, Canada, the United States, the former U.S.S.R., and the former Yugoslavia, record the state, province, or territory after the place-name. Abbreviate the state, province, or territory following Appendix B.

> Preferred name: *Chicago (Ill.)*
> Preferred name: *Washington (D.C.)*
> Preferred name: *Ottawa (Ont.)*
> Preferred name: *Latah Soil and Water Conservation District (Idaho)*
> Preferred name: *San Juan (P.R.)*

Places in the British Isles. For England, Northern Ireland, Scotland, and Wales, do not record the larger jurisdiction as part of the preferred name.

> Preferred name: *England*
> Preferred name: *Northern Ireland*

For other places within the British Isles, record *England, Northern Ireland, Scotland,* or *Wales* as appropriate.

> Preferred name: *London (England)*
> Preferred name: *Powys (Wales)*

Overseas territories, dependencies, etc. Do not record the name of the larger jurisdiction as part of the preferred name for overseas territories, dependencies, etc.

Preferred name: *Isle of Man*
Preferred name: *French Guiana*

Places in other jurisdictions. For all other places below the national level, add the name of the country and apply the abbreviation guidelines in Appendix B where applicable.

Preferred name: *Rome (Italy)*
Preferred name: *Far North Province (Cameroon)*
Preferred name: *Queenstown-Lakes District (N.Z.)*

Places with the same name. If there are two or more places within the same larger jurisdiction that have the same name, include in the preferred name a word or phrase that is commonly used to distinguish them.

Preferred name: *Alhama de Almería (Spain)*
Preferred name: *Alhama de Granada (Spain)*

If no such word exists, record an intervening jurisdiction to distinguish them.

Preferred name: *Farnham (Dorset, England)*
Preferred name: *Farnham (Essex, England)*
Preferred name: *Oakdale (Stearns County, Minn.)*
Preferred name: *Oakdale (Washington County, Minn.)*

Places within cities, etc. If recording the name of a place within a city or town, add the name of the city along with the larger jurisdiction that is typically recorded with the city, applying abbreviation conventions where applicable.

Preferred name: *Hyde Park (Chicago, Ill.)*
Preferred name: *Chelsea (London, England)*
Preferred name: *Quartier latin (Paris, France)*
Preferred name: *Tamaki (Auckland, N.Z.)*

Variant Name for the Place

Variant name for the place is defined as *a name or form of name by which a place is known that differs from the name or form of the name chosen as the preferred name.* The variant name for the place can be taken from any source. Following are some examples of when the variant name for the place may be useful for access.

Preferred name: *St. John's (N.L.)*
Variant name: *Saint John's (N.L.)* (expanded form)

Preferred name: *Lower Downtown (Denver, Colo.)*
Variant name: *Lo Do (Denver, Colo.)* (abbreviated form)
Variant name: *LoDo (Denver, Colo.)* (abbreviated form without spacing)

Preferred name: *R.A.F. Kenley (England)*
Variant name: *RAF Kenley (England)* (initialism without full stops)

Preferred name: *Quartier latin (Paris, France)*
Variant name: *Latin Quarter (Paris, France)* (different language form)

Preferred name: *Pio XII (Brazil)*
Variant name: *Pio Doze (Brazil)* (different recording of the numeral)

Preferred name: *Albania*
Variant name: *People's Socialist Republic of Albania* (different form)

Preferred name: *Dalles (Or.)*
Variant name: *The Dalles (Or.)* (initial article included)

Preferred name: *Cabbagetown (Toronto, Ont.)*
Variant name: *Toronto (Ont.). Cabbagetown* (city section recorded as a subdivision of the city)

RDA 16.4 Constructing Access Points to Represent Places

RDA refers to Chapter 11 for constructing access points for places-names used as conventional names for governments. The following examples show the authorized and variant access points representing places, along with the relevant MARC coding.

151	$a United States
451	$a US
451	$a U.S.
451	$a Estados Unidos
151	$a Quartier latin (Paris, France)
451	$a Latin Quarter (Paris, France)
451	$a Paris (France). $b Quartier latin

CONCLUSION

This chapter outlined the guidelines for recording the attributes of persons, families, corporate bodies, and places. It detailed the relevant MARC coding for the variable authority fields used for recording these attributes and explained when and how to incorporate some of these attributes into authorized and variant access points. This chapter concludes the portion of RDA devoted to recording the attributes of FRBR and FRAD entities. The next two chapters address the relationships among the entities. Of note are the relationships between Group 1 entities (work, expression, manifestation, and item) and Group 2 entities (person, family, and corporate body). In MARC, the relationship between a Group 1 entity and a Group 2 entity is often conveyed by adding the authorized access point for the Group 2 entity to the record for the Group 1 entity. Now that we have learned how to construct access points for persons, families, and corporate bodies, we can focus our attention on recording these relationships in bibliographic records. These and other relationships are outlined in the next chapter.

7

Recording Relationships

RDA Sections 5–10 comprise twenty-one chapters that provide instructions on recording relationships among the various FRBR and FRAD entities. Each section is devoted to a specific category of relationships. Specifically:

- RDA Section 5, "Recording Primary Relationships between Work, Expression, Manifestation & Item" (Chapter 17), offers guidelines on recording the primary relationships among Group 1 entities.
- RDA Section 6, "Recording Relationships to Persons, Families & Corporate Bodies" (Chapters 18–22), provides instructions on recording the responsibility relationships between Group 1 and Group 2 entities.
- RDA Section 7, "Recording Relationships to Concepts, Objects, Events & Places" (Chapter 23), serves as a placeholder for future instructions on recording subject relationships between works and Group 3 entities.
- RDA Section 8, "Recording Relationships betweenWorks, Expressions, Manifestations & Items" (Chapters 24–28), provides instructions on recording relationships between Group 1 entities at the same hierarchical level.
- RDA Section 9, "Recording Relationships between Persons, Families & Corporate Bodies" (Chapter 29–32), provides instructions on recording the relationships between Group 2 entities.
- RDA Section 10, "Recording Relationships between Concepts, Objects, Events & Places" (Chapter 33–37), serves as a placeholder for future guidelines on recording the relationships between Group 3 entities.

RDA Sections 5–10 all provide instructions that support the "find" user task.

RDA's first chapter on relationships, Chapter 17, "General Guidelines on Recording Primary Relationships," provides guidelines for recording the relationship between a work and the expression through which it is realized, the relationship between an expression and the manifestation in which it is embodied, and the relationship between a manifestation and the item by which it is exemplified. Recording these types of relationships would be more applicable in a database implementation scenario in which each of the entities was described in a separate record. However, in the current MARC environment, recording primary relationships is moot because the bibliographic record is essentially a composite of all the Group 1 entities. Therefore, the guidelines in Chapter 17 are not covered here.

RDA Chapter 23 is intended to provide guidelines on recording the subject matter of a work, but it is currently a placeholder. RDA Chapters 33–37 are intended to provide instructions on recording related concepts, related objects, related events, and related places, but these chapters are also placeholders. Therefore, Chapter 23 and Chapters 33–37 are not covered in this book.

This chapter of this book begins by detailing the instructions in RDA Section 6 (Chapters 18–22), which provide guidelines for recording the relationships among persons, families, and corporate bodies and the works, expressions, manifestations, and items for which they are responsible. It then covers RDA Section 8 (Chapters 24–28), detailing the instructions therein for recording the relationships between two works, between two expressions, between two manifestations, and between two items. Finally, it discusses RDA Section 9 (Chapters 29–32), which provides guidelines for recording related persons, related families, and related corporate bodies.

Many elements in RDA Sections 6, 8, and 9 can be taken from any source. If the source of information for an element differs from this pattern, it is noted.

RDA SECTION 6: RECORDING RELATIONSHIPS TO PERSONS, FAMILIES & CORPORATE BODIES

RDA Section 6 comprises five chapters: Chapters 18–22. Chapter 18 provides general guidelines that pertain to the remaining chapters. Chapter 19 addresses the relationship between a work and the Group 2 entities responsible for its creation. Chapter 20 addresses the relationship between an expression and the Group 2 entities responsible for its realization. Chapter 21 addresses the relationship between a manifestation and the Group 2 entities responsible for its production. Finally, Chapter 22 addresses the relationship between an item and the Group 2 entities responsible for its ownership.

In MARC, the way to represent the relationship between a resource and the person, family, or corporate body responsible for it is to record the authorized access point for the Group 2 entity in the bibliographic record of the resource. The access point for the Group 2 entity should be constructed according to guidelines in RDA Chapters 9–11 (described in chapter 6 of this book).

Information on the person, family, or corporate body associated with a work, expression, manifestation, or item should be taken from statements appearing on the preferred sources of information in manifestations that embody the work, as outlined in RDA instruction 2.2.2 (described in chapter 4 of this book). For most standard resources this will be the title page, the title screen, a permanently affixed label, or some other location, depending on the resource. If those preferred sources bear insufficient information, the following sources of information should be used (in order of preference): other prominent statements within the resource, information within the content of the resource, or other sources.

RDA CHAPTER 18: GENERAL GUIDELINES ON RECORDING RELATIONSHIPS TO PERSONS, FAMILIES & CORPORATE BODIES ASSOCIATED WITH A RESOURCE

As do other introductory chapters in RDA, Chapter 18 contextualizes the content of the four chapters that follow. It explains the terminology used in the chapters; outlines the functional objectives and principles met by the instructions in the chapters; names the RDA Section 6 elements that are core; explains the two conventions used for recording responsibility relationships; provides instructions on how to address a change in responsibility for multipart monographs, serials and integrating resources; and provides instructions for the chapter's sole element: relationship designators. The discussion that follows addresses the conventions for recording responsibility relationships, changes in responsibility, and relationship designators.

Recording Responsibility Relationships

Recording Conventions

RDA describes two methods for recording responsibility relationships. The first method is to record the identifier for the person, family, or corporate body, which is less common in the current RDA implementation scenario. The second, more common method is to provide the access point for the person, family, or corporate body. This method is covered more extensively in this book. In addition, a relationship designator can be provided to further clarify the relationship.

Change in Responsibility

For multipart monographs and serials with a change in responsibility, additional access points can be added for persons, families, and corporate bodies associated with the later parts or issues, if considered important for access. For integrating resources, access points for persons, families, and corporate bodies associated with the most recent iteration can be added, if considered important for access. Access points for persons, families, and corporate bodies associated with earlier iterations of integrating resources may also be retained, if considered important for access.

RDA 18.5 Relationship Designator

Relationship designator is defined as *a designator that indicates the nature of the relationship between a resource and a person, family, or corporate body associated with that resource represented by an authorized access point and/or identifier.* RDA Appendix I has an open list of relationship designators for the various levels of responsibility for a resource (e.g., creator, contributor, producer, owner, etc.). One or more of these terms may be assigned as appropriate to indicate the nature of the relationship. If none of the terms is sufficient or appropriate, another concise term may be devised. When used to explicate a responsibility relationship, designators are generally recorded in bibliographic records in subfield $e of MARC fields 100, 110, 700, and 710 and in the $j of MARC fields 111 and 711.

Although not core, relationship designators can help clarify the role a person, family, or corporate body has played in the creation, realization, production, or ownership of a resource.

```
100   1_  $a Bailey, David, $d 1938– $e photographer.
245   10  $a Goodbye baby & amen : $b a saraband for the sixties /
          $c David Bailey & Peter Evans.
700   1_  $a Evans, Peter, $d 1933– $e author.
```

The $e is a repeatable field. Thus, as many relationship designators may be added as applicable, even if they reflect different levels of responsibility. For example, if a musical group both writes songs for an album (creates a work) and performs on the album (contributes to an expression), one relationship designator can be added for the "creation" aspect and a second for the "contribution" aspect."

```
100   1_  $a Coldplay (Musical group), $e lyricist, $e performer.
245   10  $a Parachutes / $c Coldplay.
```

Because RDA is a content standard rather than a display standard, RDA Chapters 19–22 do not depict the relationship designator in the examples. In fact, they do not mention relationship designators at all. However, to show the designators in context, they are included in the discussion on Chapters 19–22 as well as in other relationship chapters covered in this book.

RDA CHAPTER 19: PERSONS, FAMILIES, AND CORPORATE BODIES ASSOCIATED WITH A WORK

RDA Chapter 19 provides guidelines on recording the relationships between Group 2 entities and the works they create. It also gives instructions for recording Group 2 entities other than creators who are responsible for a work. The following discussion covers highlights from Chapter 19 and provides examples of the relevant MARC fields and, in some examples, relationship designator terms.

RDA 19.2 Creator

Creator is a core element for the first creator named. It is defined as *a person, family, or corporate body responsible for the creation of a work.* If recording the access point for a single creator, a principal creator, or a first-named creator, use MARC bibliographic field 100 with a 0 or 1 in the first indicator for persons, field 100 with a 3 in the first indicator for families, and field 110 or 111 for corporate bodies. If applicable, add one or more relationship designators that reflect responsibility for the intellectual or artistic creation of the work. The following are examples from the open list of relationship designators in RDA Appendix I.2.1: *artist, author, cartographer, compiler, composer, enacting jurisdiction, filmmaker, interviewer, interviewee, lyricist, photographer,* and *screenwriter.*

    100   1_ $a Hemingway, Ernest, $d 1899–1961, $e author.
    245   14 $a The sun also rises / $c by Ernest Hemingway.

    100   3_ $a Austen (Family : $g Austen, Jane, 1775–1817)
    245   10 $a Austen papers, 1704–1856 / $c edited by R.A. Austen-Leigh.

    110   1_ $a Maine.
    245   10 $a Maine.gov : $b official Web site of the state of Maine.

For subsequently named creators, use the 7XX fields that correspond to the 100, 110, and 111 fields mentioned above.

    100   1_ $a Zim, Herbert S. $q (Herbert Spencer), $d 1909–1994,
          $e author.
    245   10 $a Birds : $b a guide to the most familiar American birds /
          $c by Herbert S. Zim and Ira N. Gabrielson ; illustrated by
          James Gordon Irving.
    700   1_ $a Gabrielson, Ira Noel, $d 1889–1977, $e author.

    100   3_ $a Short (Family : $g Ohio)
    245   10 $a Short-Harrison-Symmes family papers, 1760–1878 (bulk
          1800–1860).
    700   3_ $a Harrison (Family : $c Ohio)
    700   3_ $a Symmes (Family : $g Symmes, John Cleves, 1742–1814)

    110   2_ $a Canadian Botanical Association.
    245   10 $a Directory of the Canadian Botanical Association & Canadian
          Society of Plant Physiologists.
    710   2_ $a Canadian Society of Plant Physiologists.

Two or more creators may be jointly responsible for a work and can perform the same role (such as coauthors) or different roles (such as a composer and a lyricist).

Same role

100　1_ $a Gumbley, Warren, $d 1962– $e author.
245　10 $a Management of wetland archaeological sites in New Zealand / $c Warren Gumbley, Dilys Johns, and Garry Law.
700　1_ $a Johns, Dilys, $e author.
700　1_ $a Law, Garry, $e author.

Different roles

100　1_ $a Shinozaki, Mamoru, $d 1908–1991, $e interviewee.
245　10 $a My wartime experiences in Singapore / $c Mamoru Shinozaki ; interviewed by Lim Yoon Lin.
700　1_ $a Lim, Yoon Lin, $e interviewer.

100　1_ $a Gorney, Jay, $d 1896–1990, $e composer.
245　10 $a You gotta wanna (once in a while) / $c music by Jay Gorney and Henry Souvaine ; lyric by Edgar Harburg.
700　1_ $a Souvaine, Henry, $e composer.
700　1_ $a Harburg, E. Y. $q (Edgar Yipsel), $d 1896–1981, $e lyricist.

A person, family, or corporate body can be considered a creator of an aggregate work if the editing, selecting, and arrangement of the content essentially yields a new work.

100　1_ $a Adams, Phillip, $e compiler.
245　14 $a The Penguin book of jokes from cyberspace / $c collected by Phillip Adams and Patrice Newell.
700　1_ $a Newell, Patrice, $d 1956– $e compiler.

A person, family, or corporate body can be considered a creator of a revised work if the content or nature of the work is changed substantially.

100　1_ $a Bell, Florence.
245　10 $a Great expectations / $c Charles Dickens ; retold by Florence Bell.

Corporate Bodies as Creators

A corporate body can be considered a creator of a work if the work falls into one or more of the following categories:

i. Administrative works dealing with aspects of the corporate body itself, such as its internal policies, procedures, or finances; its officers, staff, or membership (such as directories); or its resources (such as catalogs).

110　2_ $a Kiowa Indian Tribe of Oklahoma.
245　10 $a Annual report / $c Kiowa Tribe of Oklahoma.

```
110   2_ $a Northern Pacific Railway Company
245   10 $a Northern Pacific Railway Company records, 1864–1957.
```

  ii. Works reflecting the collective thought of the body (such as committee reports and official statements of position on external policies and standards).

```
110   1_ $a Zambia.
245   14 $a The national conservation strategy for Zambia / $c prepared
         by the Government of the Republic of Zambia with assistance from
         . . .
```

  iii. Works that record hearings conducted by legislative, judicial, governmental, and other corporate bodies.

```
110   1_ $a New York (State). $b Insurance Department
245   10 $a Welfare and pension fund public hearing
```

  iv. Works reporting the collective activity of a conference, expedition, or event.

```
111   2_ $a Janus Conference on Research Library Collections $d (2005 :
         $c Cornell University Library)
245   10 $a Janus Conference on Research Library Collections :
         $b managing the shifting ground between writers and readers :
         October 9–11, 2005, Cornell University Library.
```

  v. Works resulting from the collective activity of a performing group that goes beyond mere performance.

```
110   2_ $a Living Theatre (New York, N.Y.)
245   10 $a Paradise now / $c collective creation of the Living Theatre ;
         written down by Judith Malina and Julian Beck.
```

  vi. Cartographic works from corporate bodies whose responsibility goes beyond mere publication or distribution.

```
110   2_ $a Ordnance Survey of Ireland.
245   10 $a Cork city street map and index : $b scale 1:15,000 /
         $c Ordnance Survey of Ireland.
```

  vii. Legal works that are laws of a political jurisdiction; decrees of a head of state, chief executive, or ruling executive body; bills and drafts of legislation; administrative regulations; constitutions and charters; court rules; treaties and international agreements; and charges to juries, indictments, court proceedings, and court decisions.

110   1_ $a Richmond (Va.)
245   10 $a Building code of the city of Richmond, Virginia.

110   1_ $a Illinois. $b Department of Public Health.
245   10 $a Rules and regulations for recreational areas : $b prescribed
      under the Recreational Area Licensing Act, chapter 111 1/2, para-
      graphs 761–792 inclusive.

110   1_ $a Maine.
245   10 $a Joint agreement between the state of Maine and the province
      of New Brunswick.
710   1_ $a New Brunswick.

A government or religious official can be considered a creator of a work if the resource is one of the following types of official communications:

viii. Official communications written by heads of state, heads of government, heads of dependent or occupied territories, and heads of international bodies. Such communications include proclamations, executive orders, and messages to legislatures.

110   1_ $a United States. $b President.
245   10 $a Economic report of the President transmitted to the Congress.

ix. Official communications issued from popes, patriarchs, bishops, and other religious officials. Such communications include orders, decrees, pastoral letters, and official messages to councils.

110   2_ $a Catholic Church. $b Pope.
245   10 $a Papal thought on the state : $b excerpts from encyclicals and
      other writings of recent popes / $c edited by Gerard F. Yates.

RDA 19.3 Other Person, Family, or Corporate Body Associated with a Work

Other person, family, or corporate body associated with a work is a core element when used for constructing the authorized access point for representing the work. It is defined as *a person, family, or corporate body associated with a work other than as a creator*. It includes addressees of correspondence, honorees of festschriften, cinematographers, directors, film producers, sponsoring bodies, issuing bodies, and institutions hosting an exhibition or event. It is usually recorded in MARC bibliographic field 700 with a 0 or 1 in the first indicator for persons, field 700 with a 3 in the first indicator for families, and field 710 for corporate bodies. In a few cases, it is recorded in the 1XX fields that correspond to the 700 and 710 fields mentioned above. This is particularly the case for some legal and religious works.

245   00 $a Music in the classic period : $b essays in honor of Barry S. Brook / $c [edited by] Allan W. Atlas.

700   1_ $a Brook, Barry S. $e honouree.

100   1_ $a Brooks, William, $d 1803–1863, $e plaintiff.

245   14 $a The case of William Brooks versus Ezekiel Byam and others, in equity, in the Circuit Court of the United States, for the First Circuit–District of Massachusetts.

Other Person, Family, or Corporate Body Associated with Legal Works

Other person, family, or corporate body associated with legal works is a core element when used for constructing the authorized access point for representing the work. The following examples represent some of the instances in which another person, family, or corporate body associated with a legal work can be recorded.

Jurisdiction governed by a law or regulation promulgated by a different jurisdiction

245   10 $a Code of the public local laws of Worcester County : $b article 24 of the Code of public local laws of Maryland ... / edited by Carl N. Everstine.

710   1_ $a Worcester County (Md.), $e jurisdiction governed.

Issuing agency or agent

245   10 $a Virginia occupational safety and health standards for general industry (29 CFR part 1910) / $c as adopted by the Safety and Health Codes Commission of the Commonwealth of Virginia ; issued by the Department of Labor and Industry.

710   1_ $a Virginia. $b Department of Labor and Industry, $e issuing body.

Courts governed by rules

110   1_ $a United States. $b Tax Court, $e court governed.

245   10 $a Rules of practice and procedure of United States Tax Court.

Non-jurisdictional bodies governed by constitutions

245   10 $a Charter of Columbus Savings Bank, incorporated by special act of Legislature of the state of Georgia, December 24, 1888.

710   2_ $a Columbus Savings Bank (Columbus, Ga.)

Criminal proceedings, appeals, and indictments

110   2_ $a Meteor (Ship), $e defendant.

245   10 $a Report of the case of the steamship Meteor, libelled for alleged violation of the Neutrality Act / $c edited by F.V. Balch.

100   1_ $a Brooks, William, $d 1803–1863, $e plaintiff.
245   14 $a The case of William Brooks versus Ezekiel Byam and oth-
      ers, in equity, in the Circuit Court of the United States, for the
      First Circuit–District of Massachusetts.
700   1_ $a Byam, Ezekiel, $d 1796–1863, $e defendant.

Charges to juries, judicial decisions, and judicial opinions
245   10 $a Judge Merrick's charge to the jury, in the Dalton divorce
      case.
700   1_ $a Dalton, Benjamin Franklin, $e plaintiff.

Other Person, Family, or Corporate Body Associated with a Religious Work

Other person, family, or corporate body associated with a religious work is a core element when used for constructing the authorized access point for representing the
work. The following examples represent instances in which another person, family,
or corporate body associated with a religious work can be recorded.

Denominational Body Associated with a Creed, Etc.
245   04 $a The confession of faith and catechisms : $b the Westmin-
      ster Confession of Faith and catechisms as adopted by the Ortho-
      dox Presbyterian Church : with proof texts.
710   2_ $a Orthodox Presbyterian Church.

Church or Denominational Body Associated with a Liturgical Work
110   2_ $a Church of England.
245   14 $a The communion in Coventry Cathedral.
710   2_ $a Coventry Cathedral.

Body within a Church, Etc., Associated with a Liturgical Work
110   2_ $a Church of England.
245   14 $a The communion in Coventry Cathedral.
710   2_ $a Coventry Cathedral.

RDA CHAPTER 20: PERSONS, FAMILIES, AND
CORPORATE BODIES ASSOCIATED WITH AN EXPRESSION

RDA Chapter 20 provides guidelines on recording the relationships between Group
2 entities and the expressions to which they have contributed. It has only one
element—*contributor*—which is described below.

RDA 20.2 Contributor

Contributor is defined as *a person, family, or corporate body contributing to the realization of a work through an expression.* Contributors include editors, illustrators,
performers, translators, writers of added commentary, arrangers of music, and com-

posers of additional parts of music. For recording the access point for a contributor, use MARC bibliographic field 700 with a 0 or 1 in the first indicator for persons, field 700 with a 3 in the first indicator for families, and field 710 for corporate bodies. If applicable, add one or more relationship designators that reflect responsibility for contributing to the realization of the expression. The following are examples from the open list of relationship designators in RDA Appendix I.3.1: *actor, arranger of music, composer (expression), editor, editor of compilation, illustrator, narrator, performer, singer, translator,* and *writer of added commentary.*

```
245   10 $a Anatomy of the human body / $c by Henry Gray.
250      $a 25th edition / $b edited by Charles Mayo Goss.
700   1_ $a Goss, Charles Mayo, $d 1899– $e editor.

245   10 $a Syrinx : $b for flute and piano : flute solo / $c Claude
         Debussy ; with piano accompaniment by Daniel Kelley.
700   1_ $a Kelley, Daniel, $e composer (expression)

245   10 $a Birds : $b a guide to the most familiar American birds / $c by
         Herbert S. Zim and Ira N. Gabrielson ; illustrated by James Gordon
         Irving.
700   1_ $a Irving, James Gordon, $e illustrator.

245   10 $a Fathers and sons / $c Ivan Turgenev ; translated by Rosemary
         Edmonds.
700   1_ $a Edmonds, Rosemary, $e translator.

245   00 $a Peter go ring dem bells : $b Negro spiritual / $c arranged by
         Florence B. Price.
700   1_ $a Price, Florence, 1887–1953, $e arranger.

245   10 $a Any day now : $b Bob Dylan's songs / $c sung by Joan Baez.
700   1_ $a Baez, Joan, $e singer.

245   00 $a Orchestral suites of the British Isles.
710   2_ $a Edmonton Symphony Orchestra, $e performer.
700   1_ $a Mayer, Uri, 1946– $e conductor.

245   10 $a The charge to the jury and the sentence by Judge Theodoric
         R. Westbrook in the case of Hilaire Latrimouille / $c reported by
         James M. Ruso, court stenographer.
700   _1 $a Ruso, James M., $e court reporter.

245   10 $a Treaties and other international agreements of the United
         States of America, 1776–1949 / $c compiled under the direction of
         Charles I. Bevans.
700   1_ $a Bevans, Charles I. (Charles Irving), $d 1908–1986,
         $e compiler.
```

RDA CHAPTER 21: PERSONS, FAMILIES, AND CORPORATE BODIES ASSOCIATED WITH A MANIFESTATION

RDA Chapter 21 provides guidelines on recording the relationships between Group 2 entities and the manifestations they have produced, published, distributed, or manufactured. These relationships can be recorded in MARC bibliographic field 700 with a 0 or 1 in the first indicator for persons, field 700 with a 3 in the first indicator for families, and fields 710 and 711 for corporate bodies.

If applicable, one or more relationship designators may be added to reflect responsibility for the manifestation. General relationship designators are not provided for producers, publishers, distributors, or manufacturers, perhaps because it is unusual, except in specialized cataloging, to provide access points for entities with these general roles. Specific designators for manufacturers are listed in RDA Appendix I.4 and include *engraver*, *etcher*, *lithographer*, and *platemaker*, among others. Specific designators for publishers and distributors are also listed and include *broadcaster* and *film distributor*, respectively.

RDA 21.2 Producer of an Unpublished Resource

Producer of an unpublished resource is defined as *a person, family, or corporate body responsible for inscribing, fabricating, constructing, etc., a resource in an unpublished form.*

```
245   00 $a Annabella / $c produced by Thomas A. Edison.
264   _0 $a [United States?] : $b Thomas A. Edison, $c 1897.
700   1_ $a Edison, Thomas A. $q (Thomas Alva), $d 1847–1931.
```

RDA 21.3 Publisher

Publisher is defined as *a person, family, or corporate body responsible for publishing, releasing, or issuing a resource.*

```
245   00 $a Stanwood area and Camano Island street map.
264   _1 $a Sedro-Woolley, Washington : $b Published by Sizemore
         Enterprises in conjunction with the Stanwood & Camano Island
         Chambers of Commerce, $c [2003]
710   2_ $a Sizemore Enterprises.
```

RDA 21.4 Distributor

Distributor is defined as *a person, family, or corporate body responsible for distributing a resource.*

```
245   00 $a Detailed ear model.
264   _1 $a [Hamburg, Germany] : $b 3B Scientific, $c 2000.
264   _2 $a Waco, TX: $b Distributed by Health Edco, $c [date of distri-
         bution not identified]
```

700 1_ $a Health Edco, Inc.

245 00 $a This film is not yet rated / $c IFC presents in association with Netflix and BBC ; a Chain Camera production ; produced by Eddie Schmidt; directed by Kirby Dick.
264 _1 $a [United States?] : $b [publisher not identified], $c [2007]
264 _2 $a Santa Monica, CA : $b Distributed by Genius Entertainment, $c [2007]
710 2_ $a Genius Entertainment, $e film distributor.

RDA 21.5 Manufacturer

Manufacturer is defined as *a person, family, or corporate body responsible for printing, duplicating, casting, etc., a resource in a published form.*

245 04 $a The blues, a musical journey / $c Vulcan Productions and Road Movies Production in association with Cappa Productions & Jigsaw Productions ; series producer, Alex Gibney.
264 _1 $a New York : $b Sony Music Entertainment, $c [2003]
264 _3 $a [Place of manufacture not identified] : $b Manufactured by Columbia Music Video, $c [date of manufacture not identified]
710 2_ $a Columbia Music Video (Firm)

RDA 21.6 Other Person, Family, or Corporate Body Associated with a Manifestation

Other person, family, or corporate body associated with a manifestation is defined as *a person, family, or corporate body other than a producer, publisher, distributor, or manufacturer associated with a manifestation.* When adding an access point for this element, one or more terms from the list of relationship designators for manufacturers can also be added.

245 00 $a Woodcock shooting / $c from nature and on stone by F.F. Palmer ; lith. of N. Currier N.Y.
264 _1 $a New York : $b Currier & Ives, $c [1852]
700 1_ $a Currier, Nathaniel, $d 1813–1888, $e lithographer.

245 00 $a Red book on work incentives : $b a summary guide to social security and supplemental security income work incentives for people with disabilities / $c developed by Social Security Administration, Office of Disability, Office of Supplemental Security Income.
264 _1 $a [Baltimore, Maryland?] : $b Social Security Administration, $c 1998.
500 $a "Embossed by American Printing House for the Blind, Louisville, Kentucky."
710 2_ $a American Printing House for the Blind (Louisville, Ky.), $e braille embosser.

RDA CHAPTER 22: PERSONS, FAMILIES, AND CORPORATE BODIES ASSOCIATED WITH AN ITEM

RDA Chapter 22 provides guidelines on recording the relationships between Group 2 entities and items they currently own, items they previously owned, items for which they serve as custodians, or items they altered in some way. These relationships can be recorded in MARC bibliographic field 700 with a 0 or 1 in the first indicator for persons, field 700 with a 3 in the first indicator for families, and fields 710 and 711 for corporate bodies. If applicable, one or more relationship designators can be added to reflect responsibility for the item. Relationship designators for owners include *current owner, depositor, donor, former owner,* and *seller.* Relationship designators for other persons, families, or corporate bodies associated with an item include *annotator, autographer, binder, curator, inscriber,* and *restorationist,* among others.

RDA 22.2 Owner

Owner is defined as *a person, family, or corporate body having legal possession of an item (i.e., a specific copy or instance of a resource).*

> 245   14 $a The other house / $c by Henry James.
> 264   _1 $a London : $b William Heinemann, $c 1896.
> 500 $a This copy once in the Grolier Club Library and has their book-plate. $CLU
> 710   2_ $a Grolier Club. $b Library, $e former owner.

RDA 22.3 Custodian

Custodian is defined as *a person, family, or corporate body having legal custody of an item (i.e., a specific copy or instance of a resource).*

> 245   10 $a Ebenezer Reformed Church records, 1867–1979.
> 264   _1 $a [Holland, Michigan] : $b Ebenezer Reformed Church, $c 1867–1979.
> 500 $a Ownership retained by Ebenezer Reformed Church. Joint Archives of Holland serves as custodian.
> 710   2_ $a Joint Archives of Holland.

RDA 22.4 Other Person, Family, or Corporate Body Associated with an Item

Other person, family, or corporate body associated with an item is defined as *a person, family, or corporate body other than an owner or custodian associated with an item.*

> 245   14 $a 100 botanical specimens from Meadville and vicinity / $c collected and presented to Allegheny College, by Ralph B. Reitz.
> 264   _1 $a [Pennsylvania] : $b Ralph B. Reitz, $c [1889]
> 700   1_ $a Reitz, Ralph B., $e collector.

RDA SECTION 8: RECORDING RELATIONSHIPS BETWEEN WORKS, EXPRESSIONS, MANIFESTATIONS & ITEMS

RDA Section 8 comprises five chapters: Chapters 24–28. Chapter 24 provides general guidelines that frame the content of the remaining chapters. Chapter 25 addresses the relationship between one work and another work. Chapter 26 addresses the relationship between one expression and another expression. Chapter 27 addresses the relationship between one manifestation and another manifestation. Finally, Chapter 28 addresses the relationship between one item and another item.

In MARC, these relationships can be represented by adding the access point for one entity to the bibliographic or authority record for the other entity or by adding a note describing the relationship to the bibliographic record. When adding an access point for a work or expression, it should be constructed according to guidelines in RDA Chapter 6 (described in chapter 5 of this book).

RDA CHAPTER 24: GENERAL GUIDELINES ON RECORDING RELATIONSHIPS BETWEEN WORKS, EXPRESSIONS, MANIFESTATIONS, AND ITEMS

RDA Chapter 24 provides general information for application of the guidelines in RDA Chapters 25–28. It explains the terminology used in the chapters; outlines the functional objectives and principles addressed by the guidelines in each chapter; addresses core elements (of which there are none for these type of relationships); explains the four conventions for recording relationships between works, expressions, manifestations, and items; and provides instructions for Chapter 24's four elements: *relationship designators*, *numbering of part*, *source consulted*, and *cataloguer's note*. The following discussion addresses the conventions for recording relationships between works, expressions, manifestations, and items. Then it covers the four elements.

Conventions for Recording Relationships between Works, Expressions, Manifestations, and Items

RDA describes four methods for recording relationships between works, expressions, manifestations, and items. The first method is to record the identifier for the related work, expression, manifestation, or item.

> University of Western Australia law review = ISSN 0042–0328
> ISBN 978–1–74146–163–3

The second method is to add the authorized access point for the related work or expression onto the record being cataloged.

700   1_ $a Shakespeare, William, $d 1564–1616. $t Taming of the shrew.
700   1_ $a Goncourt, Edmond de, $d 1822–1896. $t Frères Zemganno.
       $l English.

The third method is to provide a structured description (full or partial) of the related work, expression, manifestation, or item (using the same order of elements used for the resource being described).

500      $a Reprint of: Venice / by Cecil Roth.—Philadelphia: The Jewish
         Publication Society of America, 1930.

The fourth method is to provide an unstructured description (full or partial) of the related work, expression, manifestation, or item (written as a sentence or paragraph).

500      $a Activities are based on the book How the brain learns,
         by David A. Sousa, 3rd edition, 2006.

RDA 24.5 Relationship Designator

Relationship designator is defined as *a designator that indicates the nature of the relationship between works, expressions, manifestations, or items represented by authorized access points, descriptions, and/or identifiers.* RDA Appendix J has an open list of relationship designators for the four types of relationships outlined in RDA Section 8. One or more of these terms may be added to indicate the nature of the relationship. If none of the terms is sufficient, catalogers may devise another concise term. When used for referencing related works, related expressions, related manifestations, and related items, relationship designators are generally recorded in the $i of 7XX bibliographic fields and of 5XX authority fields.

RDA 24.6 Numbering of Part

Numbering of part is defined as *a designation of the sequencing of a part or parts within a larger work. Numbering of part may include a numeral, a letter, any other character, or the combination of these, with or without an accompanying caption (volume, number, etc.) and/or a chronological designation.* Record numbering as it appears on the resource. Follow the guidelines for numbers expressed as numerals or words in RDA 1.8. Also, follow the capitalization guidelines in RDA Appendix A.3.2 and the abbreviation guidelines in RDA Appendix B.5.5. Appendix A.3.2 instructs not to capitalize other terms associated with titles of works (such as "volume" and "number"). Appendix B.5.5 instructs to abbreviate "volumes" to "v." and "number" to "no." Thus, a series statement appearing on the source as:

DENTAL CLINICS OF NORTH AMERICA
Volume 56—Number 4

would be recorded in an access point as follows:

830   _0 $a Dental clinics of North America ; $v v. 56, no. 4.

RDA 24.7 Source Consulted

Source consulted is defined as *a resource used in determining the relationship between works, expressions, manifestations, or items.* For citing the sources used for determining a relationship, provide the data in MARC authority field 670 for information that is found or 675 for information that is not found.

670      $a ISSN portal, viewed January 13, 2006: $b (Australasian studies in history and philosophy of science, ISSN 0929–6425; continued by Studies in history and philosophy of science (Dordrecht),
ISSN 1871–7381).

RDA 24.8 Cataloguer's Note

Cataloguer's note is defined as *an annotation that might be helpful to those using or revising the relationship data, or creating an authorized access point representing a work or expression.* It maps to MARC authority field 667.

667      $a Not related to: Technical report series (Tennessee Valley Au-
thority)

RDA CHAPTER 25: RELATED WORKS

RDA Chapter 25 provides guidelines on recording the relationships between one work and a related work. It also outlines the four conventions used for referencing related works. The following discussion highlights the instructions in Chapter 25, providing examples of the relevant MARC fields and relationship designator terms.

RDA 25.1 Related Work

Related work is defined as a work related to the resource being described (e.g., an adapta-tion, commentary, supplement, sequel, part of a larger work). For most cases, a relationship designator can be added to specify the nature of the relationship between two works. RDA Appendix J provides an open list of over one hundred terms, including *adaptation of (work), continued by (work), continues (work), critique of (work), in series (work), parody of (work), prequel to, supplement to (work),* and *sequel to.* Most relationship designators for related works are recorded in the subfield $i of 7XX bibliographic fields or of 5XX authority fields. Because the MARC field tags generally do not specify the relationship involved, the relationship designator can be useful for conveying the precise nature of the relationship between two works. However, there are a few cases in which the designator is not needed because the nature of the relationship is specified by the field tag itself. The following are examples.

The designator *contains (work)* is already specified by recording a "2" in the second indicator of a 7XX field of the bibliographic record.

        245   10 $a Dance of wild Irravel ; Paean; Symphony no. 3 / $c Sir Ar-
              nold Bax.
        700   12 $a Bax, Arnold, $d 1883–1953. $k Sketches. $t Dance of wild
              Irravel.
        700   12 $a Bax, Arnold, $d 1883–1953. $t Paean; $o arranged.
        700   12 $a Bax, Arnold, $d 1883–1953. $t Symphonies, $n no. 3.

The designators *continues (work)* and *continued by (work)* are specified by using MARC bibliographic fields 780 and 785, respectively.

        245   00 $a Jane's intelligence review pointer.
        780   00 $t Pointer

        245   00 $a Pointer.
        785   00 $t Jane's intelligence review pointer

The designator *in series (work)* is specified by recording the information in the 8XX fields of the bibliographic record.

        245   00 $a India literacy atlas.
        810   2_ $a Central Institute of Indian Languages. $t CIIL linguistic atlas
              series.

Identifier for the Related Work

RDA shows four methods for referencing a related work. One method that is less common in the current MARC environment is to reference the identifier for the related work.

        Supplement to: Novum Testamentum = ISSN 0048–1009

Authorized Access Point Representing the Related Work

Another method for referencing a related work is to add the authorized access point for the related work to the MARC authority record for the work being cata-loged. In some cases, the access point may be added to the bibliographic record, using MARC bibliographic field 730 or field 700, 710, or 711 with a subfield $t. As mentioned previously, relationship designators for works, if used, are placed in the subfield "i" of the appropriate MARC field. As with all relationship designators in RDA Appendix J, the first letter of each term (e.g., "parody of (work)") appears in lowercase in the Appendix. However, catalogers encountering records in the U.S. national authority file (LCNAF) will see the first letter capitalized, which is standard practice for catalogers contributing to this file.

245 10 $a Great expectations / $c Charles Dickens ; retold by Florence Bell.

700 1_ $i Adaptation of (work): $a Dickens, Charles, $d 1812–1870. $t Great expectations.

245 10 $a Bored of the rings : $b a parody of J.R.R. Tolkien's The lord of the rings / $c by Henry N. Beard and Douglas C. Kenney of The Harvard lampoon.

700 1_ $i Parody of (work): $a Tolkien, J. R. R. $q (John Ronald Reuel), $d 1892–1973. $t Lord of the rings.

245 00 $a Microsoft multimedia Mozart : $b the Dissonant quartet : an illustrated, interactive musical exploration.

700 1_ $i Analysis of (work): $a Mozart, Wolfgang Amadeus, $d 1756–1791. $t Quartets, $m strings, $n K. 465, $r C major

245 00 $a Plays from Black Australia / $c Jack Davis, Eva Johnson, Richard Walley, Bob Maza ; with an introduction by Justine Saunders.

700 12 $a Davis, Jack, $d 1917–2000. $t Dreamers.

700 12 $a Johnson, Eva. $t Murras.

700 12 $a Walley, Richard. $t Coordah.

700 12 $a Maza, Bob, $d 1939–2000. $t Keepers.

245 10 $a Understanding voice problems : $b a physiological perspective for diagnosis and treatment / $c Raymond H. Colton and Janina K. Casper ; edited by Rebecca Leonard.

830 _0 $a Communication disorders.

In some cases, an access point for the related work may be added to the authority record for a work. In this case, the related work would be recorded in MARC authority field 530 or field 500, 510, or 511 with a subfield $t.

130 _0 $a 21 Jump Street (Motion picture)

530 _0 $w r $i Motion picture adaptation of (work): $a 21 Jump Street (Television program)

Structured Description of the Related Work

The third method for referencing a related work is to add a structured description in field 500 or 505 of the bibliographic record.

245   00 $a Gone with the wind / $c by Margaret Mitchell.
500        $a Sequel: Scarlett: the sequel to Margaret Mitchell's Gone with
           the wind / by Alexandra Ripley.—New York, NY: Warner Books,
           1991.

245   00 $a Voices from Ariel: $b ten-minute plays reflecting the Jewish
           experience: a collection of ten short plays / $c compiled and edited
           by Julianne Bernstein and Deborah Baer Mozes.
505   0_ $a 'Til death do us plots / by Julianne Bernstein—Class act / by
           Michael Elkin—Where's your stuff? / by Daniel Brenner—Foot ped-
           dler / by Vivian Green—Smoke / by Louis Greenstein—
           Single Jewish female / by Julianne Bernstein—In spite of everything
           / by Hindi Brooks—Ger (the convert) / by Leslie B. Gold and Louis
           Greenstein—Golden opportunity / by Julianne
           Bernstein—Interview with a scapegoat / by Louis Greenstein

Unstructured Description of the Related Work

The fourth method is to provide an unstructured description in field 500 of the
bibliographic record.

500        $a Author's adaptation of his Russian text.

RDA 25.2 Explanation of Relationship

Explanation of relationship is defined as *information elaborating on or clarifying the
relationship between a work represented by an authorized access point and/or identifier
and a related work.* Explanation of relationship can be recorded in Complex Name
References fields in the MARC authority format.

100   1_ $a Reger, Max, $d 1873–1916. $t Dies irae
500   1_ $a Reger, Max, $d 1873–1916. $t Requiem (Mass)
664        $a For this movement included in the composer's unfinished
           Requiem search under $b Reger, Max, 1873–1916. $t Requiem
           (Mass)

RDA CHAPTER 26: RELATED EXPRESSIONS

RDA Chapter 26 provides guidelines on recording the relationships between one
expression and an associated expression and outlines the four conventions for referencing related expressions. The following discussion highlights the instructions
in Chapter 26, providing examples of the associated MARC fields and the relevant
relationship designator terms.

RDA 26.1 Related Expression

Related expression is defined as *an expression related to the expression represented
by an identifier, an authorized access point, or a description (e.g., a revised version,*

a translation). A relationship designator can be added to specify the nature of the relationship between two expressions. As with designators for related works, RDA Appendix J provides an open list of over one hundred terms for relating expressions, including *contains (expression), illustrations for (expression), musical variations (expression), revision of,* and *translation of.* Relationship designators for relating expressions are generally recorded in the subfield $i of 7XX bibliographic fields or of 5XX authority fields.

As with related works, RDA's examples show four different methods for referencing related expressions.

Identifier for the Related Expression

> Revised as: Library of Congress control number: no2008127546

Authorized Access Point Representing the Related Expression

> 245 10 $a The long exile / $c Georges Simenon ; translated from the French by Eileen Ellenbogen.
> 700 1_ $i Translation of: $a Simenon, Georges, $d 1903–1989. $t Long cours.
>
> 245 10 $a Roget's Thesaurus of English words and phrases.
> 250 $a New edition / $b completely revised and modernized by Robert A. Dutch.
> 700 1_ $i Revision of: $a Roget, Peter Mark, $d 1779–1869. $t Thesaurus of English words and phrases.
>
> 100 1_ $a Shakespeare, William, $d 1564–1616. $t Romeo and Juliet. $l Spanish
> 500 1_ $i Translation of: $a Shakespeare, William, $d 1564–1616. $t Romeo and Juliet.

Structured Description of the Related Expression

> 500 $a Revision of: Biology of fishes / Carl E. Bond.—Second edition.—Fort Worth: Saunders College Publishing, [1996]

Unstructured Description of the Related Expression

> 500 $a Revised and shortened version of the author's thesis (Ph.D.)—Yale University, 1982.

RDA 26.2 Explanation of Relationship

Explanation of relationship is defined as *information elaborating on or clarifying the relationship between an expression represented by an authorized access point and/ or identifier and a related expression.* Explanation of relationship can be recorded in Complex Name References fields in the MARC authority format, such as field 663 subfield $a.

> 663 $a For the separately published parts revised for this compilation, see $b Gunston, Bill. $t Illustrated guide to the modern Soviet Air Force $b Illustrated guide to weapons of the modern Soviet ground forces $b Jordan, John. $t Illustrated guide to the modern Soviet Navy

RDA CHAPTER 27: RELATED MANIFESTATIONS

RDA Chapter 27 provides guidelines on recording the relationships between associated manifestations. It discusses the three conventions for referencing related manifestations, which are covered in the following discussion. Examples of relevant MARC encoding and relationship designators are provided.

RDA 27.1 Related Manifestation

A related manifestation is defined as *a manifestation related to the resource being described (e.g., a manifestation in a different format)*. A relationship designator can be added to specify the nature of the relationship between two manifestations. RDA Appendix J provides an open list of over two dozen terms, including *also issued as*, *accompanied by (manifestation)*, and *reproduction of (manifestation)*.

RDA's examples show three different methods for referencing related manifestations.

Identifier for the Related Manifestation

> Also issued as: ISBN 978–0–06128–533–2

Structured Description of the Related Manifestation

> 245   10 $a History of the Jews in Venice / $c Cecil Roth.
> 264   _1 $a New York: $b Schocken Books, $c 1975.
> 500 $a Reprint of: Venice / by Cecil Roth.—Philadelphia: The Jewish Publication Society of America, 1930.

Unstructured Description of the Related Manifestation

> 530 $a Issued also in Blu-ray Disc format.

RDA CHAPTER 28: RELATED ITEM

RDA Chapter 28 provides guidelines on referencing related items and describes three conventions for recording this information. The discussion that follows highlights these details, showing examples of MARC coding and relationship designators.

RDA 28.1 Related Item

Related item is defined as *an item related to the resource being described (e.g., an item used as the basis for a microform reproduction)*. A relationship designator can be added to specify the nature of the relationship between two items. RDA Appendix J provides an open list of over a dozen terms, including *bound with, preservation facsimile of (item)*, and *reprint of (item)*.

RDA's examples show three methods for referencing related manifestations.

Identifier for the Related Item

> Facsimile of: Bodleian Library: MS. Junius 11

Structured Description of the Related Item

> 501 $a Bound with: Report of the Committee on the District of Columbia in relation to the city of Washington : read in Senate, February 2, 1835.—[Washington] : [publisher not identified], [1835] (City of Washington: Printed at the Globe Office, 1835) $5 CLU

Unstructured Description of the Related Item

> 500 $a Reproduction of original from Harvard Law School Library.
> 500 $a Library's copy bound with 11 other songs. $5 CLU

RDA SECTION 9: RECORDING RELATIONSHIPS BETWEEN PERSONS, FAMILIES, AND CORPORATE BODIES

RDA Section 9 comprises four chapters: Chapters 29–32. Chapter 29 provides background information for contextualizing the instructions in Chapters 30–32. Chapter 30 offers instructions on recording related persons. Chapter 31 offers instructions on recording related families. Finally, Chapter 32 offers instructions on recording related corporate bodies.

In MARC, these relationships can be represented by adding the access point for the person, family, or corporate body into a 5XX field of the authority record for another entity. When adding the access point for the person, family, or corporate body, it should be constructed according to guidelines in RDA Chapters 9–11 (described in chapter 6).

RDA CHAPTER 29: GENERAL GUIDELINES ON RECORDING RELATIONSHIPS BETWEEN PERSONS, FAMILIES, AND CORPORATE BODIES

RDA Chapter 29 offers introductory information that frames the rest of Section 9. It defines the terminology that appears in Chapters 30–32; highlights the functional objectives and principles addressed by the chapters; notes the lack of core elements in the chapters; explains the two conventions for recording related persons, related families, and related corporate bodies; and provides instructions for the chapter's three elements: *relationship designators, source consulted,* and *cataloguer's note.* The following discussion addresses the conventions for recording related persons, related families, and related corporate bodies, and then covers the three elements.

Conventions for Recording Relationships between Persons, Families, and Corporate Bodies

RDA describes two methods for recording related persons, related families, and related corporate bodies. The first (and currently less common) method is to record the identifier for the person, family, or corporate body. The second method is to provide the access point for the person, family, or corporate body, which is more common in the current implementation scenario and is thus covered in more depth here. A relationship designator may be added to further explicate the nature of the relationship.

RDA 29.5 Relationship Designator

Relationship designator is defined as *a designator that indicates the nature of the relationship between persons, families, or corporate bodies represented by authorized access points and/or identifiers.* RDA Appendix K has an open list of relationship designators for the three types of relationships covered in Section 9. One or more of these terms may be assigned as appropriate. If none of the terms is sufficient, the cataloger may devise a concise term to clarify the relationship. When used in access points for referencing related persons, families, and corporate bodies, relationship designators are recorded in the $i of the 5XX authority fields.

RDA 29.6 Source Consulted

Source consulted is defined as *a resource used in determining the relationship between persons, families, or corporate bodies.* For citing the sources used for determining a relationship, provide the data in MARC authority field 670 for information that is found or 675 for information that is not found.

> 670 $a Familia de Yan desde 1719 Pagsanjaniaguna, 2005 $b (page 47: family changed its surname "De La Resurección" to "Yan" in 1849; lived in Pagsanjan, Philippines)

RDA 29.7 Cataloguer's Note

Cataloguer's note is defined as *an annotation that might be helpful to those using or revising the relationship data, or creating an authorized access point representing a related person, family, or corporate body.* It maps to MARC authority field 667.

667     $a King has written seven novels under the pseudonym Richard
Bachman and one short story under the pseudonym John Swithen.

RDA CHAPTER 30: RELATED PERSONS

RDA Chapter 30 provides guidelines on referencing related persons and describes two conventions for recording this information. The following discussion details these guidelines and provide examples of relevant MARC coding and relationship designator terms.

RDA 30.1 Related Person

Related person is defined as *a person who is associated with the person, family, or corporate body represented by an authorized access point and/or identifier (e.g., a collaborator, a member of a family, a founder of a corporate body). Related persons include separate identities established by an individual (either alone or in collaboration with one or more other individuals).* When using an authorized access point for a related person, record the information in MARC authority field 500 with a 0 or 1 in the first indicator. A relationship designator can be added to specify the nature of the relationship between a person and a related entity. RDA Appendix K offers an open list of terms, which include *alternate identity, real identity, family member, progenitor, group member,* and *incumbent.*

RDA shows two methods for referencing a related person.

Identifier for the Related Person

Library of Congress control number: n 50035608

Authorized Access Point Representing the Related Person

100   1_ $a Dodgson, Charles Lutwidge, $d 1832–1898
500   1_ $w r $i Alternate identity: $a Carroll, Lewis, $d 1832–1898

100   1_ $a Carroll, Lewis, $d 1832–1898
500   1_ $w r $i Real identity: $a Dodgson, Charles Lutwidge, $d 1832–1898

100   3_ $a Boyd (Family : $g Boyd, John David, 1839–1917)
500   1_ $w r $i Progenitor: $a Boyd, John David, $d 1839–1917

110   2_ $a Monolake (Musical group)
500   1_ $w r $i Group member: $a Henke, Robert, $d 1969–
500   1_ $w r $i Group member: $a Behles, Gerhard, $d 1969–

RDA 30.2 Explanation of Relationship

Explanation of relationship is defined as *information elaborating on or clarifying the relationship between a person, family, or corporate body represented by an authorized access point and/or identifier and a related person.* Explanation of relationship can be recorded in Complex Name References fields in the MARC authority format.

```
100   1_ $a Gray, E. Conder, $d 1839–1905
500   1_ $w nnnc $a Japp, Alexander H. $q (Alexander Hay), $d 1839–
      1905
500   1_ $w nnnc $a Page, H. A., $d 1839–1905
663      $a For works of this author written under his real name, search
         also under $b Japp, Alexander H. (Alexander Hay), 1839–1905.
         $a For works written under another pseudonym, search also under
         $b Page, H. A., 1839–1905.
```

Note on the example above: the subfield $w is a "control subfield" that contains codes that can be used to affect the display of the field.

RDA CHAPTER 31: RELATED FAMILIES

RDA Chapter 31 offers instructions on referencing related families and describes two conventions for recording this information. The following discussion covers these guidelines and show the relevant MARC encoding and relationship designators.

RDA 31.1 Related Family

Related family is defined as *a family that is associated with the person, family, or corporate body represented by an authorized access point and/or identifier (e.g., a person's family, a family that owns the controlling interest in a corporate body).* When using an authorized access point for a related family, record it in MARC authority field 500 with a 3 in the first indicator. A relationship designator can be added to specify the nature of the relationship between a family and a related entity. RDA Appendix K offers an open list of terms, which include *descendants, descendant family, founding family,* and *sponsoring family.*

RDA shows two methods for referencing a related family.

Identifier for the Related Family

```
Union List of Artist Names ID: 500092478
```

Authorized Access Point Representing the Related Family

```
100   1_ $a Carroll, Charles N. $q (Charles Negus), $d 1817–1902
500   3_ $w r $i Descendant family: $a Carroll (Family : $g Carroll,
      Charles N. (Charles Negus), 1817–1902)
```

100 3_ $a Nayak (Dynasty : $d 18th century : $c Madurai, India)
500 3_ $w r $i Descendant family: $a Nayak (Dynasty : $c Thanjavure, India)

110 2_ $a Berith Salom (Organization)
500 3_ $w r $i Founding family: $a Spanjaard (Family)

RDA 31.2 Explanation of Relationship

Explanation of relationship is defined as *information elaborating on or clarifying the relationship between a person, family, or corporate body represented by an authorized access point and/or identifier and a related family.*

663     $a Marcel Duchamp was the last surviving member of the Duchamp family of artists.

RDA CHAPTER 32: RELATED CORPORATE BODIES

RDA Chapter 32 provides instructions on referencing related corporate bodies. It also outlines the two conventions for recording related corporate bodies. The following discussion covers these details and offers examples of MARC coding and the relevant relationship designators.

RDA 32.1 Related Corporate Body

Related corporate body is defined as *a corporate body that is associated with the person, family, or corporate body represented by an authorized access point and/or identifier (e.g., a musical group to which a person belongs, a subsidiary company). Related corporate bodies include corporate bodies that precede or succeed the body represented by an authorized access point and/or identifier as the result of a change of name.* When using an authorized access point for a related person, record the information in MARC authority field 510 or 511. A relationship designator can be added to specify the nature of the relationship between a corporate body and a related entity. RDA Appendix K offers an open list of terms, including *founded organization, hierarchical subordinate, hierarchical superior, predecessor*, and *successor*, among others.

RDA shows two methods for referencing a related corporate body.

Identifier for the Related Corporate Body

Library of Congress control number: no2007001419

Authorized Access Point Representing the Related Corporate Body

100 1_ $a Behles, Gerhard, $d 1969–
510 2_ $a Monolake (Musical group)

```
100   3_ $a Spanjaard (Family)
510   2_ $w r $i Founded organization: $a Berith Salom (Organization)


110   2_ $a California Library Association. $b Technical Services Chapter
510   2_ $w r $i Hierarchical superior: $a California Library Association
```

For corporate bodies that are predecessors or successors to other corporate bodies, the MARC coding already conveys this information. However, catalogers may
choose to explain the relationship using a designator.

```
110   2_ $a College of Surgeons of Australasia
510   2_ $w b $a Royal Australasian College of Surgeons


110   2_ $a Royal Australasian College of Surgeons
510   2_ $w a $a College of Surgeons of Australasia
```

OR

```
110   2_ $a College of Surgeons of Australasia
510   2_ $w r $i Successor: $a Royal Australasian College of Surgeons


110   2_ $a Royal Australasian College of Surgeons
510   2_ $w r $i Predecessor: $a College of Surgeons of Australasia
```

CONCLUSION

This chapter discussed the various relationships involving Group 1 entities (works,
expressions, manifestations, and items) and Group 2 entities (persons, families, and
corporate bodies). It detailed the instructions in RDA Section 6 for recording the relationships between Group 1 and Group 2 entities, the instructions in RDA Section 8
for recording the relationships between Group 1 entities, and the instructions in RDA
Section 9 for recording the relationships between Group 2 entities. It demonstrated the
relevant MARC coding for each type of relationship, which sometimes involved bibliographic fields and sometimes authority fields. It also elucidated the role of relationship
designators and offered examples of how they can be used to clarify the nature of certain
relationships. Because some of the information for referencing related entities can appear in authority records, certain introductory chapters (namely RDA Chapters 24 and
29) contain elements, like *source consulted* and *cataloguer's note*, in order to contextualize
and justify the referencing of relationships. This was noted where applicable.

Because this chapter focused on the remaining chapters of RDA, it concludes part
II of this book. Part III ties together parts I and II, coupling the differences (and
the rationale for these differences) mentioned in part I with the specific instructions
delineated in part II to provide details of the similarities and differences between
AACR2 and RDA. Using this as a foundation, the reader will be shown how to
construct full RDA records in the MARC context.

III

APPLYING RDA IN THE MARC ENVIRONMENT

8

Creating and Intepreting Bibliographic Records for Books

Part I of this book provided a background and rationale to help contextualize some of the differences between AACR2 and RDA. Part II focused on RDA in and of itself, detailing the instructions and showing the associated MARC coding. Part III attempts to bring everything together, revisiting FRBR concepts where relevant, providing specific details on changes between AACR2 and RDA, and ultimately showing how it all plays out in the MARC environment.

This chapter details the most important concepts needed when cataloging a book using RDA and MARC. It discusses the most common MARC fields—old and new—that a cataloger will typically find in an RDA record. Significant differences between AACR2 and RDA are noted along the way. At the end of the chapter, these differences are examined holistically through the comparison of three pairs of records, with each pair describing a different book. One record in each pair has been created using AACR2; the other record has been created using RDA. It is hoped that the reader will emerge from this chapter with a solid foundation that can be used as the basis for cataloging books using RDA.

CORE ELEMENTS AND BEYOND

Before populating the MARC record, one needs to know which fields are required and which are optional but useful. The following discussion covers both the core elements and the elements that are beyond core, but may be useful for providing information about books.

Core Elements (RDA 0.6)

All resources have a set of core elements which, if applicable, must be present in the record. Following is a list of core elements in MARC tag order:

020 – Identifier for the Manifestation
1XX – Principal or first named creator
245 $a, $c – Title proper, Statement of responsibility relating to title proper
250 $a – Designation of edition, Designation of a named revision of an edition
264 _1 – Publication statement
264 _2 – Distribution statement (if publication information is missing)
264 _3 – Manufacture statement (if publication, distribution, and copyright information are missing)
264 _4 – Copyright date (if publication and distribution date are missing)
300 $a – Extent
336 – Content type
338 – Carrier type
490 – Series statement

Noncore Elements of Relevance to Books

Many elements that are not core may still be added to the bibliographic record if the cataloger deems them useful for describing books. The following elements may commonly be found in bibliographic records for a book, even though they are beyond core:

245 $b – Other title information
300 $b – Illustrative content, Colour content
300 $c – Dimensions
337 – Media type
504 – Supplementary content
505 – Related work (whole-part relationship)
7XX – Additional creators; contributors
830 – Related work (in series relationship)

FILLING OUT THE MARC
BIBLIOGRAPHIC RECORD FOR BOOKS

There are various aspects of the MARC record that have nothing to do with AACR2 or RDA. The following discussion is not meant to be an exhaustive review of how to complete an entire MARC bibliographic record; it is only meant to focus on those fields of relevance to RDA. The MARC fields that have associated elements in RDA are discussed in MARC tag order so that the reader can have an easily navigable, ready reference source of information while working through the MARC record. The reader is encouraged to use the chapters in part II of this book for more information on these elements (such as source of information and other details) if necessary, as well as the *RDA Toolkit*.

Recording the Mode of Issuance (RDA 2.13)

Leader 07—Bibliographic Level

Most of the Leader positions in MARC 21 will be coded the same in RDA as in AACR2. Leader position 07, defined as Bibliographic Level, is one of those that will be coded the same. However, unlike AACR2, RDA has an element that maps to Leader position 07: *Mode of issuance* (element 2.13). Around half a dozen options exist in MARC for Leader position 07, but only three map to RDA, as follows:

m *for single units and for multipart monographs*
s *for serials*
i *for integrating resources*

For print monographs, the position should be coded "m."

Coding the Record as RDA

Leader 18—Descriptive Cataloging Form

Leader position18, defined as Descriptive Cataloging Form, has different coding in RDA than in AACR2. In AACR2 it is coded "a" for AACR2. In RDA the position is coded "i" for "ISBD punctuation included" or {blank} for "Non-ISBD." Many cataloging agencies use ISBD punctuation, so most RDA records will likely have an "i" in Leader position18. Seeing an "i" rather than an "a" in Leader position18 can serve as a signal that the record is not an AACR2 record, and that it *may* instead be an RDA record. Note that an "i" in Leader position18 can *also* signal a pre-AACR2 record containing ISBD punctuation.

Field 040 $e—Descriptive Conventions

The way to definitively code an RDA record is to record *rda* in the 040 field subfield $e. To standardize the location of the subfield $e and to ensure its detection among multiple listings of agencies, the recommended best practice is to record the subfield $e between the subfield $b and the first subfield $c.

040    $a XXX $b eng **$e rda** $c XXX

The combination of recording "i" in Leader position 18 and "rda" in the 040 subfield $e is accepted practice for indicating that the record has been created using RDA. This record coding practice differs from that employed to identify a record created using AACR2, which only required recording "a" in Leader position18.

AACR2

>   Desc   a

RDA

>   Desc   i
>   040 $a XXX $b eng **$e rda** $c XXX

Field 020—Identifier for the Manifestation (RDA 2.15)

The identifier for the manifestation can map to many different fields. The most common identifier for the print monograph is the international standard book number, or ISBN. RDA instructs the cataloger to record ISBN numbers and other identifiers in accordance with the prescribed display format, if applicable.

>   020 $a 978–90–70002–34–3
>   020 $a 978 1 85604 693 0

However, in some cataloging utilities (such as OCLC), the number is normalized though the deletion of intervening hyphens and spaces.

>   020 $a 9789070002343
>   020 $a 9781856046930

Fields 100, 110, and 111—Creators (RDA 19)

In both AACR2 and RDA, the criteria for determining authorship are largely the same. However, one notable difference between the standards is the terminology used with respect to the 1XX bibliographic fields. Because of the *objective of flexibility*, RDA does not carry over the term "main entry." However, MARC terminology still bears the vestiges of this inherited "card catalog" term. The 100, 110, and 111 fields generally map to RDA element 19.2 for the creator of a work, although in a few cases involving legal and religious works, these fields may map to element 19.3 for another person, family, or corporate body associated with a work.

Relationship Designators for Creators

Another difference is in the use of relationship designators. Although AACR2 allowed for the optional addition of designations of function to access points, in practice these designations were not widely applied. When catalogers record relationship designators for creators (RDA 18.5), they support RDA's *principle of relationships*. Relationship designators are strongly recommended in U.S. cooperative cataloging ventures. Thus, catalogers may see relationship designators much more often in RDA records than they are accustomed to seeing in AACR2 records.

The most common relationship designators that may be recorded in the 1XX fields of book records are *author, compiler, interviewer,* and *interviewee.* Following are examples:

    100   1_ $a Neff, Daniel, $d 1955– $e author.
    100   1_ $a Winston, James, $e compiler.

Collaborative Works and the Elimination of the "Rule of Three" (RDA 6.27.1.3)

Similarly to AACR2, in RDA, if there are two or three creators, the principal or first-named creator is recorded in the 1XX field.

    100   1_ $a Barrus, Nancy Wilson.
    245   10 $a Handbook for must and wine analysis / $c by Nancy Wilson Barrus & James A. Evans.

However, RDA differs from AACR2 when there are more than three creators. In AACR2, if there are more than three authors, the first author is entered into the 7XX field and the remaining authors are omitted. In RDA, the first named creator is recorded in the 1XX, regardless of the number of creators named on the preferred source.

AACR2

    245   00 $a Medical insurance : $b an integrated claims process approach / $c Joanne D. Valerius, Nenna L. Bayes, Cynthia Newby, Janet I.B. Seggern.
    700   1_ $a Valerius, Joanne.

RDA

    100   1_ $a Valerius, Joanne, $e author.
    245   10 $a Medical insurance : $b an integrated claims process approach / $c Joanne D. Valerius, Nenna L. Bayes, Cynthia Newby, Janet I.B. Seggern.

Fictitious Persons

AACR2 instructed catalogers to enter a work fictitiously attributed to a person under the name of the true author (if he or she was known) or under the title. It also instructed against making an added entry for the name of the fictitious person. In RDA, such an instruction would conflict with the *principle of attribution,* which states that responsibility relationships should reflect attribution stated on the resource (or in reference sources) "irrespective of whether the attribution of responsibility is accurate." This results in a change from omitting fictitious persons altogether in AACR2 to adding them in a position of prominence in the 100 field in RDA.

AACR2

> 100   1_ $a Schulz, Charles M. $q (Charles Monroe), $d 1922–2000.
> 245   10 $a Dr. Snoopy's advice to pet owners / $c by Dr. Snoopy ;
> illustrations by Charles M. Schulz.

RDA

> 100   1_ $a Snoopy, $c Dr., $e author.
> 245   10 $a Dr. Snoopy's advice to pet owners / $c by Dr. Snoopy ;
> illustrations by Charles M. Schulz.
> 700   1_ $a Schulz, Charles M. $q (Charles Monroe), $d 1922–2000,
> $e illustrator.

Fields 130, 1XX/240, and 1XX/245—Authorized Access Points for Works and Expressions

Differences in Terminology

As with the 1XX fields in general, field 130 (or field 240 which is used in conjunction with the other 1XX fields) involves a difference in terminology. The MARC terminology retains the AACR2 "uniform title," whereas in RDA this concept would be referred to as the "preferred title" for the work or expression (under RDA 6.27).

Compilations of Works by Different Creators (RDA 6.27.1.4)

For compilations of works by multiple authors and that have a collective title, RDA is similar to AACR2. Application of the guidelines in both standards results in the recording of the collective title in the 245 and omitting a 1XX.

> 245   00 $a Anthologie de la poésie baroque française /
> $c textes choisis et présentés par Jean Rousset.

Where AACR2 and RDA differ is in the treatment of such compilations when there is no collective title. AACR2 instructs the cataloger to enter the compilation under the author of the first named work (MARC 1XX field) and to make added entries (7XX fields with a subfield $t) for the remaining works. In RDA, the default instruction under 6.27.1.4 is to construct an access point for the first named work (MARC 7XX field) along with the other works.

RDA 2.3.2.9, which provides guidelines for recording the title of a resource that lacks a collective title, is similar to the corresponding AACR2 rule, in which all the titles are recorded. However, RDA also provides an alternative approach, which is to devise a collective title. Whichever approach is chosen, there would be no 1XX field in a record for a resource consisting of compilations of works by multiple creators.

AACR2

```
100   1_ $a Vizinczey, Stephen, $d 1933–
240   10 $a In praise of older women
245   10 $a In praise of older women / $c Stephen Vizinczey.
      Feramontov / Desmond Cory. The graveyard shift / Harry Patterson.
700   12 $a Cory, Desmond, $d 1928– $t Feramontov.
700   12 $a Patterson, Harry, 1929– $t Graveyard shift.
```

RDA

```
245   00 $a In praise of older women / $c Stephen Vizinczey.
      Feramontov / Desmond Cory. The graveyard shift / Harry Patterson.
700   12 $a Vizinczey, Stephen, $d 1933– $t In praise of older women.
700   12 $a Cory, Desmond, $d 1928– $t Feramontov.
700   12 $a Patterson, Harry, 1929– $t Graveyard shift.
```

OR

```
245   00 $a [Three novels].
505   0_ $a In praise of older women / Stephen Vizinczey—Feramontov /
      Desmond Cory—The graveyard shift / Harry Patterson.
```

OR

```
245   00 $a [Three novels].
505   0_ $a In praise of older women / Stephen Vizinczey—Feramontov /
      Desmond Cory—The graveyard shift / Harry Patterson.
700   12 $a Vizinczey, Stephen, $d 1933– $t In praise of older women.
700   12 $a Cory, Desmond, $d 1928– $t Feramontov.
700   12 $a Patterson, Harry, 1929– $t Graveyard shift.
```

Compilations of Works by the Same Creator (RDA 6.2.2.10)

RDA also differs from AACR2 with respect to the treatment of compilations of works written by the same author. For compilations of two works by the same author, AACR2 instructs the cataloger to "use the uniform title of the work that [occurred] first in the item" and to "make a name-title added entry using the uniform title of the second work." The following example illustrates application of this rule in MARC:

```
100   1_ $a Dickens, Charles. $d 1812–1870.
240   10 $a Hard times
245   10 $a Dickens' new stories.
505   0_ $a Hard times—Pictures from Italy.
700   1_ $a Dickens, Charles. $d 1812–1870. $t Pictures from Italy.
```

In contrast, RDA 6.2.2.10.3 simply instructs the cataloger to construct access points for each work, although it offers as an alternative to record the conventional collective title for the compilation instead of or in addition to constructing the access points for each work. Applying the default instruction along with instruction RDA 6.27.1.2 would result in the following:

```
100   1_ $a Dickens, Charles. $d 1812–1870.
245   10 $a Dickens' new stories.
505   0_ $a Hard times—Pictures from Italy.
700   1_ $a Dickens, Charles. $d 1812–1870. $t Hard times.
700   1_ $a Dickens, Charles. $d 1812–1870. $t Pictures from Italy.
```

If applying the alternative under RDA 6.2.2.10.3, either of the following would result:

```
100   1_ $a Dickens, Charles. $d 1812–1870.
240   10 $a Works. $k Selections.
245   10 $a Dickens' new stories.
505   0_ $a Hard times—Pictures from Italy.
```

              OR

```
100   1_ $a Dickens, Charles. $d 1812–1870.
240   10 $a Works. $k Selections.
245   10 $a Dickens' new stories.
505   0_ $a Hard times—Pictures from Italy.
700   1_ $a Dickens, Charles. $d 1812–1870. $t Hard times.
700   1_ $a Dickens, Charles. $d 1812–1870. $t Pictures from Italy.
```

AACR2 and RDA have similar guidelines for compilations that are (or purport to be) the complete works of a creator. These guidelines apply to works in a single form or in various forms as well as to compilations of three or more (but not all) of a creator's works that are in a single form.

```
100   1_ $a Maugham, W. Somerset $q (William Somerset),
         $d 1874–1965.
240   10 $a Works
245   14 $a The complete works of Somerset Maugham.

100   1_ $a Maugham, W. Somerset $q (William Somerset),
         $d 1874–1965.
240   10 $a Short stories
245   10 $a Complete short stories of W. Somerset Maugham.

100   1_ $a Maugham, W. Somerset $q (William Somerset),
         $d 1874–1965.
```

```
240   10 $a Short stories. $k Selections
245   10 $a Seventeen lost stories / $c by W. Somerset Maugham; com-
         piled by Craig V. Showalter.
```

However, RDA differs from AACR2 when it comes to compilations of three or more (but not all) of a creator's works that are in various forms. In AACR2 the cataloger is instructed to "use the collective title *Selections* . . . for works in various forms." The following example illustrates application of this rule:

```
100   1_ $a Maugham, W. Somerset $q (William Somerset),
         $d 1874–1965.
240   10 $a Selections
245   14 $a The Somerset Maugham pocket book.
```

RDA 6.2.2.10.3 instructs the cataloger to apply the guideline under RDA 6.2.2.10.1 and to record the word *Works* before the word *Selections*. Applying these instructions with instruction RDA 6.27.1.2 would result in the following:

```
100   1_ $a Maugham, W. Somerset $q (William Somerset),
         $d 1874–1965.
240   10 $a Works. $k Selections
245   14 $a The Somerset Maugham pocket book.
```

Translations and Resources Comprising Two or More Language Expressions (RDA 6.11, 6.27.3, and 26.1)

As AACR2 did, RDA instructs the cataloger to add an access point for the original language of the expression if a resource is a translation.

```
100   1_ $a Lessius, Leonardus, $d 1554–1623.
240   10 $a Hygiasticon. $l English
245   10 $a Hygiasticon, or, A treatise of the means of health and long
         life . . .
```

If there are two or more language expressions, however, AACR2 and RDA guidelines diverge. In AACR2, if a resource comprises two different language expressions of the same work, the cataloger would add both languages to the heading for the uniform title and separate the languages with an ampersand. In RDA, the cataloger would add an access point for the first named language expression and, if considered important for access, the cataloger would add a separate access point for the second language expression. If a resource comprises three or more different language expressions, the cataloger would add the word *Polyglot* to the uniform title in AACR2, whereas in RDA the cataloger would add an access point for the first listed expression and optionally add separate access points for the remaining expressions.

Two expressions, one in the original language:

AACR2

    100   1_ $a Caesar, Julius.
    240   10 $a De bello civili. $l English & Latin
    245   10 $a De bello civili = $b Civil wars / $c Julius Caesar.

RDA

    100   1_ $a Caesar, Julius.
    245   10 $a De bello civili = $b Civil wars / $c Julius Caesar.
    700   12 $a Caesar, Julius. $t De bello civili. $l Latin.
    700   12 $a Caesar, Julius. $t De bello civili. $l English.

Three expressions, none in the original language:

AACR2

    100   1_ $a Einhorn, Erich.
    240   10 $aPražský hrad. $l Polyglot
    245   10 $a Prague Castle = $b Le Château de Prague = Die Prager Burg
          / $c Erich Einhorn.

RDA

    100   1_ $a Einhorn, Erich.
    245   10 $a Prague Castle = $b Le Château de Prague = Die Prager Burg
          / $c Erich Einhorn.
    700   12 $a Einhorn, Erich. $t Pražský hrad. $l English.
    700   12 $a Einhorn, Erich. $t Pražský hrad. $l French.
    700   12 $a Einhorn, Erich. $t Pražský hrad. $l German.

Field 245 Subfield $a—Title Proper (RDA 2.3)

RDA shares many similarities with AACR2 with respect to the title proper. Both allow abridgment of a lengthy title proper if it "can be done without loss of essential information." Also, alternative titles are still treated as part of the title proper.

    245   00 $a Lacan and Lévi-Strauss, or The return to Freud, 1951–1957.

Introductory words not intended to be part of the title are not transcribed.

    245   04 $a The HMO salary survey.
    246   3_ $a Warren surveys presents the HMO salary survey

Symbols and other characters that cannot be reproduced by the facilities available to the cataloger are replaced by a description of the symbol enclosed in square brackets.

> 245   00 $a Robust H [proportional to] stabilization of stochastic hybrid systems with Wiener process
> *Symbol for "proportional to" appears on source of information.*

Titles comprising only the name of a person, family, or corporate body are recorded as the title proper.

> 245   10 $a White Earth Health Center.

Statements of responsibility or names of publishers that are integral to the title are transcribed in the title proper.

> 245   00 $a Mosby's review for the pharmacy technician certification examination.

Titles of parts, sections, and supplements that are not grammatically linked to the title of the larger resource are transcribed after the main title, with a full stop separating them.

> 245   00 $a Neurobiology of cytokines. $n Part A.

One of the areas in which RDA differs from AACR2 with respect to the title proper is in the transcription of the punctuation marks ". . ." and "[ ]." In AACR2, these are replaced by "—" and "( )," respectively, whereas in RDA they are transcribed as they appear.

AACR2

> 245   00 $a And then forgot to tell us why— : $b a look at the campaign against river blindness in West Africa.

RDA

> 245   00 $a And then forgot to tell us why. . . : $b a look at the campaign against river blindness in West Africa.

Another change involves a different treatment of inaccuracies. AACR2 instructs the catalogers to follow inaccuracies "either by *[sic]* or by *i.e.* and the correction in brackets." Because this in essence interrupts the transcription, two variant titles are added: both the inaccurate title (interrupted) and the corrected title. In RDA, interrupting the transcription with corrections would violate the *principle of representation*. Thus, the title proper is transcribed as it appears on the source and, if considered important for access, a variant title can be added for the corrected title.

AACR2

> 245 10 $a Statisical [i.e. Statistical] methods in bioinformatics : $b an introduction / $c Warren J. Ewens, Gregory R. Grant.
> 246 3_ $a Statisical methods in bioinformatics
> 246 3_ $a Statistical methods in bioinformatics

RDA

> 245 10 $a Statisical methods in bioinformatics : $b an introduction / $c Warren J. Ewens, Gregory R. Grant.
> 246 1_ $i Title should read: $a Statistical methods in bioinformatics

Field 245 Subfield $b—Parallel Title Proper (RDA 2.3.3)

RDA's instructions for transcribing the parallel title proper are largely the same as those in AACR2.

> 245 00 $a Strassenkarte der Schweiz = $b Carte routière de la Suisse.
> 246 31 $a Carte routière de la Suisse

One notable difference involves the source of information for parallel titles proper. In AACR2, the prescribed source of information was the same for all elements in the "title and statement of responsibility" area, which included the title proper and the parallel title proper. RDA decouples the sources of information for the title proper and the parallel title proper. While the source of information for the title proper has a defined set of hierarchal preferences, the source of information for the parallel title proper can be taken from any source within the resource. In AACR2, if only the title proper appeared on the title page and the parallel title proper appeared on the cover, only the title proper could be transcribed in the 245. However, in RDA the parallel title proper in such a scenario can now be transcribed in the 245, even if it comes from a difference source within the resource.

AACR2

> 245 00 $a Migración y salud: $b los hijos de migrantes mexicanos en Estados Unidos
> 246 15 $a Migration and health : $b the children of Mexican immigrants in the U.S.

RDA

> 245   00 $a Migración y salud : $b los hijos de migrantes mexicanos en Estados Unidos = Migration and health: the children of Mexican immigrants in the U.S.
>
> 246   15 $a Migration and health : $b the children of Mexican immigrants in the U.S.

Field 245 Subfield $b—Other Title Information (RDA 2.3.4)

RDA shares many similarities with AACR2 when it comes to transcription of other title information. As with titles proper, both standards allow abridgment of lengthy other title information if it "can be done without loss of essential information." Both standards also instruct the cataloger to transcribe a statement of responsibility or the name of a publisher that is integral to the other title information as other title information.

> 245   10 $a Neutron capture therapy : $b proceedings of the Second International Symposium on Neutron Capture Therapy held on October 18, 19, and 20, 1985, at Teikyo University, Tokyo.

However, RDA differs from AACR2 in that it limits the scope of resources to which other title information can be supplied. AACR2 allowed the cataloger to supply a "brief addition as other title information" if the title proper needed explanation. This rule was in AACR2 Chapter 1 ("General Rules for Description"), which meant it could be applied to all types of resources. This general rule was not carried over into RDA. Instead, RDA identifies only two types of resources for which other title information can be supplied: cartographic resources and moving images.

AACR2

> 245   10 $a Longfellow : $b [selections].

RDA

> 245   10 $a Longfellow.
> 500 $a Selection of Longfellow's writings.

Field 245 Subfield $c—Statement of Responsibility (RDA 2.4)

Because of RDA's *principle of representation*, the statement of responsibility is one of the areas of major change from AACR2. However, there are still some similarities. In AACR2, a word or short phrase can be added in brackets if the role of the person, family, or corporate body named in a statement of responsibility is not clear from the source of information and needs clarification. RDA retained this guideline, which complements its *principle of relationships*.

245   00 $a Piers Plowman / $c [edited by] Elizabeth Salter.

One of the areas in which AACR2 and RDA differ with respect to statements of responsibility is the omission or abridgment of data. AACR2 required omission of intervening text in the statement of responsibility, such as titles of address, titles of honor, degrees, and institutional affiliations. RDA *allows* omission of these data as an option, but the default instruction in RDA 2.4.1.4 is to transcribe the statement "in the form in which it appears on the source of information." This is in line with the *principle of representation*.

AACR2

245   10 $a Concussive brain trauma : $b neurobehavioral impairment and maladaptation / $c Rolland S. Parker.

RDA

245   10 $a Concussive brain trauma : $b neurobehavioral impairment and maladaptation / $c Rolland S. Parker, Ph.D., F.A.P.A., Consulting Neuropsychologist, Adjunct Professor of Clinical Neurology, NYU Medical School, New, NY.

AACR2 also required abridgment of a statement of responsibility if there were more than three entities performing the same function. In such cases, only the first-named person or corporate body was transcribed, while the others were omitted. The omission was indicated with the mark of omission (. . .) and the recording of *et al.* in brackets. Again, RDA allows this omission as an option, but the default guideline is to transcribe all that are named. If the optional omission is applied, instead of the mark of omission and recording *et al.*, the spelled-out number of entities being omitted must be recorded following the formula: *[and # others]*.

AACR2

245   10 $a Creating conditions for scaling up access to life skills based sexual and reproductive health education and condom services : $b strengthening safe sex decision-making / $c study conducted and report prepared by Ismat Bhuiya...[et al.].

RDA

245   10 $a Creating conditions for scaling up access to life skills based sexual and reproductive health education and condom services : $b

strengthening safe sex decision-making / $c study conducted and report prepared by Ismat Bhuiya, Ubaidur Rob, K.M. Zahiduzzaman, Asiful Haidar Chowdhury, Haribondhu Sarma, K.M. Amanur Rahman.

OR

245   10 $a Creating conditions for scaling up access to life skills based sexual and reproductive health education and condom services : $b strengthening safe sex decision-making / $c study conducted and report prepared by Ismat Bhuiya [and five others].

Another notable difference is in the treatment of noun phrases. In AACR2, if a noun phrase in conjunction with statements of responsibility was indicative of the nature of the work, it was treated as other title information. In RDA, such noun phrases are always treated as part of the statement of responsibility.

AACR2

245   10 $a Characters from Dickens : $b dramatized adaptations / $c by Barry Campbell.

RDA

245   10 $a Characters from Dickens / $c dramatized adaptations by Barry Campbell.

Field 246—Variant Title (RDA 2.3.6)

Variant titles are generally handled similarly in AACR2 and RDA. Following are a few examples of when variant titles might be added if considered important for access.

245   00 $a Lacan and Lévi-Strauss, or The return to Freud, 1951–1957.
246   30 $a Return to Freud, 1951–1957

245   04 $a The HMO salary survey.
246   3_ $a Warren surveys presents the HMO salary survey

245   10 $a Statisical methods in bioinformatics : $b an introduction / $c Warren J. Ewens, Gregory R. Grant.
246   1_ $i Title should read: $a Statistical methods in bioinformatics

245   00 $a Qualificação da saúde suplementar : $b nova perspectiva no process de regulação do setor = Supplementary health qualification.
246   31 $a Supplementary health qualification

Field 250—Edition Statement (RDA 2.5)

Designation of Edition

As AACR2 did, RDA instructs the cataloger to consider words like "edition," "issue," "release," "level," "state," or "update" (or their equivalents in another language) as evidence that such a statement is a designation of edition. Both AACR2 and RDA also instruct to add an appropriate word in brackets if the statement contains letter(s) and/or numbers(s) without accompanying words.

> 250 $a Fourth [edition].

One of the main changes from AACR2 is RDA's instruction for transcribing the designation of edition. AACR2 instructed the cataloger to abbreviate the edition statement according to conventions outlined in the appendix on abbreviations. In contrast, RDA instructs the cataloger to transcribe the designation of edition as it appears on the source, in keeping with the *principle of representation*. Thus, the designation of edition would only be abbreviated if it appeared that way on the source.

AACR

> 250 $a 1st American ed.
> 250 $a 7th ed.

RDA

> 250 $a First American edition.
> 250 $a 7th ed.   *abbreviated on the source*

Designation of a Named Revision of an Edition

Both *designation of edition* and *designation of a named revision of an edition* are core elements. The same similarities and differences already mentioned apply to the designation of a named revision of an edition. The following is an example of how a designation of a named revision of an edition would be transcribed in AACR2 and RDA.

AACR2

> 250 $a 1st American ed., new enl. revision.

RDA

> 250 $a First American edition, new enlarged revision.

Field 264—Production Statement, Publication Statement, Distribution Statement, Manufacture Statement, and Copyright Date (RDA 2.7–2.11)

One of the most substantial changes from AACR2 involves information about the production, publication, distribution, and manufacture of resources. In AACR2, this information was collectively referred to as the "Publication, Distribution, etc., Area." It involved over a dozen different types of information, all crammed into half a dozen subfields within MARC field 260. RDA defines twenty-one elements for these attributes. To accommodate this higher level of granularity, a new field was created: bibliographic field 264. Table 8.1 shows the different subfields and indicators that map from the RDA elements to field 264.

Table 8.1.   Field 264 Indicator Values and Subfields

Indicator	Subfield $a		Subfield $b		Subfield $c
264 _0	Place of Production	Parallel Place of Production	Producer's Name	Parallel Producer's Name	Date of Production
264 _1	Place of Publication	Parallel Place of Publication	Publisher's Name	Parallel Publisher's Name	Date of Publication
264 _2	Place of Distribution	Parallel Place of Distribution	Distributor's Name	Parallel Distributor's Name	Date of Distribution
264 _3	Place of Manufacture	Parallel Place of Manufacture	Manufacturer's Name	Parallel Manufacturer's Name	Date of Manufacture
264 _4					Copyright Date

Production Statement

The production statement is a new element introduced by RDA. Whereas AACR2 instructed the cataloger to include only a date in the production statement for unpublished resources, such as manuscripts, RDA fleshes out the rest of the field, adding instructions for *place of production, parallel place of production, producer's name,* and *parallel producer's name*. The following example from RDA illustrates how a production statement might be useful.

> *Typewritten carbon, "copied from Doctor Barry's typescript by Robert Hitchman, April 27, 1952"*
> 264   _0 $a [Place of production not identified] : $b Robert Hitchman, $c 1952.

Distribution Statement

Because the distribution statement has its own field indicator, it is transcribed in a separate field from the publication statement rather than in a second pair of $a and $b subfields within the same field as the publication statement.

AACR2

> 260 $a Stockholm : $b Grammofon AB BIS ; $a New York: $b Distributed by Qualiton Imports, $c 1999.

RDA

> 264   _1 $a Stockholm : $b Grammofon AB BIS, $c 1999.
> 264   _2 $a New York : $b Distributed by Qualiton Imports, $c [1999]

Manufacture Statement

Because the manufacture statement has its own field indicator, it is transcribed in a separate field from the publication statement rather than in the $e, $f, and $g subfields within the same field as the publication statement.

AACR2

> 260 $a [S.l. : $b s.n., $c 1970] $e (London : $f High Fidelity Sound Studios)

RDA

> 264   _1 $a [Place of publication not identified] : $b [publisher's name not identified], $c [date of publication not identified]
> 264   _3 $a London : $b High Fidelity Sound Studios, $c 1970.

Copyright Date

In AACR2, if information about the date of publication or the date of distribution were unknown, catalogers could supply a copyright date in its place. In RDA, information about the date of publication is always core, whether it is known or unknown. If the copyright date is given, it is provided in addition to (rather than in lieu of) information about the date of publication. When the copyright date is recorded, it is preceded by the copyright symbol. If the copyright symbol cannot be reproduced with the facilities available, the word *copyright* is recorded instead.

AACR2

> 260 $a Berlin : $b Verlag, $c c2005.

RDA

    264   _1 $a Berlin : $b Verlag, $c [date of publication not identified]
    264   _4 $c ©2005

      OR

    264   _1 $a Berlin : $b Verlag, $c [date of publication not identified]
    264   _4 $c copyright 2005

Fictitious Information

A difference between AACR2 and RDA that is common to all of the statements is the treatment of fictitious information. In AACR2, if information related to the publication, distribution, or manufacture was known to be fictitious or erroneous, the cataloger was instructed to follow it with the corrected information in brackets. In keeping with its *principle of accuracy*, RDA carries over the importance of making such corrections, but instructs the cataloger to do so in a separate note.

AACR2

    260      $a Paris : $b Impr. Vincent, $c 1798 [i.e. Bruxelles : Moens, 1883]

RDA

    264   _1 $a Paris : $b Impr. Vincent, $c 1798
    500      $a Actually published in Brussels by Moens in 1883.

264 Subfield $a

Place of production, place of publication, place of distribution, and place of manufacture share similar guidelines, many of which were carried over from AACR2.

As AACR2 did, RDA allows addition of a larger jurisdiction in brackets after the name of a local place-name if considered important for identification.

AACR2

    260    $a Dublin [Ireland]

RDA

    264   _1 $a Dublin [Ireland]

Also similar to AACR2, if the place of production, publication, distribution, or manufacture is absent, a probable place can be supplied in brackets if certain (followed by a question mark, if uncertain).

AACR2

    260    $a [Chicago]

RDA

    264 _1 $a [Chicago]

One of the changes from AACR2 is that RDA does not prescribe omission of a larger jurisdiction, such as a state or country, that appears with the local place on the source of information. AACR2 instructed catalogers to omit the larger jurisdiction unless its retention was thought to aid in identification or distinction from similarly named places. In line with its *principle of representation*, RDA instructs catalogers to transcribe the larger jurisdiction as it appears on the source.

AACR2

    260    $a Portland

RDA

    264 _1 $a Portland, OR, USA

Another change is that RDA does not prescribe abbreviation of the larger jurisdiction when spelled out on the source of information, as AACR2 did.

AACR2

    260    $a Portland, Or.

RDA

    264 _1 $a Portland, Oregon

Still another difference is that RDA does not limit the number of places that can be transcribed and does not prescribe inclusion of a place that is in the home country of the cataloging agency. In RDA, the first place is core, but other listed places may also be transcribed, with no preference prescribed for the agency's home country.

AACR2

> 260 $a London ; $a New York   *cataloging agency in the U.S.*

RDA

> 264   _1 $a London

>   OR

> 264   _1 $a London ; $a New York ; $a Ontario

Finally, RDA differs from AACR2 in its instructions for indicating that there is no place named on the source and that it cannot be determined. In AACR2, the cataloger was instructed to record *s.l.*, the abbreviation for the Latin phrase "sine loco." This conflicts with RDA's aim to make information clearer to users by minimizing the use of abbreviations and Latin expressions. Thus, RDA instructs the cataloger to record *place of publication not identified* (or *place of distribution not identified*, etc.) in brackets.

AACR2

> 260 $a [S.l.]

RDA

> 264   _1 $a [Place of publication not identified]

264 Subfield $b

As AACR2 did, RDA instructs the cataloger to retain words or phrases that indicate function (other than solely publishing) as they appear on the source of information.

AACR2

> 260 $a Montreal : $b SAGE Publications on behalf of McGill University, $c 2002.

RDA

> 264   _1 $a Montreal : $b SAGE Publications on behalf of McGill University, $c 2002.

Also like AACR2, RDA instructs catalogers to add a term that clarifies the function of the producer, publisher, distributor, or manufacturer if it is not clear from the source of information.

AACR2

> 260 $a London : $b Macmillan : $b Educational Service [distributor], $c 1982.

RDA

> 264   _1 $a London : $b Macmillan, $c 1982.
> 264   _2 $a London : $b Educational Service [distributor], $c 1982.

One of the ways that RDA differs from AACR2 is that it does not instruct the cataloger to give the name of the producer, publisher, distributor, or manufacturer in the shortest form by abbreviating or omitting words, but to transcribe the information as it appears on the source.

AACR2

> 260 $a New York : $b Springer Pub. Co. ; $a Portland, Mne. : $b Distributed by Townsend, $c 1998.

RDA

> 264   _1 $a New York : $b Springer Publishing Company, $c 1998.
> 264   _2 $a Portland, Maine : $b Distributed by Townsend, Inc., $c [1998?]

Finally, RDA also differs from AACR2 in how it instructs catalogers to record information explaining the absence of a publisher's name (or distributor's name, etc.). In AACR2, the cataloger was instructed to record *s.n.*, the abbreviation for the Latin phrase "sine nomine." In RDA, the cataloger is instructed to record *publisher not identified* (or *distributor not identified*, etc.) in brackets. If the cataloger needs to indicate that both the place and the publisher (distributor, manufacturer, etc.) are not identified, he or she must record the information for each in a separate set of brackets.

AACR2

> 260 $a [S.l.: $b s.n., $c 2004?]

RDA

> 264   _1 $a [Place of publication not identified] : $b [publisher not identified], $c [2004?]

264 Subfield $c

When it comes to the date, one major difference between AACR2 and RDA is that information on the date of publication must always be recorded, whether or not it is known. If the date of publication is absent, it can be inferred from another source (such as the date of distribution, copyright date, or date of manufacture) and recorded in brackets. Alternatively, *date of publication not identified* can be recorded in the first 264 subfield $c, and another date (e.g. date of distribution, copyright date, or date of manufacture) can be recorded in the subfield $c of a separate 264 field.

When the date of publication is present on the source:

AACR2

    260       $a Amsterdam : $b Academic Press, $c 2001.

RDA

    264   _1 $a Amsterdam : $b Academic Press, $c 2001.

When the date of publication is absent from the source, but the copyright date is available:

AACR2

    260       $a New York : $b Apress, $c c1998.

RDA

    264   _1 $a New York : $b Apress, $c [date of publication not identified]
    264   _4 $c ©1998

        OR

    264   _1 $a New York : $b Apress, $c [1998]

When the date of publication is absent from the source, but the date of manufacture is available:

AACR2

    260       $a New York : $b Apress, $c [1998] $e (Buffalo: $f Mayer Printers)

RDA

    264   _1 $a New York : $b Apress, $c [date of publication not identified]
    264   _3 $a Buffalo : $b Mayer Printers, $c 1998.

        OR

    264   _1 $a New York : $b Apress, $c [1998]

These examples show the options for recording core information. The cataloger can opt to go "beyond core" and record both the date of publication and the copyright date or date of manufacture (or all three, if applicable and desired).

264   _1 $a New York : $b Apress, $c [1998]
264   _4 $c ©1998

OR

264   _1 $a New York : $b Apress, $c [1998]
264   _3 $a Buffalo : $b Mayer Printers, $c 1998.

OR

264   _1 $a New York : $b Apress, $c [1998]
264   _3 $a Buffalo : $b Mayer Printers, $c 1998.
264   _4 $c ©1998

If none of the subelements within a 264 statement is identified, such information is recorded in separate pairs of brackets, as follows:

264   _1 $a [Place of publication not identified]: $b [publisher not identified], $c [date of publication not identified]

Note that the Library of Congress, in conjunction with the Program for Cooperative Cataloging, has issued policy statements (LC-PCC PS for RDA 2.8.2.6 and 2.8.6.6) encouraging catalogers to supply place and date of publication if possible.

Field 300

Field 300 Subfield $a–Extent of Text (RDA 3.4.5)

Most of RDA's guidelines for recording information about the extent of a text were carried over from AACR2. The main difference lies in spelling out information that was formerly abbreviated in AACR2 and fully explaining in words, rather than brackets, when pages are unnumbered.

300	$a A-T pages	*20 pages numbered in letters*
300	$a 99 pages	*pages numbered as words*
300	$a 257 pages	*pages numbered: i-vii, 8–257*
300	$a pages 248–405	*numbering is part of a larger sequence*
300	$a 197, that is, 179 pages	*correction of recorded (not transcribed) information within the same field is acceptable*
300	$a 1 folded sheet (6 pages)	
300	$a iv, 77, 78, iv pages	*pages numbered in opposite directions*

As AACR2 did, RDA has a default instruction that says not to record the number of pages, leaves, or columns in an unpaged resource unless referencing one or more of them in a note. It then offers an optional provision, which allows the cataloger to record this information anyway. If the information is recorded, it can be done in one of three ways. Methods *a* and *b* are analogous to the methods in AACR2.

Method a (if the pagination is readily ascertainable)

      300      $a 40 unnumbered pages

Method b (if the pagination is not readily ascertainable)

      300      $a approximately 400 pages

Method c

      300      $a 1 volume (unpaged)

RDA also retained AACR2's guideline to disregard pages, leaves, or columns in an unnumbered sequence unless the sequence comprises a substantial part of the resource or if part of the sequence is being referenced in a note. RDA offers an optional provision allowing for this information to be recorded anyway, and it can be recorded in one of three methods, the first two of which were carried over from AACR2.

Method a

      300      $a xiii, 10 leaves, 50 unnumbered pages

Method b

      300      $a 47, approximately 200 pages

Method c

      300      $a vi, 24 leaves, unnumbered sequence of pages

RDA's instructions for recording complicated and irregular paging were also carried over from AACR2. There are three options for recording this information, as illustrated below.

Method a

      300      $a 800 pages in various pagings

Method b

    300       $a 583 pages, 84 pages, 133 variously numbered pages

Method c

    300       $a 1 volume (various pagings)

Field 300 Subfield $b—Illustrative Content (RDA 7.15) and
Colour Content (RDA 7.17)

As AACR2 did, RDA excludes alphanumeric tables from the definition of illustrative content and instructs the cataloger to disregard illustrated title pages and other minor illustrations. The main difference from AACR2 is in the spelling out of words like *facsimiles, genealogical tables, illustrations,* and *portraits.* Also, RDA expands the list of types of illustrative content to include *charts, graphs, illuminations,* and *photographs.* Another difference is that RDA appears not to have carried over AACR2's guideline that instructed catalogers to record *all [name of illustration type]* or *chiefly [name of illustration type]* (as in *all ill., chiefly maps,* etc.). Finally, RDA allows the cataloger to record the type of illustrative content in place of or in addition to the generic term *illustrations.*

    300       $a 405 pages : $b illustrations

        OR

    300       $a 405 pages : $b charts, graphs, maps

        OR

    300       $a 405 pages : $b illustrations, charts, graphs, maps

RDA carried over the AACR2 guideline instructing catalogers to explain if the illustrative content is in color. It also allows the cataloger to specify the degree of color and to say whether the illustrative content is in some color or is chiefly in color. With *colour content,* the main difference is in the spelling out of "color" or "colour." Cataloging agencies in the United States have the option to choose the American English form of the spelling.

    300       $a 25 leaves : $b color illustration
    300       $a xi, 188 pages : $b illustrations (chiefly color), maps (some color)

Field 300 Subfield $c—Dimensions of Volumes (RDA 3.5.1.4.14)

As AACR2 did, RDA instructs the cataloger to record the height in cm if it is greater than 10 cm and to record it in mm if it is less than 10 cm. RDA also carried over AACR2's guideline that instructs the cataloger to record the *height x width* if the width is either less than half of the height or is greater than the height.

> 300 $a xi, 240 pages : $b color maps ; $c 24 cm
> 300 $a 50 pages ; $c 85 mm
> 300 $a 207 leaves : $b illustrations ; $c 25 x 10 cm

In terms of dimensions of volumes, the major change is that in RDA *cm* and *mm* are symbols, which are not automatically followed by stops. (In AACR2, they were treated as abbreviations and always terminated in a stop, regardless of context.) In RDA, if field 300 ends with the symbol "cm," because of ISBD conventions, the field may or may not terminate in a stop depending on what follows. In ISBD, field 300 corresponds to Area 5, and field 490 corresponds to Area 6. Area 6 is supposed to be preceded by a "point, space, dash, space (. -)" if present. This affects the MARC coding of field 300. If there is a series statement in field 490, the field 300 terminates in a stop. If there is no series statement in field 490, then a stop is not recorded.

> 300 $a 151 leaves ; $c 28 cm
> {No series statement}

> 300 $a 25 pages : $b illustrations (some color) ; $c 24 cm.
> 490   0_ $a Health report ; $v 3

Field 336—Content Type (RDA 6.9)

Field 336 is a new field introduced in MARC to accommodate the RDA element *content type*. Content type, *media type*, and *carrier type* collectively replace the general material designation in AACR2. Although this replacement brings about change for all types of materials, the change is particularly significant for print monographs, because the general material designation was generally never used for these types of resources. In RDA, all resources must at least be described in terms of their content type and carrier type, because these types are core elements.

For books, the content type term is *text*, which is recorded in subfield $a. When the MARC cataloger records this term, he or she must also specify that the term is an RDA vocabulary term and record "rdacontent" in subfield $2 of the same field.

> 336 $a text $2 rdacontent

Catalogers may optionally add subfield $b for the content type code "txt," though it is not required.

> 336 $a text $b txt $2 rdacontent

Field 337—Media Type (RDA 3.2)

Field 337 was introduced in MARC to accommodate the RDA element *media type*. For books the media type term is *unmediated*, which is recorded for content intended to be perceived without the aid of an intermediating device. *Media type* is not a core element, but catalogers may routinely find this information in bibliographic records along with *content type* and *carrier type*. When describing the media type, catalogers must record this term in the subfield $a and record *rdamedia* in the subfield $2.

> 337 $a unmediated $2 rdamedia

Catalogers may optionally add the media type code "n" (for "unmediated") in a subfield $b.

> 337 $a unmediated $b n $2 rdamedia

Field 338—Carrier Type (RDA 3.3)

Field 338 was created to accommodate the RDA element *carrier type*. For books the carrier type term is *volume*, which is recorded in subfield $a. The term *rdacarrier* must also be recorded in a $2.

> 338 $a volume $2 rdacarrier

Catalogers may optionally add a $b and record the carrier type code "nc" for "volumes."

> 338 $a volume $b nc $2 rdacarrier

Field 490—Series Statement (RDA 2.12)

Field 490 Subfield $a—Title Proper of Series (2.12.2)

Many of the guidelines for recording the title proper of a series are similar in AACR2 and RDA.

> 490   0_ $a Essential public health

As AACR2 did, RDA treats numbering that is an integral part of the title proper of the series as part of the title proper.

> 490   0_ $a WALS—the fifth James A. Shannon lecture

Field 490 Subfield $x—ISSN of Series (RDA 2.12.8)

ISSN of series is treated similarly in RDA and in AACR2.

> 490   0_ $a Biorheology, $x 0006–355X ; $v volume 20, number 5

One notable difference is that in RDA, the ISSN of the main series is retained, even if there is a separate ISSN for the subseries.

AACR2

> 490   0_ $a Janua linguarum. $a Series maior, $x 0075–3114

RDA

> 490   0_ $a Janua linguarum, $x 0446–4796. $a Series maior, $x 0075–3114

Field 490 Subfield $v—Numbering within Series (RDA 2.12.9)

RDA guidelines for numbering within a series are similar to those in AACR2.

> 490   0_ $a The Richard and Hinda Rosenthal lecture ; $v 2007
> 490   0_ $a RSC drug discovery series, $x 2041–3203 ; $v 2–3

If a new sequence of numbering is accompanied by wording that differentiates the sequence, such as "new series," both AACR2 and RDA instruct the cataloger to include the wording.

> 490   0_ $a UCLA symposia on molecular and cellular biology ; $v new series, v. 3

Because numbering within a series is a transcribed element, much of the change from AACR2 is due to RDA's *principle of representation*. For example, unlike AACR2, RDA does not instruct the cataloger to abbreviate designations such as "volumes" and "number" unless they are already abbreviated on the resource.

AACR2

> 490   0_ $a Health communication, $x 2153–1277 ; $v v. 4

RDA

> 490   0_ $a Health communication, $x 2153–1277 ; $v volume 4

AACR2

> 490   0_ $a DHHS publication ; $v no. (PHS) 2012–1983

RDA

> 490   0_ $a DHHS publication ; $v no. (PHS) 2012–1983
> *abbreviation appears on the source*

RDA also instructs the cataloger to correct inaccuracies in a separate note field, rather than in field 490 as in AACR2.

AACR2

> 490   0_ $a International perspectives on aging ; $v 1 [i.e. 2]

RDA

> 490   0_ $a International perspectives on aging ; $v 1
> 500 $a Series numbering should read: 2.

Field 490 Subfield $a—Title Proper of Subseries (RDA 2.12.10)

As with the main series, the title proper of the subseries is treated similarly in AACR2 and RDA.

> 490   0_ $a The NIH director's Wednesday afternoon lectures. NIH director's sixth astute clinician lecture

There may be some transcription differences between AACR2 and RDA where the latter does not prescribe abbreviations or other adjustments, as the former does.

AACR2

> 490   0_ $a Theorie und Forschung ; $v Bd. 20. $a Psychologie ; $v Bd. 8

RDA

> 490   0_ $a Theorie und Forschung ; $v Band 20. $a Psychologie ; $v Band 8

As in AACR2, in RDA if a phrase such as a new series appears with an unnumbered series on the source of information, then the phrase is recorded as a subseries title.

> 490   0_ $a Royal Historical Society studies in history. New series

If the phrase appears with a numbered series, then the phrase is recorded as part of the numbering of the series.

> 490   0_ $a Inaugural lecture ; $v new series, number 131

Field 490 Subfield $x—ISSN of Subseries (RDA 2.12.12)

There are largely no differences between AACR2 and RDA with respect to the ISSN of subseries.

> 490   0_ $a Janua linuarum, 0446–4796. $a Series maior, $x 0075–3114

Field 490 Subfield $v—Numbering within Subseries (RDA 2.12.17)

As with numbering within a series, the differences between AACR2 and RDA when it comes to numbering within a subseries stem from the *principle of representation*. Captions consist of abbreviations only if they appear as abbreviations on the source of information, and inaccuracies are corrected in notes rather than within the same line.

```
490   0_  $a Sciences. Physics ; $v TSP 1
490   0_  $a Temas actuales ; $v 3. $a Bolsillo ; $v número 7
500       $a Subseries numbering should read: 8.
```

Field 500—Note on Manifestation or Item (RDA 2.20)

General notes can be provided in field 500 to describe various aspects of print monographs, and the guidelines are largely the same in AACR2 and RDA. Following are some examples:

```
Note on Title
   500   $a Caption title.
   500   $a Volumes 3–5 have title: Outsider's indoor delight.
   500   $a The word "Brain" in the title appears with an X through it.
Note on Statement of Responsibility
   500   $a Editor attributed as author.
Note on Edition Statement
   500   $a Edition statement on colophon varies: Shohan.
Note on Publication Statement
   500   $a Actually published in Dublin.
Note on Series Statement
   500   $a Series numbering should read: vol. 421.
```

Fields 500 and 504—Supplementary Content (RDA 7.16)

The guidelines for recording supplementary content are largely the same in AACR2 and RDA except for a few transcription differences. When cited alone, indexes are recorded in field 500, often in the following style:

```
500       $a Includes index.
```

If a resource has more than one index, the following can be recorded:

```
500       $a Includes indexes.
```

If the resource has a bibliography by itself or in concert with an index, an explanatory note is given in field 504, often along one the following styles:

```
504       $a Includes bibliographical references.
504       $a Includes bibliographical references and index.
```

If the resource has a single bibliography, the page range can be added. RDA examples precede the page range with a colon; Library of Congress practice is to enclose the page range in parentheses. This note uncover a difference from AACR2 in that RDA spells out rather than abbreviates the word "pages" in the bibliographical note.

AACR2 as written

> 504 $a Includes bibliographical references: p. 204–212.

AACR2 as interpreted by the Library of Congress

> 504 $a Includes bibliographical references (p. 204–212).

RDA as written

> 504 $a Includes bibliographical references: pages 204–212.

RDA as interpreted by the Library of Congress

> 504 $a Includes bibliographical references (pages 204–212).

Fields 700, 710, and 711—Creators, Contributors, and Other Responsible Entities (RDA 19–22)

While the 1XX field generally maps to the principal or first-named creator, the 7XX field maps to the remaining elements that represent responsibility relationships. These relationships include other creators, other entities responsible for a work, entities responsible for an expression (or contributors), and entities whose relationship with a resource is at the manifestation or item level. Table 8.2 shows relationship designators for some common types of responsibility relationships.

Table 8.2. Common Relationship Designators for Print Monographs

Creator	Other Person, Family, or Corporate Body Responsible for a Work	Entity Responsible for an Expression (Contributor)	Entity Responsible for a Manifestation	Entity Responsible for an Item
author	honoree	editor	book designer	annotator
compiler	host institution	editor of compilation	engraver	autographer
interviewer	issuing body	illustrator	lithographer	curator
interviewee	sponsoring body	translator	printer	inscriber

The relationship designators for creators are the same whether they involve the 1XX field or the 7XX field.

```
100  1_ $a Pattison, Luc D., $e author.
700  1_ $a Flynt, Rachel, $d 1970– $e author.

100  1_ $a Pollock, Gillian, $e compiler
700  1_ $a Humphreys, Donovan, $e compiler.
```

Unlike AACR2, RDA does not limit the number of added entries for creators when there are more than three.

```
700  1_ $a Morrison, Daniel, $e author.
700  1_ $a Park, Lionel, $e author.
700  1_ $a Gomez, Anastasia C., $e author.
700  1_ $a Gray, Jared I., $e author.
```

Field 8XX—Related Works in Series (RDA 25.1)

One important relationship between two resources is that between a work and the series in which it is issued. This relationship is typically conveyed by recording the authorized access point for the series onto the record of the work within the series. Series access points are generally recorded in field 830, although in some cases they may be conveyed using a combination of field 800 or 810 and a subfield $t.

Title proper of series and *Numbering within series* are core elements, so it is required to record this information in a 490 field whenever there is a series statement. If the cataloger wants to trace the series, he or she can also add the authorized access point for the work in an 8XX field if the series is already established. If the series does not yet exist, the cataloger can establish one by creating an authority record.

The purpose of recording series in 8XX fields is to collocate all the parts of a series under the same standard title, regardless of how each series statement appears in its individual form. Thus, it is very common to encounter a 490 field with a different form from the 8XX field. The 490 field reflects the information as it appears on the resource, whereas the 8XX adheres to stricter parameters in order to support collocation. So while RDA retains many of the same abbreviations and other adjustments with respect to the 8XX field, it instructs the cataloger to transcribe the information as it appears when it comes to the 490 field. The result is that the 8XX field will likely play an even greater role in standardizing the form used for grouping together members within the same series.

```
490  1_ $a New library of psychoanalysis
830  0_ $a New library of psychoanalysis.

490  1_ $a Health communication, $x 2153–1277 ; $v volume 4
830  0_ $a Health communication (New York, N.Y.) ; $v v. 4. $x 2153–1277

490  1_ $a Theorie und Forschung. Psychologie ; $v Band 8
830  0_ $a Theorie und Forschung. $p Psychologie ; $v Bd. 8.
```

BIBLIOGRAPHIC RECORD COMPARISONS

Following are three full-record comparisons between AACR2 and RDA. The first example shows a record for a work issued as part of a series, the second shows a collaborative work written by four authors, and the final example shows three language expressions of a work embodied in the same manifestation. The records are all cataloged according to standards established by the Program for Cooperative Cataloging and the Library of Congress, which include RDA core elements and elements that "go beyond core." These conventions are shown here to promote standardization of practices in an increasingly shared bibliographic environment.

Case 1: Work in a Series

In looking at the first comparison case, we see much of the same information in both records. Starting from the top, we see that most of the Leader and 008 information is the same, including Leader position 07 ("Bibliographic Level"), because the mode of issuance is "m" whether the record is AACR2 or RDA.

Case 1.   Bibliographic Record: Work in Series

AACR2

LDR	01520cam a2200385 a 450
008	101029s2010 gw a b 000 0 eng
010	2010554020
040	XXX $c XXX
020	9783866283183
020	3866283180
041 0_	eng $b ger
042	pcc
050 00	TK5103.4875 $b .C47 2010
100 1_	Christen, Thomas, $d 1979-
245 10	Multi-mode delta-sigma A/D-converters for multi-standard wireless receivers / $c Thomas Christen.
250	1st ed.
260	Konstanz : $b Hartung-Gorre Verlag, $c 2010.
300	xiv, 197 p. : $b ill. ; $c 21 cm.
490 1_	Series in microelectronics, $x 0936-5362 ; $v v. 208
546	Summaries in English and German.
500	Originally presented as the author's thesis (doctoral)--Eidgenössische Technische Hochschule Zürich, 2010.
504	Includes bibliographical references (p. 175–188).
650 _0	Software radio.
650 _0	Modulators (Electronics) $x Design and construction.
650 _0	Analog-to-digital converters $x Design and construction.
830 _0	Series in microelectronics ; $v v. 208. $x 0936-5362.

Case 1.   Bibliographic Record: Work in Series

RDA

LDR	01520cam a2200385 i 450
008	101029s2010 gw a b 000 0 eng
010	2010554020
040	XXX **$b eng $e rda** $c XXX
020	9783866283183
020	3866283180
041 0_	eng $b ger
042	pcc
050 00	TK5103.4875 $b .C47 2010
100 1_	Christen, Thomas, $d 1979-
245 10	Multi-mode delta-sigma A/D-converters for multi-standard wireless receivers / $c Thomas Christen.
250	**First edition.**
264 _1	Konstanz : $b Hartung-Gorre Verlag, $c 2010.
300	xiv, 197 **pages** : $b **illustrations** ; $c 21 cm.
336	**text $2 rdacontent**
337	**unmediated $2 rdamedia**
338	**volume $2 rdacarrier**
490 1_	Series in microelectronics, $x 0936-5362 ; $v **volume** 208
546	Summaries in English and German.
500	Originally presented as the author's thesis (doctoral)--Eidgenössische Technische Hochschule Zürich, 2010.
504	Includes bibliographical references (**pages** 175-188).
650 _0	Software radio.
650 _0	Modulators (Electronics) $x Design and construction.
650 _0	Analog-to-digital converters $x Design and construction.
830 _0	Series in microelectronics ; $v v. 208. $x 0936-5362.

The first difference we encounter is in Leader position 18 field (LDR 18), or the *Descriptive Cataloging Form*. We see that the LDR 18 is coded "a" in the AACR2 record and "i" in the RDA record. This makes sense, because the RDA record is not an AACR2 record, and the variable fields in this particular RDA record include ISBD punctuation. If the record did not include ISBD punctuation, then the field would be coded {blank} for "no ISBD punctuation."

Moving down to the variable fields, the first difference encountered involves the 040 field. To definitively identify the record as an RDA record, a subfield $e must be added with the code "rda." Many cooperative cataloging participants will also add an additional 040 subfield $b coded with the designation "eng" to represent "English" as the language of cataloging. Although technically this convention did not stem from RDA instructions, it is an increasing practice that has gained momentum with the advent of RDA implementation. In cooperative cataloging ventures, it is becoming standard practice to add the language of cataloging into the subfield $b, and the preferred order is to record "$e rda" immediately after "$b eng."

Chapter 8

The next notable difference involves information in the 250 field subfield $a, or the *designation of edition* field. Here the designation of edition is spelled out as it appears on the source of information in the RDA record (in compliance with the *principle of representation*), rather than abbreviated according to AACR's abbreviation conventions.

The next noticeable difference involves a different MARC value; information that is coded in the 260 field in AACR2 is coded in the 264 field in RDA. Moreover, the RDA record has a 264 2nd indicator value of "1" to indicate that the information given is the publication statement, while the AACR2 record cannot offer such granular information because the 2nd indicator is not defined in the 260 field.

Moving on from the 264 field, we see the 300 field, which involves different abbreviation conventions between the two sets of records. Whereas AACR2 prescribed the abbreviation of words like "pages" and "illustrations," these abbreviation prescriptions were not carried over into RDA. As a result, these terms are spelled out in the RDA version of the record. Also worth noting is that, in the case of this record example, the 300 field terminates with a stop in both the AACR2 version and the RDA version, because the record has a series statement.

The next difference involves the presence of 336, 337, and 338 fields in the RDA record, which are noticeably absent from the AACR2 record. For this record example, the cataloger chose to include only the required subfields, and he or she recorded the term in the subfield $a and the source in the subfield $2. If the cataloger desired, he or she also could have recorded the appropriate code in the subfield $b.

The next field involving a difference is the 490 field. In AACR2, a caption word like "volume" was routinely abbreviated to "v." following Appendix B. In RDA, such abbreviations occur only if found on the source of information. In the case of this book, the word "volume" was found spelled out on the resource, so that is how it was transcribed into the RDA record.

Moving down to the 504 field, one notices a minor difference between the two records. In the AACR2 version of the record, "pages" is abbreviated, in keeping with AACR2 abbreviation conventions, whereas it is spelled out in the RDA version of the record.

Finally worthy of note is the 830 field, which shows identical abbreviations between AACR2 and RDA. This is because unlike the 490 field, the 830 field retains many of the abbreviation conventions from AACR2 to promote collocation of works.

Case 2: Collaborative Work Written by Four Authors

As in the first case scenario, much of the information in the second record comparison reveals similar information in both record versions, including the coding of Leader 07 as "m" for this single-unit monograph. The first major difference is Leader 18, which, as in the first comparison, is coded "i" for ISBD punctuation in the RDA record rather than "a" for "AACR2" in the AACR2 record. Also, in the 040 variable field, one sees the "$e rda" in the RDA record, which is absent from the AACR2 record.

Case 2. Bibliographic Record: Collaborative Work Written by Four Authors

AACR2

LDR   02716cam a2200457 a 450
008   101110s2012 nyua 001 0 eng
010   2010047906
040   XXX $c XXX
020   9780073374918
020   0073374911
042   pcc
043   n-us---
050 00 HG9383 $b .B39 2012
245 00 Medical insurance : $b an integrated claims process approach / $c Joanne D. Valerius...[et al.].
250   5th ed.
260   New York, NY : $b McGraw-Hill, $c c2012.
300   1 v. (various pagings) : $b ill. ; $c 28 cm.
500   Includes index.
505 0_ Introduction to the medical billing cycle -- HIPAA, HITECH, and medical records -- Patient encounters and billing information -- Diagnostic coding : introduction to ICD- 9-CM and ICD-10-CM -- Procedural coding: introduction to CPT -- Procedural coding : introduction to HCPCS -- Visit charges and compliant billing -- Health care claim preparation and transmission -- Private payers/ Blue Cross and Blue Shield -- Medicare -- Medicaid -- TRICARE and CHAMPVA -- Workers' compensation and disability -- Payments (RAs/EOBs), appeals, and secondary claims -- Patient billing and collections -- Primary case studies -- RA/EOB/secondary case studies -- Hospital billing and reimbursement.
650 _0 Health insurance.
650 _0 Health insurance claims $z United States.
650 _0 Health insurance $z United States.
650 _2 Insurance Claim Reporting $z United States.
650 _2 Insurance, Health $z United States.
700 1_ Valerius, Joanne.

Case 2. Bibliographic Record: Collaborative Work Written by Four Authors

RDA

LDR	02716cam a2200457 i 450
008	101110t20122012nyua 001 0 eng
010	2010047906
040	XXX $b eng $e rda $c XXX
020	9780073374918 (pbk.: acid-free paper)
020	0073374911 (pbk.: acid-free paper)
042	pcc
043	n-us---
050 00	HG9383 $b .B39 2012
100 1_	Valerius, Joanne, $e author.
245 10	Medical insurance : $b an integrated claims process approach / $c Joanne D. Valerius, RHIA, MPH, Director, Health Information Management Certificate Program, Oregon Health & Science University, Nenna L. Bayes, BBA., M.Ed., Professor, Program Coordinator of Office Systems Administration, Ashland Community and Technical College, Cynthia Newby, CPC, CPC-P, Janet I.B. Seggern, M.Ed., M.S., CCA Professor of Business, Lehigh Carbon Community College.
250	Fifth edition.
264 _1	New York, NY : $b McGraw-Hill, $c [2012]
264 _4	$c ©2012
300	1 volume (various pagings) : $b illustrations ; $c 28 cm
336	text $2 rdacontent
337	unmediated $2 rdamedia
338	volume $2 rdacarrier
500	Includes index.
505 0_	Introduction to the medical billing cycle—HIPAA, HITECH, and medical records—Patient encounters and billing information—Diagnostic coding: introduction to ICD-9–CM and ICD-10–CM—Procedural coding: introduction to CPT—Procedural coding: introduction to HCPCS—Visit charges and compliant billing—Health care claim preparation and transmission—Private payers/Blue Cross and Blue Shield—Medicare—Medicaid—TRICARE and CHAMPVA—Workers' compensation and disability—Payments (RAs/EOBs), appeals, and secondary claims—Patient billing and collections—Primary case studies—RA/EOB/secondary case studies—Hospital billing and reimbursement.
650 _0	Health insurance.
650 _0	Health insurance claims $z United States.
650 _0	Health insurance $z United States.
650 _2	Insurance Claim Reporting $z United States.
650 _2	Insurance, Health $z United States.
700 1_	Bayes, Nenna L., $e author.
700 1_	Newby, Cynthia, $e author.
700 1_	Seggern, Janet I. B., $e author.

The next difference encountered involves the date bytes: "Type of Date/Publication Status," "Date 1," and "Date 2" in the 008 field. In AACR2, if a publication date were absent, a copyright date could be supplied in its place with no need to mention the publication date. In RDA, information about the publication date must be provided whether a publication date is present or not. Moreover, a copyright date can be supplied in addition to a publication date, which was less common in the AACR2 environment. In RDA, it may be more common to see both a publication date in one 264 field and a copyright date in a separate 264 field. This will lead to more situations in which the "Type of Date/Publication Status" byte is coded as "t" for "Publication date and copyright date" rather than "s" for "Single known date/probable date." It also means that catalogers may encounter copyright dates recorded in the "Date 2" byte with greater frequency in RDA than in AACR2, even if the publication and copyright dates are the same.

The next important difference involves the presence of a 100 field in the RDA record, when it is absent from the AACR2 record. In AACR2, collaborative works among four or more authors would require a main entry under the title of the work and an added entry into the 7XX field for the first listed author. In RDA, the access point for the first author of a collaborative work would be added through a 1XX field, regardless of the number of collaborators. This accounts for why the first author of this collaborative work of more than three authors is in the 100 field in the RDA version and in the 700 field in the AACR2 version.

Another important difference involving the 100 field relates to the subfield $e, which contains a relationship designator for the creator in the RDA version of the record, but not in the AACR2 version. Though not core in RDA, relationship designators may be increasingly encountered in RDA records, and they may be required in some cooperative cataloging practices.

In the 245 subfield $c, one notices in the AACR2 version of the record that only the first author is listed, while the other three authors are omitted and replaced with the designation ". . .[et al.]." RDA did not carry over this instruction to omit all but first author when there are more than three listed, so one sees all authors listed in the RDA version of the record. If the cataloger preferred, he or she could have applied the optional omission under RDA instruction 2.4.1.5 and recorded "/ $c Joanne D. Valerius [and three others]." However, PCC catalogers are generally encouraged to give each responsible entity's name in the statement, which is what was done here.

The next important difference has to do with the intervening statement of responsibility data in the 245 subfield $c. In the AACR2 record, intervening data such as "Director," "Ashland Community and Technical College," "CPC-P," and "CCA Professor of Business" are omitted in compliance with AACR2 guidelines. These guidelines that mandate omission of intervening data are absent from RDA. RDA catalogers are given the option to omit the data if desired, but they are not mandated to do so. The default instruction is to transcribe the information as it appears on the resource. Thus, it will be more common to see this information in the 245 $c, as is the case in the example here.

The next difference has to do with the 250 subfield $a. As in the first record comparison, this second case scenario shows the standard abbreviation in the AACR2 records and the spelled out forms in the RDA records. However, one may also notice a subtle difference between the RDA examples. The first example shows capitalization of the first letter of the first word ("First edition"), whereas the second example shows capitalization of the first letters of both words ("Fifth Edition"). The capitalization conventions in RDA allow for transcribing the form found on the source or applying the capitalization conventions in the appendix. It is not possible to tell if "First edition" appeared that way on the resource or if it was adjusted to comply with abbreviation conventions. However, it is much easier to tell that "Fifth Edition" was transcribed to reflect the form found on the resource. With RDA, the cataloger has the choice of either form.

Another difference of note involves information in the subfield $c of the 260 and 264. In AACR2, a copyright date was allowed to substitute for an absent publication date, and the copyright symbol was represented by the letter "c." In RDA, *date of publication* is a core element; it must be accounted for and it cannot be replaced by a copyright date. Thus, the RDA record in the example includes the publication date, whereas it is ignored in the AACR2 record.

The cataloger appears to have inferred the publication date "[2012]," most likely from the copyright date "©2012." The cataloger could have chosen to record "date of publication not identified," but this would have then required the cataloger to go down a matrix of "core if" elements, such as "date of distribution" and "copyright date," before the core requirements were satisfied. Catalogers may elect to bypass this by simply inferring the publication date from other information such as the copyright date or date of manufacture. In addition, the cataloger may add the copyright date, date of manufacture, or some other date used for inferring the publication date into a separate 264 field. This additional 264 is not required as long as the date of publication is supplied, but it is allowable. In this case, the cataloger chose to add a second 264 field for the copyright date, and he or she recorded it with a copyright symbol rather than the letter "c."

In the 300 field, one sees the abbreviation of the words "volume" and "illustrations" in the AACR2 record, which are spelled out in the RDA version. One also sees that the 300 field in the AACR2 record terminates in a stop, which is noticeably absent from the RDA record. This differs from the first case scenario, in which the 300 fields in both versions terminate in a stop. In the case of the first record comparison, there was a series statement, which required a stop in the terminal position of the preceding ISBD area—the 300 field. In the case of this second record comparison, there is no series field. In RDA, terms like "cm" are considered metric symbols that do not automatically terminate in a stop. This contrasts with AACR2, which lists "centimeters" as the abbreviation "cm.," which would mandate a stop, regardless of the absence or presence of a series statement.

Thus, because there is no series statement in this record comparison, the RDA version of the record lacks a stop, which contrasts with the AACR2 version in this case.

As in the first record comparison, the RDA record includes 33X fields for the content type (text), the media type (unmediated), and the carrier type (volume), which are absent from the AACR2 record.

Finally, the RDA record ends with three 700 fields for the last three authors of this collaborative work, whereas these authors are absent from the AAC2 record. In AACR2, when more than three authors are present, all but the first are omitted. In RDA, only the first author is required, but as many additional authors may be added as desired, regardless of the number. So although the cataloger could have chosen to omit the last three authors, he or she chose to record them in addition to the first author (listed in the 100 field). Also, as with the 100 field, the cataloger of the RDA record chose to add the relationship designator "author" to each 700 field, which is absent from the AACR2 version of the record. Again, though not core, catalogers may encounter such designator terms much more commonly in the RDA context.

Case 3: Three Language Expressions of a Work Embodied in the Same Manifestation

In the final record comparison, one sees even more similarities between the AACR2 record and its RDA counterpart. The only difference in the fixed fields is the coding of Leader 07 as "a" in the AACR2 record and "i" in the RDA record. Also, in the 040 variable field, one sees the "$e rda" in the RDA record, which is absent from the AACR2 record. The RDA record includes spelled-out terms and lacks a terminal stop in the 300 field, both of which contrast with the AACR2 record. It also has the requisite 33X fields that are absent from the AACR2 record.

The most significant difference between the two records has to do with treatment of the access points involving the different language expressions. In AACR2, a manifestation embodying three or more language expressions of the same work would get an access point in a 130 field or a 100/240 combination, where the term "Polyglot" would be added to convey the multilingual nature of the language content. This practice was not carried over into RDA. When three or more languages are present in the manifestation, the original language expression is recorded if it can be determined. In this case, the original language is Moldovan, and it is recorded in a 700 field subfield $t rather than a 100/240 combination. If the original language is known, the language term can be added or omitted from the access point. In this case, the language term was omitted from the access point in the RDA record, which is in keeping with the practice of the Library of Congress (LC) and probably many other PCC institutions.

> **Case 3.   Bibliographic Record: Three Language Expressions of a Work Embodied in the Same Manifestation**
>
> **AACR2**
>
> | | |
> |---|---|
> | LDR | 01872cam a2200433 a 450 |
> | 008 | 110510s2011 mv a 000 0 eng |
> | 010 | 2011472184 |
> | 040 | XXX $c XXX |
> | 020 | 9789975696418 |
> | 020 | 9975696414 |
> | 041 1_ | eng $a fre $a rum $h rum |
> | 042 | pcc |
> | 043 | e-mv— |
> | 050 00 | DK509.7724 $b .H56 2011 |
> | 100 1_ | Hîncu, Damian, $d 1985– |
> | 240 10 | Moldova mă doare. $l Polyglot |
> | 245 10 | Moldova mă doare : $b (mărturie) / $c Damian Hîncu ; traducere în engleză şi franceză de Damian Hîncu = Moldova hurts me : (testimony) / Damian Hîncu ; translation in English and French by Damian Hîncu = J'ai mal à la Moldavie : (témoignage) / Damian Hîncu ; traduction en anglais et en français de Damian Hîncu. |
> | 246 31 | Moldova hurts me : $b (testimony) |
> | 246 31 | J'ai mal à la Moldavie : $b (témoignage) |
> | 260 | Chişinău : $b Prut Internaţional, $c [2011] |
> | 300 | 128 p. : $b col. ill. ; $c 20 cm. |
> | 546 | Moldovan original with English and French translations. |
> | 651 _0 | Moldova $x Politics and government $y 1991– |
> | 610 10 | Moldova. $b Parlament $x Elections, 2009. |
> | 650 _0 | Riots $z Moldova. |
> | 650 _0 | Demonstrations $z Moldova. |
> | 600 10 | Hîncu, Damian, $d 1985– |

In addition to adding an access point for the original language expression, a cataloger following LC practice would add at least one additional access point for one of the translations. In this case, the language term would be retained, because the expression does not represent the original language. In the case of this RDA record, the cataloger chose to "go beyond core" and add access points for both the English-language and French-language expressions.

Case 3. Bibliographic Record: Three Language Expressions of a Work Embodied in the Same Manifestation

RDA

LDR	01872cam a2200433 i 450
008	110510s2011 mv a 000 0 eng
010	2011472184
040	XXX **$b eng $e rda** $c XXX
020	9789975696418
020	9975696414
041 1_	eng $a fre $a rum $h rum
042	pcc
043	e-mv—
050 00	DK509.7724 $b .H56 2011
100 1_	Hîncu, Damian, $d 1985–
245 10	Moldova mă doare : $b (mărturie) / $c Damian Hîncu ; traducere în engleză și franceză de Damian Hîncu = Moldova hurts me : (testimony) / Damian Hîncu ; translation in English and French by Damian Hîncu = J'ai mal à la Moldavie : (témoignage) / Damian Hîncu ; traduction en anglais et en français de Damian Hîncu.
246 31	Moldova hurts me : $b (testimony)
246 31	J'ai mal à la Moldavie : $b (témoignage)
264 _1	Chișinău : $b Prut Internațional, $c [2011]
300	128 **pages :** $b **color illustrations ;** $c 20 cm
336	**text $2 rdacontent**
337	**unmediated $2 rdamedia**
338	**volume $2 rdacarrier**
546	Moldovan original with English and French translations.
651 _0	Moldova $x Politics and government $y 1991–
610 10	Moldova. $b Parlament $x Elections, 2009.
650 _0	Riots $z Moldova.
650 _0	Demonstrations $z Moldova.
600 10	Hîncu, Damian, $d 1985–
700 12	**Hîncu, Damian, $d 1985– $t Moldova mă doare.**
700 12	**Hîncu, Damian, $d 1985– $t Moldova mă doare. $l English.**
700 12	**Hîncu, Damian, $d 1985– $t Moldova mă doare. $l French.**

CONCLUSION

This chapter showed how to populate the MARC record with bibliographic fields relevant for cataloging books in RDA. It first looked at the core elements and other elements that are useful for describing books. It next detailed the major fields commonly found in book records, highlighting both the similarities and differences between AACR2 and RDA. Finally, it looked at the bibliographic record holistically, focusing on three records that were each cataloged according to AACR2 and RDA. It compared the AACR2 with the RDA record in order to glean further insight into how RDA data play out in the bibliographic environment.

It is hoped that after reading this chapter, the reader will gain a better sense of how to catalog a book using RDA. The next chapter follows a similar course, but is targeted toward nonbook resources and is more of an overview. Both chapters aim to provide the reader with a basic understanding of how to catalog resources of all types using RDA.

9

Creating and Interpreting Bibliographic Records for Nonbook Resources

Sara Shatford Layne with the assistance of
Luiz Mendes and Hermine Vermeij

AACR2 contained chapters devoted to cataloging particular categories of library resources, categories based seemingly on the way these resources might most frequently be stored or processed in a library. When AACR2 was first published, these categories included, in addition to printed books: cartographic materials; manuscripts; music; sound recordings; motion pictures and videorecordings; graphic materials; machine-readable data files (subsequently revised as electronic resources); serials; three-dimensional artefacts and realia; microforms; and serials (subsequently revised as continuing resources). These categories have traditionally been referred to by catalogers as "nonbooks." In larger libraries, a cataloger might catalog just one or two of these categories; for example, a music cataloger might catalog scores and music sound recordings, but no other categories of resource. Although the AACR2 arrangement of cataloging rules was quite practical, it lacked a solid theoretical foundation. In addition, the AACR2 arrangement made it difficult to figure out how to catalog a resource that shared characteristics from more than one category, such as a map that was also a continuing resource or a sound recording that was also an electronic resource. With the explosion of electronic resources in the years since AACR2 was developed, the problem of resources combining characteristics of two or more of the AACR2 categories became increasingly common. RDA has made the description of nonbook resources more logical, in particular by separately identifying content, carrier, and media type and eliminating the AACR2 "GMD" or General Material Designation, as described in more detail in chapter 3 of this book. As explained in chapter 2 of this book, RDA is organized based on the FRBR entities rather than on resource format.

This chapter looks, often quite briefly, at some of the categories of resources other than books that a cataloger is likely to encounter and describes how RDA, as coded in MARC, is used to address some of the issues encountered in their cataloging. The chapter generally does not repeat the information common to records for all resources, information that is detailed in chapter 8, instead focusing on information and issues that are specific to the nonbook resources being discussed. In addition, references are made to sources that contain detailed guidance for catalogers of these materials. Almost every one of these categories of materials has its own cataloging community and specialized cataloging documentation. It is hoped that this chapter will make catalogers aware of some of the changes associated with the cataloging of these nonbook resources in RDA, as well as providing them with references to useful specialized documentation. For the ease of catalogers accustomed to AACR2, the organization of this chapter follows that of AACR2 Chapters 3–12, with the addition of a section that discusses accompanying materials and kits.

CARTOGRAPHIC RESOURCES

This section touches on some significant differences between RDA and AACR2 in the MARC environment that are particularly relevant to the cataloging of cartographic resources, analyzes a MARC bibliographic record for a published map, and concludes with references to specialized documentation and training prepared by the community of cartographic resource catalogers.

The first and most obvious difference between RDA and AACR2 with respect to cartographic resources is the use of content, media, and carrier types instead of a GMD. The second difference concerns the scale statement. The third difference is in the use of relationship designators. We look at each of these in turn.

Content/Media/Carrier Type (RDA 6.9.1.3/3.2.1.3/3.3.1.3; MARC 336/337/338 Fields)

It should be noted that although AACR2 initially listed two possible GMDs for cartographic resources ("map" for North American agencies in earlier editions of AACR2, "cartographic material" for British agencies), libraries in the United States that followed Library of Congress practice did not use either GMD. Bibliographic records for cartographic resources cataloged using RDA and MARC should contain, in a 336 field, one of the cartographic resource content types. The most commonly used content type will be "cartographic image," which is used for atlases and maps on paper as well as digital images. Other content types include "cartographic three-dimensional form," which is used for globes or relief models, and "cartographic dataset." Content type is considered a core element. Note that media type (coded in the MARC 337 field and not considered a core element) as well as carrier type (coded in the MARC 338 field and considered a core element) will be determined by the format of the cartographic resource. Consider the examples in Figure 9.1, all of which would be assigned the content type "cartographic image": a map printed or drawn on a single sheet of paper would have the carrier type "sheet"; an atlas, consisting of maps bound together as a book, would be assigned the carrier type "volume"; a digitized map available via the Internet would be assigned the carrier type "online resource." The printed map and the atlas would be assigned the media type "unmediated," whereas the digitized map would be assigned the media type "computer."

Figure 9.1. Examples of Content/Media/Carrier Type for Cartographic Resources

A Printed Map

```
336     $a cartographic resource $2 rdacontent
337     $a unmediated $2 rdamedia
338     $a sheet $2 rdacarrier
```

A Printed Atlas

```
336     $a cartographic resource $2 rdacontent
337     $a unmediated $2 rdamedia
338     $a volume $2 rdacarrier
```

A Digitized Map Available Via the Internet

```
336     $a cartographic resource $2 rdacontent
337     $a computer $2 rdamedia
338     $a online resource $2 rdacarrier
```

Scale (RDA 7.25; MARC 255/034 Fields)

Scale is a core element for cartographic resources only. In RDA, the scale statement, which is encoded in the MARC 255 field, is never enclosed in square brackets, even when it is estimated. Estimated scales are introduced by the word "approximately," not "ca.," the abbreviation for the Latin word "circa," which is not used in RDA.

Relationship Designators (RDA Appendix I)

Though relationship designators are not specific to cartographic resources, their use may pose particular problems where cartographic resources are concerned, largely because of the difficulty of describing precisely the nature of the relationship of various corporate bodies to a cartographic resource. The most commonly used relationship designators for persons or bodies associated with cartographic resources are likely to be "cartographer" and "issuing body." However, it should be remembered that relationship designators are not core and may be omitted altogether. It should also be noted that "cartographer" has a somewhat broader definition in RDA than it does in the dictionary. The RDA definition is "a person, family, or corporate body responsible for creating a map, atlas, globe, or other cartographic work." The

Merriam-Webster definition is "one that makes maps." It may therefore be appropriate to use the relationship designator "cartographer" for a corporate body responsible for creating a cartographic resource. The cartographic resources cataloging community, at the time of this writing, was still discussing policies for using relationship designators in bibliographic records for these materials.

Bibliographic Record for a Printed Map

Figure 9.2 shows an example of a bibliographic record for a printed map cataloged using RDA. The parts of the record that are different from the way the record would have looked if AACR2 had been used are in **bold**.

Figure 9.2. Bibliographic Record for a Printed Map

Type e	ELvl I	Srce d	Relf b	Ctrl	Lang fre
BLvl m	Form	GPub	SpFm	MRec	Ctry fr
CrTp a	Indx 0	Proj	DtSt s	Dates 1879	,
Desc **i**					

007	aj_aanzn
040	$a ___ $b eng **$e rda** $c _____
034 1	$a a $b 9200000
043	$a pome---
050 _ 4	$a G9260 1879 $b .S6
052	$a 9260
110 2 _	$a Société de géographie (France), **$e cartographer**.
245 1 0	$a Archipels des Salomon, des Nouvelles-Hébrides et de Santa-Cruz : $b avec la Nouvelle Calédonie et les Iles Loyalty / $c gravé par Erhard.
255	**$a Scale approximately 1:9,200,000.**
264 _ 1	**$a [Paris] : $b [Société de géographie], $c [1879]**
264 _ 3	**$a Paris : $b Impie. Erhard**
300	$a 1 map ; $c 21 x 17 **cm**
336	**$a cartographic image $2 rdacontent**
337	**$a unmediated $2 rdamedia**
338	**$a sheet $2 rdacarrier**
500	$a Relief shown by shading.
500	$a "Société de géographie. Séance du 18 Juillet 1879."
651 _ 0	$a Melanesia $v Maps.
655 _ 7	$a Maps. $2 lcgft
710 2 _	$a Erhard (Firm)

Note: Data from the LDR and 008 fields are displayed in "OCLC format" in this record, with brief labels for each data element. LDR/07 data are labeled "Desc."

LDR/07 "i" and 040 $e "rda"

See chapter 8 of this book for an explanation. Note that LDR/07 displays in this record with the label "Desc."

110 $e "cartographer"

We see here the relationship designator "cartographer" used in the access point for a corporate body. Note that the 710 field does not contain a relationship designator. Relationship designators are not core elements.

255 Field

We see here the use of the word "approximately" in an estimated scale statement. We see also the absence of brackets. Scale of cartographic resources is a core element.

264 Fields

We see here the use of two separate 264 fields. The first 264 field, with second indicator 1, gives publication information supplied or inferred by the cataloger, with the content of each subfield in its own set of square brackets. The second 264 field, with second indicator 3, gives information about the manufacture of the item. Just the first 264 field is core, but the cataloger in this case has chosen to add a second 264 field with the manufacture information in it. RDA gives the option to add the manufacture information, even when publication information has been given, if "it is considered important for identification or access" (RDA 2.10.1.4).

300 Field

Although *Dimensions* (RDA 3.5) is not a core element in RDA, the dimensions of a map are considered to be core by the Library of Congress and the cartographic resources cataloging community. Note the absence of a period following "cm" because it is a symbol, not an abbreviation. RDA 3.5.2 provides specific instructions for recording the dimensions of maps, instructions that have essentially the same results as the equivalent rules in AACR2.

336 Field

We see here the content type "cartographic image" with the appropriate $2 rdacontent, which indicates that the source of the term is the RDA controlled list of content types.

337/338 Fields. Media/Carrier Type

These fields contain the terms "unmediated" and "sheet" respectively, with the appropriate codes in the $2, indicating that the sources of the terms are the RDA controlled list of media types and carrier types.

The record shown in Figure 9.2 is the third of eleven records for cartographic resources available on the Library of Congress website at http://www.loc.gov/ catworkshop/RDA%20training%20materials/SCT%20RDA%20Records%20TG/ index.html.

Additional Information

At the time of this writing, the cartographic resources cataloging community and the Library of Congress are working on specialized documentation for cataloging cartographic resources using RDA, but the documentation has not yet been published. However, the following presentations include useful information:

"Maps the RDA Way." 2013 MAGIRT program presented by Paige Andrew and Susan Moore. PowerPoint slides from this presentation are available through the MAGIRT Lib-Guide at http://magirt.ala.libguides.com/trainingsandpresentations.
Rankin, K., and M. L. Larsgaard. "RDA for Cartographic Resources." Presented at WAML Meeting 2012, Honolulu, HI. Available at http://digitalscholarship.unlv.edu/libfacpresentation/98.
RDA and Cartographic Materials: Mapping A New Route. ALCTS webinar presented by Paige G. Andrew, September 28, 2011. Recording available at http://alcts.ala.org/ ce/0928_2011_RDA_and_Cartographic_Materials.wmv. Presentation Slides available at http://alcts.ala.org/ce/0928_2011_RDA_and_Cartographic_Materials_Slides.pptx.

MANUSCRIPTS (INCLUDING MANUSCRIPT COLLECTIONS)

The cataloging of individual textual manuscripts using RDA and MARC does not differ greatly from the cataloging of books using RDA, as described in chapter 8 of this book. The carrier type (RDA 3.3.1.3; MARC 338 field) for an individual manuscript may more often be "sheet" than volume, and the cataloger may more often need to consult the guidelines for constructing a title when none is present on the item being cataloged (RDA 2.3.2.10–RDA 2.3.2.11). These guidelines are not significantly different from the comparable rules in AACR2, with the following exception: under AACR2, devised titles are placed in square brackets to distinguish them from titles transcribed from the "chief source" of information; under RDA 2.2.4, square brackets are an option for distinguishing between devised and transcribed titles, but only for resources that would be expected to "carry identifying information" (e.g., not collections). It should be noted that the archival cataloging community in the United States has for some time omitted square brackets from devised titles for manuscript collections.

The only other significant difference between RDA and AACR2 in the MARC environment that is specific to individual manuscripts is that production information (both place of production and name of producer) can now be recorded in the MARC 264 field, in addition to the date of production. Date of production is a core element in RDA for "resources issued in an unpublished form." The inclusion of other production subelements is optional. The resulting change for manuscript or archival collections is that the dates of production of materials within such collections are encoded in the 264 subfield $d when RDA is being followed, whereas under AACR2 these dates would have been encoded in the 245 $f. For example, the 245 field of a manuscript collection cataloged using AACR2 and MARC might look like this:

> 245   10 $a Sally Maguire papers. $f 1974–1987.

Whereas the same collection cataloged using RDA and MARC would have the same data in the following two MARC fields:

> 245   10 $a Sally Maguire papers.
> 264   _0 $c 1974–1987.

Bibliographic Record for a Manuscript Dissertation

Figure 9.3 shows an example of a bibliographic record for a manuscript dissertation cataloged using RDA. The parts of the record that are different from the way the record would have looked if AACR2 had been used are in **bold**.

Figure 9.3. Bibliographic Record for a Manuscript Dissertation

Type t	ELvl K	Srce d	Aud	Ctrl	Lang eng
BLvl m	Form	Conf0	Biog	MRec	Ctry ncu
	Cont bm	GPu	LitF 0	Indx 0	
Desc **i**	Ills befo	Fest 0	DtSt s	Dates 1966	,

040	$a _____ $b eng **$e rda** $c _____
050 1 4	$a LD3921 .Arch. .H92
100 1	$a Burns, Robert Paschal, $d 1933- **$e author.**
245 1 0	$a Urban renewal : $b Southside, Raleigh, North Carolina / $c by Robert P. Burns.
264 0	**$a [Raleigh, North Carolina] : $b North Carolina State University**, $c 1966.
300	$a 34 leaves, **unnumbered leaves of plates** : $b maps, plans, **photographs** ; $c 29 cm
336	**$a text $b txt $2 rdacontent**
337	**$a unmediated $b c $2 rdamedia**
338	**$a volume $b cr $2 rdacarrier**
502	**$b** M.S. **$c** North Carolina State University, **$d** 1966.
504	$a Includes bibliographical references (leaf 34).

Note: Data from the LDR and 008 fields are displayed in "OCLC format" in this record, with brief labels for each data element. LDR/07 data is labeled "Desc."

264 Field

Second indicator "0" indicates that this field contains production information. Note that both $a and $b subfields are present, although this information is not core. Note also that the place and producer information would not have been included in the 260 field for a dissertation cataloged using AACR2, as AACR2 Chapter 4 specified that date alone be given for manuscripts in this area of the description.

502 Field

Although the 502 field is not new, it does contain new subfield codes created to correspond to the separate RDA elements for *academic degree* (subfield $b), *granting institution or faculty* (subfield $c), and *year degree granted* (subfield $d).

Other RDA Data

The remaining RDA data that are in bold—LDR/07 (labeled "Desc") "i," 040 $e rda, 100 $e author, 300 $a "unnumbered leaves of plates," 300 $b "photographs" (spelled out rather than abbreviated), the lack of a period after "cm" in the 300 $c, and the 336–337–338—are data that could be present in a record for a printed book.

The record shown in Figure 9.3 is the first of seven records for dissertations and microforms available on the Library of Congress website at http://www.loc.gov/catworkshop/RDA%20training%20materials/SCT%20RDA%20Records%20TG/index.html. The record shown in Figure 9.3 and the second record in that set are the only records in the set that are for unpublished (i.e., manuscript) dissertations. For examples of records for archival collections, on the same website is a set of seven records for archival family records.

Additional Information

The archival cataloging community has a history of devising special rules for archival collections. Indeed, RDA development was influenced by DACS (*Describing Archives: A Content Standard*), a standard in common use in the archival community. For more information about cataloging archival resources using RDA, see the following:

Cataloging Archival Materials: Using RDA with DACS. ALCTS webinar presented by Cory Nimer, May 30, 2012. Recording available at http://alcts.ala.org/ce/05302012_RDA_DAC_recording.wmv. Presentation slides: http://downloads.alcts.ala.org/ce/05302012_RDA_DACS_slides.pdf.

MUSIC

"Music" in the context of this section refers to music scores, which when cataloged using RDA in the MARC environment should receive the following 336 field, describing the content of the resource:

336      $a notated music $2 rdacontent

This section highlights some significant differences between RDA and AACR2 in the MARC environment that are particularly relevant to music cataloging, analyzes a MARC bibliographic record for a published score, and concludes with references to specialized documentation and training prepared by the community of music catalogers, as well as additional examples of records for music scores.

Following is a discussion of some of the significant differences between RDA and AACR2 in the MARC environment that are of particular interest when cataloging music scores.

Preferred Source of Title

RDA 2.2.2.2 applies to all resources composed of pages, leaves, or sheets, and therefore applies to music scores. Since music scores often have no title page, but will have both a caption title and a title page title, it is worth mentioning here that in RDA a cover title is preferred to a caption title. In AACR2, the caption title was preferred to the cover title.

Expansion of the Concept of Edition

In RDA, the term "musical presentation statement" does not appear. In RDA 2.5.2.1, "a particular voice range or format for notated music" is considered one of several different categories of "designation of edition." This means that statements such as "study score" or "Klavierauszug" are considered to be edition statements in RDA; the implication for MARC is that such statements will be recorded in the 250 field rather than in a 254 field.

Expanded Definition of Score

In RDA, the term "score" is defined to include resources such as music for an unaccompanied solo instrument that catalogers using AACR2 would have described using phrases like "p. of music." This expanded definition means that the 300 $a of bibliographic records for music cataloged using RDA will never include the "of music" phrase found in AACR2 records.

Miniature Score

The term "miniature score" is no longer used in RDA. It has been replaced with "study score."

Musical Notation Statements

RDA 7.13.3, *Form of Musical Notation*, is a core element for agencies following the Library of Congress policies. This means that statements such as "notated music" will begin to appear in bibliographic records for scores. The corresponding MARC encoding for these data is the 546 $b (field 546 is defined as "Language Note," and 546 subfield $b is "information code or alphabet"), which may seem odd at first to catalogers unaccustomed to considering music to be a "language" and the form in which it is recorded to be an "information code." However, upon consideration, a cataloger can see that this does indeed make sense.

Librettos

Although librettos are textual materials, not music, they are of course closely related to scores, and for that reason a significant change in their treatment between AACR2 and RDA is highlighted here. When cataloged using AACR2, a libretto for an opera or musical was "entered under" the name of the composer. In RDA, a libretto is considered to be the work of the librettist, not the composer. This means that the preferred access point for the work that is the libretto will consist of the authorized access point for the librettist followed by the preferred title for the opera or musical. Figure 9.4 shows an example comparing the access points for a libretto under AACR2 and under RDA.

Figure 9.4. Access Points for a Libretto Cataloged Using AACR2 and RDA

AACR2

```
100  1_ $a Sullivan, Arthur, $d 1842–1900.
240  10 $a Mikado. $s Libretto
245  10 $a The Mikado, or, The town of Titipu / $c by W.S. Gilbert.
700  10 $a Gilbert, W. S. $q (William Schwenck), $d 1836–1911.
```

RDA

```
100  1_ $a Gilbert, W. S. $q (William Schwenck), $d 1836–1911, $e author.
240  10 $a Mikado
245  10 $a The Mikado, or, The town of Titipu / $c by W.S. Gilbert.
700  1_ $i Libretto for (work): $a Sullivan, Arthur, $d 1842–1900. $t Mikado.
```

Bibliographic Record for a Printed Music Score

Figure 9.5 shows an example of a bibliographic record for a printed music score cataloged using RDA and encoded using MARC. The elements of the record that are different from the way the record might have looked if AACR2 had been used are in **bold**. Following are brief explanations of these different elements, presented in the order in which they appear in the MARC record.

Figure 9.5. Bibliographic Record for a Score

Type c	ELvl	Srce c	Audn	Ctrl	Lang zxx
BLvl m	Form	Comp zz	AccM	MRec	Ctry ilu
	Part	TrAr			
Desc **i**	FMus a	LTxt n	DtSt t	Dates 2011 ,	2009

```
040        $a ___ $b eng $e rda $c ___
020        $a 1608740196
020        $a 9781608740192
028 3 0    $a FK090003 $b Serenissima Music, Inc.
042        $a pcc
050 _4     $a M1060.J
100 1_     $a Joplin, Scott, $d 1868-1917, $e composer.
240 1_     $a Entertainer; $o arranged
245 14     $a The entertainer / $c Scott Joplin ; orchestration by Richard W.
           Sargeant, Jr.
250        $a Study score = Partitur.
264 _1     $a [Edwardsville, IL] : $b Serenissima Music, Inc., $c [2011]
264 _4     $c ©2009
300        $a 1 study score (30 pages) ; $c 25 cm
336        $a notated music $2 rdacontent
337        $a unmediated $2 rdamedia
338        $a volume $2 rdacarrier
500        $a Originally for solo piano; arranged for orchestra.
546        $b staff notation
650 _0     $a Orchestral music, Arranged.
650 _0     $a Ragtime music.
700 1_     $a Sargeant, Richard W., $c Jr., $e arranger.
```

Note: Data from the LDR and 008 fields are displayed in "OCLC format" in this record, with brief labels for each data element. LDR/07 data is labeled "Desc".

LDR/07 "i" and 040 $e "rda"

See chapter 8 of this book for an explanation. Note that LDR/07 displays in this record with the label "Desc".

100 $e "composer"

Although relator codes or terms were used in music cataloging by catalogers following AACR2, the use of these terms, now referred to as "relationship designators," has expanded in RDA. Catalogers following AACR2 would frequently have used the relator code "arr" or the relator term "arranger" for someone responsible for arranging a musical expression, but they would not normally have used the relator term "composer" or its corresponding code.

240 $o "arranged"

RDA avoids abbreviations in many instances where AACR2 accepted them. The result is that the 240 $o contains the word "arranged" rather than the abbreviation "arr."

250 Field. Edition Statement

Note that the transcribed statement "Study score = Partitur" now appears in the 250 field of the MARC bibliographic record rather than in a 254 field.

264 _1. Publication Information

Note that publication information appears in the MARC 264 field, with the second indicator "1", rather than in a 260 field. The bracketing of the 264 $c indicates that the cataloger inferred the publication date from some evidence such as a printing date.

264 _4. Copyright Date

Although the copyright date is not a core element when a publication date has been inferred, it is considered by music catalogers that a copyright date, when one appears in the resource, is a particularly important piece of information to include in bibliographic records for scores.

300 Field

Note that "study score" appears instead of "miniature score" in the extent statement in 300 subfield $a. Note also the lack of abbreviations elsewhere in the 300 field.

336 Field. Content Type

As mentioned previously, the RDA content type for music scores is "notated music."

337/338 Fields. Media/Carrier Type

As for resources discussed elsewhere, because the format of this score is a bound volume, the media and carrier types are "unmediated" and "volume" respectively.

546 Field. Language Note

As mentioned at the beginning of this section, the *Form of Musical Notation* is encoded in the MARC 546 subfield b.

The record shown in Figure 9.5 is the second of ten records for musical scores available on the Library of Congress website at http://www.loc.gov/catworkshop/ RDA%20training%20materials/SCT%20RDA%20Records%20TG/index.html. This set includes records for both manuscript and online scores as well as printed scores.

Additional Information

The Music Library Association is preparing specialized instructions for music catalogers using RDA. As of this writing, the instructions are available in the following:

Best Practices for Music Cataloging Using RDA and MARC21, Prepared by the RDA Music Implementation Task Force, Bibliographic Control Committee, Music Library Association (February 15, 2013 draft consulted). Available at http://bcc.musiclibraryassoc.org/BCC-Historical/ BCC2013/RDA_Best_Practices_for_Music_Cataloging.pdf.

Training materials are available as follows:

"Hit the Ground Running! RDA Training for Music Catalogers: A Guide to the RDA Preconference at the Music Library Association 2013 Meeting." Available at http://guides.library .cornell.edu/MLARDA2013.

SOUND RECORDINGS

"Sound recordings" in the context of this section includes both musical sound recordings and nonmusical sound recordings. When sound recordings are cataloged using RDA in the MARC environment, they should be described using one (or possibly more) of the following content types, encoded in one or more 336 $a: "performed music"; "spoken word"; or "sounds." If media type is included in the record for a sound recording, it will always have the value "audio" and be encoded in MARC 337 $a. The carrier type will of course vary, with "audio disc" being a common value that includes a range of carriers, from vinyl LPs to CDs.

This section highlights some significant differences between RDA and AACR2 in the MARC environment that are particularly relevant to the cataloging of musical sound recordings, analyzes a MARC bibliographic record for a musical sound recording, and concludes with references to additional records and to specialized documentation and training in the cataloging of sound recordings.

Following are some of the significant differences between RDA and AACR2 in the MARC environment that are of particular interest when cataloging sound recordings, especially musical sound recordings.

Preferred Source of Information

For resources that are neither book-like materials nor moving images, RDA 2.2.2.4 specifies that the preferred source is based on whether the resource is tangible or online. For tangible resources, a permanent label on the resource itself is the first choice, as it was in AACR2, with container and accompanying material the second choice if there is no textual content within the resource itself. For online resources with no textual content, embedded metadata are the preferred source.

Performers and Performing Groups

Catalogers accustomed to cataloging sound recordings using AACR2 as interpreted by the Library of Congress will also be accustomed to "entering" sound recordings under the names of these performers and performing groups. In RDA, this has changed. Unless the performers or groups are also considered to be the creators of the works being performed, their names will no longer appear in the 100 or 110 fields of the MARC records for these sound recordings. In RDA terms, the authorized access point for the sound recording work will consist of just the preferred title for the work and will not include the authorized access point for the performer or performing group.

Describing the Carrier

In RDA, the terminology for describing extent has changed from the AACR2 "sound disc" to "audio disc." In addition, the description of the carrier of a sound recording is more granular in RDA than it was in AACR2, and additional MARC fields have been developed to capture this granularity. The media/carrier types have made more granular the carrier aspect implied by the AACR2 GMD "sound recording." In addition, it is possible to encode both *Sound Characteristics* and *Digital File Characteristics* in the more granular MARC 344 and 347 fields respectively, rather than in, or in addition to, the 300 $b. Figure 9.6 shows a comparison of AACR2 to RDA carrier information for a sound recording.

Figure 9.6. Describing the Carrier for a Sound Recording Using AACR2 and RDA

AACR2

```
245   XX $a ... $h [sound recording].
300      $a 1 sound disc : $b digital
```

RDA (following Music Library Association recommendations)

```
300   $a 1 audio disc ; $c 4 3/4 in.
336   $a performed music $2 rdacontent
337   $a audio $2 rdamedia
338   $a audiodisc $2 rdacarrier
344   $a digital $2 rda
347   $a audio file $b CD audio $2 rda
```

Or, if the 300 $b is used instead of the 344 and 347 fields

```
300   $a 1 audio disc : $b CD audio ; $c 4 3/4 in.
336   $a performed music $2 rdacontent
337   $a audio $2 rdamedia
338   $a audiodisc $2 rdacarrier
```

Bibliographic Record for a Musical Sound Recording

Figure 9.7 shows an example of a bibliographic record for a musical sound recording cataloged using RDA and encoded using MARC. The elements of the record that are different from the way the record might have looked if AACR2 had been used are in **bold**. Following are brief explanations of these different elements, presented in the order in which they appear in the MARC record.

LDR/07 "i" and 040 $e "rda"

See chapter 8 of this book for an explanation. Note that LDR/07 displays in this record with the label "Desc."

Figure 9.7. Bibliographic Record for a Musical Sound Recording

Type j	ELvl	Srce c	Audn	Ctrl	Lang zxx
BLvl m	Form	Comp jz	AccM i	MRec	Ctry tu
	Part n	TrAr n			
Desc i	FMus n	LTxt	DtSt t	Dates 2007 ,	2007

007	sd_f s ngnnmmne d
040	$a ___ $b eng $e rda $c ___
024 3	$a 8691834008229
028 02	$a CD 419 $b Kalan
033 10	$a 20070608 $a 20070609 $b 7434 $c l8
041 0 _	$g eng $g tur
042	$a pcc
050 _ 4	$a M1366.S
245 00	$a Swing a la Turc.
264 _ 1	**$a Unkapanı, İstanbul : $b Kalan, $c [2007]**
264 _ 4	**$c ©2007**
300	$a 1 **audio disc** ; $c 4 3/4 in.
336	**$a performed music $2 rdacontent**
337	**$a audio $2 rdamedia**
338	**$a audiodisc $2 rdacarrier**
344	**$a digital $2 rda**
347	**$a audio file $b CD audio $2 rda**
500	$a Jazz, some of which is derived from Turkish art music.
511 0_	$a Önder Focan Group (Önder Focan; A. Şenol Filıiz; Şenova Ülker; Erdal Akyol; Cem Aksel; Ferit Odman).
500	$a All arrangements by Önder Focan.
518	**$o** Recorded **$d** 2007 June 8-2007 June 9 **$p** MMA, Istanbul.
500	$a Notes in Turkish and English inserted in container.
505 0_	$a Cici kız = Cutie / Erol Sayan (6:10) -- Lal (Oniki) / Fahir Atakoğlu (4:27) – Gönül sana tapalı = Since I've been loving you / Sadettin Kaynak (8:34) -- Geçti bahar = Spring is over / Fehmi Tokay (9:18) – Sen = You / Birol Yayla (7:25) -- Bahar geldi = Spring is here / M. Sebahattin Ezgi (12:22) -- Karlı kayı ormanı / Zülfü Livaneli (4:09) – Canberra zortlatması = Canberra tune / Önder Focan (4:33) -- Kaçsam bırakıp = If I leave you / Mehveş Hanım (6:10).
650 _ 0	$a Jazz $y 2001-2010.
700 1 _	$a Focan,Önder, $d 1955– **$e arranger of music**.
710 2 _	$ a ÖnderFocanGroup, **$e performer.**

Note: Data from the LDR and 008 fields are displayed in "OCLC format" in this record, with brief labels for each data element. LDR/07 data is labeled "Desc."

1XX Field and GMD

Note that there is no 100 or 110 field, as neither the arranger nor the performing group is considered to be the creator of this sound recording work in RDA. Note also the absence of the GMD.

264 _1. Publication Information

Note that publication information appears in the MARC 264 field, with the second indicator "1", rather than in a 260 field. The bracketing of the 264 $c indicates that the cataloger inferred the publication date, probably based on the copyright date.

264 _4. Copyright date

Although the copyright date is not a core element when a publication date has been inferred, it is common practice to include it (especially a phonogram copyright, or date, which refers to the copyright of the recorded sound), even when it is the same as the inferred publication date.

300 Field

Note that "audio disc" appears instead of "sound disc"' in the extent statement in subfield $a. Note, though, that it is still acceptable in the United States to give dimensions in inches, not centimeters, and to use the abbreviation "in." in the 300 $c.

336 Field. Content Type

As discussed previously, the RDA content type for musical sound recordings is "performed music."

337/338 Fields. Media/Carrier Type

As discussed previously, the media and carrier types are "audio" and "audio disc" respectively.

344/347 Fields

As discussed previously, the Sound Characteristics and Digital File Characteristics can be encoded here or in the 300 $b, or in both.

518 Field. Date, Time, and Place of an Event

Note the use of subfields to identify the RDA elements Date of Capture (subfield $d) and Place of Capture (subfield $p). Subfield $o is defined as "Other event information" and in this instance is used to identify the nature of the event. This is an example of MARC subfield coding developed to correspond to the increased granularity of RDA elements.

710 $e

Note the use of RDA Appendix I relationship designators "arranger of music" and "performer."

The record shown in Figure 9.7 is a slightly modified version of the fifth of eight records for musical sound recordings available on the Library of Congress website at http://www.loc.gov/catworkshop/RDA%20training%20materials/SCT%20 RDA%20Records%20TG/index.html. This set includes a record for a "78 rpm" as well as a record for a sound recording that is also a serial. Also available on the same site is a set of three records for nonmusical sound recordings.

Additional Information

As mentioned at the end of the previous section, the Music Library Association is preparing specialized instructions for music catalogers using RDA. As of this writing, the instructions, which include guidance for the cataloging of musical sound recordings, are available in the following:

Best Practices for Music Cataloging using RDA and MARC21, Prepared by the RDA Music Imple-
  mentation Task Force, Bibliographic Control Committee, Music Library Association (February
  15, 2013 draft consulted). Available at http://bcc.musiclibraryassoc.org/BCC-Historical/
  BCC2013/RDA_Best_Practices_for_Music_Cataloging.pdf.

Training materials are available as follows:

"Hit the Ground Running! RDA Training for Music Catalogers: A Guide to the RDA Preconference at the Music Library Association 2013 Meeting." Available at http://guides.library
  .cornell.edu/MLARDA2013.

MOTION PICTURES AND VIDEORECORDINGS

The scope of this section is resources for which the RDA Content type is either "two-dimensional moving image" or "three-dimensional moving image" (used for 3–D movies, for example). The content type "cartographic moving image" (used, for example, for a videorecording of satellite images of the earth) is also a possibility, but not a common one. The cataloging community that deals with these resources has had many discussions and debates about FRBR concepts and their application to moving image resources as well as ongoing discussions on RDA implementation of FRBR concepts both in and out of the MARC environment. This section does not attempt to review these discussions. Instead, it focuses on the following differences between AACR2 and RDA for moving image resources: preferred source of information as applied to moving images in RDA, the RDA elements that replace the AACR2 GMDs "motion picture" and "videorecording," and the increased granularity of some expression and manifestation elements in RDA that are relevant to the description of moving images. For the cataloger with a particular interest in moving images, references for additional information are provided at the end of the section.

Preferred Source of Information

Moving images have their own RDA guidelines (2.2.2.3) for identifying the preferred source of information. These guidelines are more explicit than the comparable guidelines in AACR2 and also specifically address intangible (i.e., online) resources. Essentially, the first choice for preferred source of information is title screen(s) or frame(s). Subsequent choices depend on whether the resource is tangible or intangible, with labels and accompanying material used for tangible resources such as a DVD, and textual content or embedded metadata used for intangible resources such as an MPEG video file. In addition, statements of responsibility and parallel titles taken from different sources within the resource can be combined into a single 245 field without using square brackets to identify which elements came from a source other than the preferred source for the title.

Content/Media/Carrier Types for Moving Images

These elements replace the AACR2 GMDs "motion picture" and "videorecording." As mentioned previously, the content type, encoded in the MARC 336 field, is one of the three content types containing the phrase "moving image." Media types that are used for resources with moving image content include "computer," "projected," and "video." Some commonly used carrier types include "online resource" (used with media type "computer"), "film reel" (used with media type "projected"), and "videodisc" (used with media type "video"). Figure 9.8 shows examples of each of these media type/carrier type combinations.

Granular Expression and Manifestation Elements

Moving image resources have a number of technical elements that under AACR2 would have been included in either the physical description (MARC 300 field) or a note (MARC 500 or 538 field). RDA has explicitly identified some of these as separate elements, and MARC coding has been developed to correspond to them. The relevant MARC fields are 344 (Sound Characteristics), 345 (Projection Characteristics of Motion Picture), 346 (Video Characteristics), and 347 (Digital File Characteristics). In these MARC fields the following RDA elements can be coded: *Presentation format*, RDA 3.17.2 (e.g., 3D) in MARC 345 subfield $a; *Projection*

**Figure 9.8.   Examples of Content/Media/
Carrier Type for Moving Images**

Streaming video

336	$a two-dimensional moving image $2 rdacontent
337	$a computer $2 rdamedia
338	$a online resource $2 rdacarrier

DVD video

336	$a two-dimensional moving image $2 rdacontent
337	$a video $2 rdamedia
338	$a videodisc $2 rdacarrier

16 mm film reel

336	$a two-dimensional moving image $2 rdacontent
337	$a projected $2 rdamedia
338	$a film reel $2 rdacarrier

Speed, RDA 3.17.3 (e.g., 48 fps) in MARC 345 subfield $b; *Video Format*, RDA 3.18.2 (e.g., VHS) in MARC 346 subfield $a; *Broadcast Standard*, RDA 3.18.3 (e.g., PAL) in MARC 346 subfield $b; *Encoding Format*, RDA 3.19.3 (e.g., Blu-ray) in MARC 347 subfield $b; and *Regional Encoding*, RDA 3.19.6 (e.g., "region 4") in MARC 347 subfield $e. These RDA elements can also continue to be included in either the MARC 300 subfield $b or the MARC 538 field, instead of or even in addition to the specific coding. For example, a single record for a DVD might contain the following 538 field for display:

> 538 $a DVD video, Dolby digital 5.1, surround, NTSC, Region 1, wide screen.

But also include the following more granular encoding for potential machine manipulation:

> 344 $a digital $b optical $g surround $h Dolby digital 5.1
> 346 $a laser optical $b NTSC
> 347 $a video file $b DVD video $e region 1

Additional Information

Best practices for the cataloging of moving images are, as of this writing, still being developed by the moving image cataloging community. Following are useful resources for more information on RDA and moving image cataloging:

The website for OLAC (Online Audiovisual Catalogers) at http://olacinc.org, especially the "Cataloging Tools & Training" section under "Publications and Training Materials->CAPC Publications," which includes, for example, detailed guidance for coping with language expressions, access points, and coding of language information in the document *Video Language Coding Best Practices*. As other best practices are developed by the moving image cataloging community, they are likely to be posted on the OLAC website.

RDA & Moving Images. ALCTS webinar presented by Kelley McGrath, March 14, 2012. Recording available at http://downloads.alcts.ala.org/ce/03142012 _RDA_Moving_Images.wmv; presentation slides available at http://down loads.alcts.ala.org/ce/03142012_RDA_Moving_Images_Slides.pptx.

GRAPHIC MATERIALS

The community of catalogers who specialize in the cataloging of graphic materials generally use their own standards, for example, *Graphic Materials: Rules for Describing Original Items and Historical Collections*, compiled by Elisabeth W. Betz (Washington, DC: Library of Congress, 1982) or its successor, *Descriptive Cataloging of Rare Materials (Graphics)*, which is expected to be available by the time this book is published. These standards have historically had a somewhat loose relationship to AACR2; it is assumed that they will continue to have a similarly loose relationship to RDA. For that reason, this section of this book is relatively brief and is limited to a discussion of some of the new RDA elements that are particularly relevant to graphic materials and their corresponding MARC encoding.

Graphic materials falling within the scope of AACR2 Chapter 8 correspond to the RDA content type "still image." At the time AACR2 was written, two sets of GMDs were created for these materials, with one set consisting of the term "graphic" and the other set of eight more specific terms, including, for example, "art original" and "slide." The result was a variation in practice. In RDA, the use of media type and carrier, as well as several explicitly defined elements and their corresponding new MARC fields, makes it possible for the cataloger to provide a more granular description of graphic materials, in particular of their physical format and characteristics.

Media/Carrier Type

The media and carrier type will reflect the physical format of the particular "still image" or graphic. The content type "still image" can be found in conjunction with a wide range of carriers within the following media types: "computer"; "microform"; "projected"; "stereographic"; "unmediated"; or even "video."

Granular Expression and Manifestation Elements

RDA defines several elements that may be particularly useful for catalogers of graphic materials, which can be encoded in the new MARC 340 field. The most obvious of these elements are *Base Material*, RDA 3.6 (e.g., paper) coded in MARC 340 $a; *Applied Material*, RDA 3.7 (e.g., ink) in MARC 340 $c; *Mount*, RDA 3.8

Figure 9.9.   Four "Physical Descriptions" of Graphic Resources Using RDA

Example 1. A set of slides depicting art works

```
300     $a 15 slides : $b color ; $c 5 x 5 cm
336     $a still image $2 rdacontent
337     $a projected $2 rdamedia
338     $a slide $2 rdacarrier
```

Example 2. A set of stereograph cards depicting landscapes

```
300     $a 6 stereographic cards
336     $a still image $2 rdacontent
337     $a stereographic $2 rdamedia
338     $a stereograph card $2 rdacarrier
```

Example 3. An etching

```
300     $a 1 print.
336     $a still image $2 rdacontent
337     $a unmediated $2 rdamedia
338     $a sheet $2 rdacarrier
340     $a paper $b 15 x 20 cm $d etching $c ink
```

Example 4. An original drawing

```
300     $a 1 drawing.
336     $a still image $2 rdacontent
337     $a unmediated $2 rdamedia
338     $a sheet $2 rdacarrier
340     $a illustration board $b 10 9/16 x 7 1/4 inches (268 x 183
        mm) $c black ink over graphite.
```

(e.g., linen) in MARC 340 $e; and *Production Method*, RDA 3.9 (e.g., etching) in MARC 340 $d. Provisions for recording these aspects of graphic materials were present in AACR2, but not at the level of granularity that is present in RDA. It is worth noting that there has for some time been provision for encoding *Base Material* and *Mount* (described respectively as Primary Support Material and Secondary Support Material) as codes in the MARC 007 field. *Dimensions* can also be recorded in MARC 340 $b or in MARC 300 $c. Figure 9.9 shows four examples of "physical descriptions" for graphic resources using RDA.

The fields shown in example 4 of Figure 9.9 are from the fourth record in the set of fifteen records for art objects and images available on the Library of Congress website at http://www.loc.gov/catworkshop/RDA%20training%20materials/SCT%20 RDA%20Records%20TG/index.html.

ELECTRONIC RESOURCES

"Electronic resources" are, in RDA terms, those resources with the media type "computer." Catalogers accustomed to AACR2 will have been using the GMD "electronic resource" for these resources. The various carrier types within this media type include "online resource" as well as terms for tangible resources, such as "computer disc." The RDA instructions relevant to electronic resources are therefore largely contained within RDA Chapter 3, "Describing Carriers."

This section highlights just three aspects of electronic resources: preferred source of information, recording extent and carrier for an online resource, and the issue of "provider-neutral" records for online resources.

Preferred Source of Information

Online resources are intangible resources, and RDA makes a distinction between tangible and intangible resources in determining the preferred source of information for resources (RDA 2.2). For intangible (online) resources, textual content found within the resource is preferred, but a second choice is embedded metadata. For tangible electronic resources, although title screens or their equivalent are preferred, there is an option in RDA for using an eye-readable label instead. The Library of Congress has selected that option for tangible (also called "direct access") electronic resources.

Recording the Extent and Carrier Type for an Online Resource

RDA 3.4.1.7.5 contains instructions for recording "subunits" of an online resource: "In some cases, a resource consists of one or more files in a format that parallels a print, manuscript, or graphic counterpart (e.g., PDF). When this occurs, specify the number of subunits by applying the instructions for extent of the appropriate parallel counterpart." What this means is that although the extent of an online resource is recorded as simply "1 online resource," it is possible, when the online resource is essentially a reproduction of another format, to record the extent of that other format as a subunit of the online resource.

> 300   1 online resource (56 p.)
> 300   1 online resource (15 maps)

Recording the media type and carrier type for an online resource is very simple, although the content type will of course depend on the nature of the resource. The media type will always be "computer," and the carrier type will always be "online resource."

> 337   computer $2 rdamedia
> 338   online resource $2 rdacarrier

Provider-Neutral Records

One issue relating to the cataloging of online resources that has not been completely resolved at the time of this writing is what are called "provider-neutral records" for serials that have the carrier type "online resource." It is the practice of catalogers in the United States to create just one record that represents all online versions (or manifestations) of an expression. Normally, in the MARC environment, catalogers create bibliographic records at the level of the manifestation whether they are using AACR2 or RDA. That is, one bibliographic record describes one manifestation. A provider-neutral record, however, can be seen as being at the expression level. It essentially describes the online expression of the work and can be used for any online manifestation of that expression. Just how this practice of creating provider-neutral records will be reconciled with RDA as implemented in the MARC environment has yet to be determined.

THREE-DIMENSIONAL ARTEFACTS AND REALIA

"Three-dimensional artefacts and realia" in AACR2 terminology encompasses the RDA carrier types "object" (media type "unmediated") and "microscope slide" (media type "microscopic"). Content types vary, depending on other attributes of the resource. For example, an object designed to be perceived through touch would have the content type "tactile three-dimensional form." But the more common content type will probably be simply "three-dimensional form." Catalogers accustomed to AACR2 may have used either the GMD "object" for these resources or more specific terms, including "game," "model," or "microscope slide." The RDA instructions relevant to three-dimensional artefacts and realia are therefore largely contained within RDA Chapter 3, "Describing Carriers." There are few differences between AACR2 and RDA that are specific to objects. Aside from the replacement of the GMD by the carrier type "object" or "microscopic slide" with the corresponding media types, the differences are all those that have been seen in the records for other resources.

Bibliographic Record for a Hand-Painted Plate

Figure 9.10 shows an example of a bibliographic record for a hand-painted plate. The record was created using RDA and encoded using MARC. The elements of the record that are different from the way the record might have looked if AACR2 had been used are in **bold**. Following are brief explanations of these different elements, presented in the order in which they appear in the MARC record.

Figure 9.10. Bibliographic Record for a Hand-Painted Plate

Type r	ELvl I	Srce d	Audn	Ctrl	Lang fre
BLvl m	Form	GPub	Time nnn	MRec	Ctry fr
Desc **i**	TMat r	Tech n	DtSt s	Dates 1910 ,	

040	$a ___ $b eng **$e rda** $c ___	
024 8	$a Fuld	
245 0 0	$a French opera plate featuring Rossini's "Le Barbier de Seville".	
264	**0**	**$a Limoges, France, $c [1910?]**
300	$a 1 plate**.**	
336		**$a three-dimensional form $2 rdacontent**
337		**$a unmediated $2 rdamedia**
338		**$a object $2 rdacarrier**
340		**$b 8 1/2 inches (190 mm) diameter $c faience**
500	$a Hand painted plate from the house of Parry and Vieille, Limoges, France, signed by the artist G. Gastiano. Part of a series of plates featuring whimiscal musical, probably opera, scenes.	
520 0	$a French "sujets musicaux" plate, a pictorial representation of Rossini's opera, "Le Barbier de Seville," with sheet music to match.	
561 1	$a James Fuld.	
562	$a Signed by the artist G. Gastiano in lower right; back stamp in gold: PV in a circle.	
650 4	$a 1910.	
600 1 0	$a Rossini, Gioacchino, $d 1792–1868. $t Barbiere di Siviglia.	
655 0 7	$c v $a plates (dishes) $2 aat	
655 0 7	$c v $a faience (earthenware) $2 aat	
655 0 7	$c v $a back stamps $2 aat	
700 1	$a Gastiano, G., **$e artist.**	
700 1	**$i Related to (work):** $a Rossini, Gioacchino, $d 1792–1868. $t Barbiere di Siviglia.	
700 1	$a Fuld, James J., $d 1916–2008, **$e former owner.**	
710 2	$a Parry Vieille (Firm), **$e manufacturer.**	
752	$a France $d Limoges	

Note: Data from the LDR and 008 fields are displayed in "OCLC format" in this record, with brief labels for each data element. LDR/07 data are labeled "Desc."

LDR/07 "i" and 040 $e "rda"

See chapter 8 of this book for an explanation. Note that LDR/07 displays in this record with the label "Desc".

264 field. Production information

The cataloger has decided that this plate is unpublished (264 1st indicator has the value "0"), and therefore just the date of production is core. The cataloger has, however, also included the place of production in the record.

336/337/338. Content/Media/Carrier Types

The content type for this resource is "three-dimensional form," the most generic of the content types for objects. The media and carrier types are, respectively "unmediated" and "object," as they would be for an object of any content type.

340 field. Physical characteristics

The cataloger has chosen to encode the dimensions in 340 subfield $b and the applied material in the 340 subfield $c, rather than in the 300 field of the record.

700 $e. Relationship designators for persons and corporate bodies

These first two terms (artist, former owner) are found in RDA Appendix I; the third term (manufacturer) is from the *MARC Code List for Relators* (http://www.loc.gov/marc/relators/). Although "artist" is normally a creator relationship, which would mean that the artist's name would be encoded in a MARC 100 field rather than a 700 field, in this particular instance the artist has not functioned as a creator, but is closer in function to an illustrator or illuminator. However, there is no truly appropriate term in the list of relationship designators, which highlights the problems faced by catalogers of objects that have sometimes complex relationships with the persons or bodies that contributed to their creation or current state.

700 $i. Relationship designators for works, etc.

The cataloger supplied this particular relationship designator, which does not appear in the list of such designators in RDA Appendix J. As with the relationship designators for persons and corporate bodies discussed previously, this highlights the problem of selecting an appropriate relationship designator from the available list.

The record in Figure 9.10 is the first record in the set of fifteen records for art objects and images available on the Library of Congress website at http://www.loc.gov/catworkshop/RDA%20training%20materials/SCT%20RDA%20Records%20TG/index.html.

Additional Information

For additional information on RDA and the cataloging of three-dimensional objects, see the following:

Cataloging Three-Dimensional Objects and Kits with RDA. ALCTS webinar presented by Kelley McGrath, March 28, 2012. Recording available at http://alcts.ala.org/ce/03282012_3D_Kits_RDA.wmv. Presentation slides available at http://downloads.alcts.ala.org/ce/03282012_RDA_3D_Kits_Slides.pdf.

MICROFORMS [AND OTHER REPRODUCTIONS]

"Microforms" are, in RDA terms, those resources with the media type "microform." Catalogers using AACR2 will have been accustomed to using the same term, "microform," as the GMD for these resources. The RDA guidelines that are specific to microforms are therefore largely contained within RDA Chapter 3, "Describing Carriers." The various carrier types within this media type are very similar to the specific material designations in AACR2 for this class of resource: microfiche, microfilm reel, etc.

Microforms are often reproductions of resources previously existing in another format, frequently textual resources. RDA is not very different from AACR2 *as written* with respect to the cataloging of microforms. However, cataloging practice in the United States for the last thirty years has followed the Library of Congress, which did not implement AACR2 as written with respect to microform reproductions. The difference centered on the focus of the description, in particular with respect to publication information and physical description. In both AACR2 and RDA, the focus of the description is on the reproduction, with a note giving information about the original; in Library of Congress practice the reverse was true, the focus of the description being on the original, with a note giving information about the reproduction. With the implementation of RDA, libraries in the United States, led by the Library of Congress, are focusing on describing the reproduction. The RDA preferred source of information for microforms of materials originally issued on pages, leaves, sheets, or cards is a title page or its image; although there is an option for choosing an eye-readable header (RDA 2.2.2.2) instead, the Library of Congress is not choosing that option.

Bibliographic Record for a Microform Reproduction of a Text

Figure 9.11 shows an example of a bibliographic record for a microform reproduction cataloged using RDA and encoded using MARC. The elements of the record that are different from the way the record might have looked if AACR2 *as implemented by the Library of Congress* had been used are in **bold**. Following are brief explanations of these different elements, presented in the order in which they appear in the MARC record.

Figure 9.11. Bibliographic Record for a Microform Reproduction of a Text

Type a	ELvl	Srce c	Audn	Ctrl	Lang ukr
BLvl m	Form b	Conf 0	Biog	MRec	Ctry sz
	Cont bc	GPub	LitF 0	Indx 0	
Desc **i**	Ills	Fest 0	DtSt **r**	**Dates 1986 ,**	**1959**

```
007      he_amb--bucu
040      $a ___ $b eng $e rda $c ___
066      $c (N $c (Q
042      $a pcc
043      $a e-un---
050    4 $a DK508.73 $b .H46 1986
```

⌐245 0 0 $a Генеральний опис Лівобережної України 1765-1769 pp : $b покажчик
        населених пунктів / $c редактор І.Л. Бутич ; покажчик склали Л.А. Попова,
        К.Г. Ревнивцева.

└245 0 0 $a Heneral'nyĭ opys Livoberezhñoĭ Ukraïny 1765-1769 rr : $b pokazhchyk
        naselenykh punktiv / $c redaktor I.L. Butych ; pokazhchyk sklaly L.A. Popova,
        K.H. Revnyvtseva.

264   1 $a Zug : $b Inter Documentation Company, $c 1986.

300 $a 2 microfiches ; $c 11 x 15 cm

336 $a text $2 rdacontent

337 $a microform $2 rdamedia

338 $a microfiche $2 rdacarrier

```
500      $a On microfiche header: R-14, 636.
651    0 $a Ukraine (Hetmanate : 1648-1782) $x Sources $v Bibliography ǂv Catalogs.
650    0 $a Cities and towns $z Ukraine $x Sources $v Bibliography $v Catalogs.
610  2 0 $a TSentral'nyĭ derzhavnyĭ istorychnyĭ arkhiv URSR u m. Kyievi $v Catalogs.
```

⌐700 1 $a Бутич, І. Л. $q (Іван Лукич)
└700 1 $a Butych, I. L. $q (Ivan Lukych)

⌐700 1 $a Попова, Л. А.
└700 1 $a Popova, L. A.

⌐700 1 $a Ревнивцева, К. Г.
└700 1 $a Revnyvtseva, K. H.

776 0 8 $i Reproduction of (manifestation): $a Heneral'nyĭ opys Livoberezhñoĭ
        Ukraïny 1765-1769 rr $d Kyïv : TSentral'nyĭ derzhavnyĭ istorychnyĭ arkhiv
        URSR u m. Kyievi, 1959 $h 184 pages

LDR/07 "i" and 040 $e "rda"

See chapter 8 of this book for an explanation. Note that LDR/07 displays in this record with the label "Desc".

008 Dates

Note that the microform is coded as a reprint, and the date of the microform reprint as well as the original are given in the 008 field.

245 Field

Note the absence of the GMD "$h [microform]."

264 Field

The publication information is for the *microform*, not for the original publication (RDA 2.8.1.3).

300 Field

The elements in this field describe the *microform*, not the original publication.

336 Field. Content Type

The content type is "text," and it is not affected by the fact that it has been reproduced in microform.

337/338 Fields. Media/Carrier Type

These are "microform" and "microfiche" respectively.

776 field. Additional Physical Form Entry

The AACR2 "note on the original" (or on the reproduction, for those libraries following Library of Congress practice), which would have been encoded in the MARC 534 field (MARC 533 field for a note on the reproduction), has been replaced by very similar data encoded in the MARC 776 field and introduced with the explicit relationship designator "Reproduction of (manifestation)."

The record shown in Figure 9.11 is the seventh record in a set of eight records for microforms of non-Western monographs available on the Library of Congress website at http://www.loc.gov/catworkshop/RDA%20training%20materials/SCT%20 RDA%20Records%20TG/index.html.

CONTINUING RESOURCES

Continuing resources encompass serials and integrating resources. In RDA, which does not use the term "continuing resource," these are both modes of issuance, defined as "a categorization reflecting whether a resource is issued in one or more parts, the way it is updated, and its intended termination" (RDA 1.1.3). As described in chapter 4 of this book, mode of issuance is encoded in the MARC leader byte 07: "s" for serial and "i" for integrating resource.

The application of RDA to the cataloging of serials and integrating resources has results that are very similar to the application of AACR2. However, there are certain characteristics that, if not unique to continuing resources, are certainly more common to these resources. It can be useful to know where the instructions for coping with these characteristics occur in RDA and how the instructions are different, if they are, from the corresponding rules in AACR2, all of which were found in Chapter 12 of AACR2. Following is a brief discussion of the most significant of these characteristics.

Changes to Serials and Integrating Resources

RDA 1.6.2 summarizes the kinds of changes that require a new description for a serial; RDA 1.6.3 summarizes the kinds of changes that require a new description for an integrating resource. RDA 2.3.2.12–13 gives specific instructions for dealing with changes in the title proper of a serial. The results of these rules are essentially the same as the comparable rules in Chapter 12 of AACR2.

Numbering of Serials (RDA 2.6)

Numbering of serials is a core element in RDA. It is also an element in which the RDA principle of representation has the potential for creating differences between RDA and AACR2. For example, depending on how numbering actually appeared on the first issue, there could be the following difference between the way numbering is recorded in the 362 field of a record for a serial cataloged using AACR2 and RDA:

AACR2

    362   1_ $a Began with v. 59, no. 1 (Feb. 2007).

RDA

    362   1_ $a Began with Volume 59, number 1 (February 2007).

Recording Relationships Between Serial Titles

RDA Section 8 contains guidelines for recording relationships between Group 1 entities, which includes serial titles. These relationships are commonly encoded in MARC 77X fields. As described in chapter 7 of this book, the MARC encoding can substitute for explicit relationship designators. For example the MARC 780 field corresponds to the relationship designator "continues . . .," and the MARC 785 field corresponds to the relationship designator "continued by . . . "

Additional Information

The community of serials catalogers in the United States commonly follows the guidelines developed by CONSER for cataloging these resources, specifically the CONSER Standard Record or CSR. As of this writing, the relevant CONSER documentation is being revised to incorporate RDA changes. Relevant documentation is available online through the CONSER home page (http://www.loc.gov/aba/pcc/conser/; see especially *CONSER RDA Cataloging Checklist and Core Elements*).

A set of sample records for serials and websites [integrating resources] is available on the Library of Congress website at http://www.loc.gov/catworkshop/RDA%20training%20materials/SCT%20RDA%20Records%20TG/index.html. Also informative is the ALCTS webinar *RDA and Serials Catalogers: Will Our Work Really Change?* presented by Steve Shadle on March 2, 2011. Recording available at http://alcts.ala.org/ce/0302_11_RDA_Serials_Catalogers.wmv.

ACCOMPANYING MATERIAL AND KITS

What was called accompanying material in ACCR2 is now considered a particular kind of related manifestation in RDA. RDA provides three options for "recording relationships to related manifestations": Identifier; Structured description of the manifestation; or Unstructured description of the manifestation (RDA 27.1.1.3, described in more detail in chapter 7 of this book), but as of this writing, RDA lacks specific instructions for, or examples of, recording the "accompanying material" relationship. In default of specific instructions, catalogers using MARC in the United States can follow the guidance embodied in the LC/PCC PS for RDA 3.1.4, which provides the option of using multiple 300 fields or following the AACR2 practice of using a single 300 field with the accompanying material described in the subfield $e. If no description of the carrier is deemed necessary, accompanying material can always be described in a note in a 500 field. The use of either multiple 300 fields or the 300 $e can be seen as an implementation of the RDA option for a "Structured description of the related manifestation." RDA Appendix J does include the relationship designator "accompanied by (manifestation)" for use when an access point is created for accompanying material.

Another aspect, however, of describing accompanying material using RDA in a MARC environment is whether and how to record the content/media/carrier type of the accompanying material, if these are different from the content/media/carrier type of the primary resource. There are two possible approaches, if multiple content/media/carrier types are to be recorded:

1. Repeat the $a within one instance of each field, as for example (for a score with an accompanying CD):

    336     $a notated music $a performed music $2 rdacontent

2. Repeat the field for each instance of the $a, as for example:

336      $a notated music $2 rdacontent
336      $a performed music $2 rdacontent

Cataloging communities in the United States are currently recommending that the field be repeated, but also that the subfield $3 be used to identify the manifestation to which the field applies. However, no formal guidelines have been developed at the time of this writing. Figure 9.12 shows what the 300 and 336/337/38 fields might look like in a record for a score with an accompanying CD, if either of the practices just described is followed. Note that the 336/337/338 fields are identical, although different choices were made with respect to the 300 fields.

Figure 9.12.   Score with Accompanying Audio Disc: 300/336/337/338 Fields

Single 300 field with $e for accompanying material

300	$a 1 score (33 pages) ; $c 30 cm + $e 1 audio disc (36 min., 59 sec. : digital, CD audio, stereo ; 4 3/4 in.)
336	$3 score $a notated music $2 rdacontent
336	$3 audio disc $a performed music $2 rdacontent
337	$3 score $a unmediated $2 rdamedia
337	$3 audio disc $a audio $2 rdamedia
338	$3 score $a volume $2 rdacarrier
338	$3 audio disc $a audio disc $2 rdacarrier

Two 300 fields, one for the score, one for the accompanying audio disc

300	$a 1 score (33 pages) ; $c 30 cm
300	$a 1 audio disc (36 min., 59 sec.) : $b digital, CD audio, stereo ; $c 4 3/4 in.
336	$3 score $a notated music $2 rdacontent
336	$3 audio disc $a performed music $2 rdacontent
337	$3 score $a unmediated $2 rdamedia
337	$3 audio disc $a audio $2 rdamedia
338	$3 score $a volume $2 rdacarrier
338	$3 audio disc $a audio disc $2 rdacarrier

Note: The cataloger has chosen, in both these examples, to include the *Sound characteristics* and *Digital File Characteristics* of the audio disc in the 300 field rather than in the specialized 344 and 347 fields.

Related to the issue of accompanying material is the issue of kits. AACR 2 included "kit" (or "multimedia") as a GMD, defined as "an item containing two or more categories of material, no one of which is identifiable as the predominant constituent of an item." RDA does not include "kit" or a comparable term as a carrier type. However, RDA 3.1.4, "Resources Consisting of More Than One Carrier Type," does include the AACR2 option of using a general term, such as "various pieces," in recording the extent of such a resource, in addition to the option of recording separately the extent of each constituent item. In summary, there appear to be just two options for recording the extent of what used to be called a kit:

1. Use a general term like "various pieces" to record the extent in a single 300 field.
2. Use multiple 300 fields to record the extent, one for each carrier present in the kit.

With respect to recording content/media/carrier type in the MARC 336/337/338 fields, if a general term such as "various pieces" is used to describe the extent, the instructions found in RDA 6.9.1.3, 3.2.1.3, and 3.3.1.3 suggest that the content/media/carrier type that applies to the "predominant" or "most substantial" part of the resource be recorded. If the option to use multiple 300 fields is chosen by the cataloger, the issues of recording content/media/carrier types for the different elements in the kit are the same as for recording these elements for a resource with an accompanying manifestation, and the use of the $3 is suggested for identifying which content/media/carrier types apply to which components of the kit.

For additional discussion of the issues of RDA and the cataloging of kits, see the following:

Cataloging Three-Dimensional Objects and Kits with RDA. ALCTS webinar presented by Kelley McGrath, March 28, 2012. Recording available at http://alcts.ala.org/ce/03282012_3D _Kits_RDA.wmv. Presentation slides available at http://downloads.alcts.ala.org/ce/03282012 _RDA_3D_Kits_Slides.pdf.

CONCLUSION

This chapter has identified basic differences between AACR2 and RDA in the cataloging of nonbook resources, reviewed sample MARC records or sample MARC fields for some of these resources, and identified sources of information that can help the cataloger who needs more detailed instructions for particular resources.

Together with chapter 8 of this book, it is hoped that this chapter will have given the reader a basic understanding of some of the issues associated with the creation and interpretation of MARC bibliographic records using RDA and provided sources for gaining additional specialized information regarding the cataloging of nonbook resources.

10

Creating and Interpreting Authority Records

Chapters 8 and 9 of this book looked at bibliographic records for books and nonbook resources and focused on the areas of change from AACR2 to RDA. This chapter does the same for authority records. We first highlight the major areas of difference between AACR2 and RDA with respect to the construction of access points, then look at authority records and the various fields beyond the authorized access point.

Many of the changes from AACR2 to RDA have been accompanied by the creation of MARC authority fields to accommodate RDA data that did not exist in the AACR2 environment. This chapter covers these new MARC fields in detail, identifying the fields and subfields used to record specific attributes. It also describes how to construct and record RDA authority data in accord with policies developed by the cooperative cataloging community in the United States, specifically the policies developed by the Library of Congress in cooperation with the Program for Cooperative Cataloging (PCC) for those agencies that contribute authority records to the national authority file. These policies are generally recorded as LC-PCC *Policy Statements* (hereafter LC-PCC PS); the national authority file is commonly referred to as LCNAF (an acronym for Library of Congress Name Authority File).

The chapter concludes with a look at eight authority records in which the results of applying RDA are examined and differences between AACR2 and RDA are identified. This review of records highlights the differences between the two standards and showcases the increased granularity that RDA brings to authority data. After reading this chapter, the reader will have a solid foundation for interpreting RDA authority data and creating authority records.

CHANGES IN THE CONSTRUCTION OF ACCESS POINTS

In order to search for records representing persons, families, corporate bodies, works, expressions, and places in an authority file, such as Library of Congress Authorities (http://authorities.loc.gov), one needs to know how access points for these entities are constructed using RDA. The construction of these access points is covered in chapters 5 and 6 of this book, but not in the context of how these constructions compared to headings formulated under AACR2. Here we highlight the differences between AACR2 and RDA with respect to the construction of access point construction.

Two of the major changes that a cataloger will encounter in RDA are a much smaller number of instances in which abbreviations are used and the eliminaton of Latin terminology. These can be seen with most of the Group 1 and Group 2 entities.

Persons

AACR2

   100   1_ $a Belloy, Pierre de, $d ca. 1540–1613

RDA

   100   1_ $a Belloy, Pierre de, $d approximately 1540–1613

Corporate Bodies

AACR2

   110   1_ $a South Dakota. $b Dept. of Public Safety

RDA

   110   1_ $a South Dakota. $b Department of Public Safety

Works

AACR2

   130   _0 $a Bible. $p O.T.

RDA

   130   _0 $a Bible. $p Old Testament

Expressions

AACR2

> 100   1_ $a Townshend, Pete. $t Songs. $k Selections; $o arr.

RDA

> 100   1_ $a Townshend, Pete. $t Songs. $k Selections; $o arranged

There are, however, a few exceptions to this. The most notable is the continued abbreviation of certain place-names in the qualifiers of access points.

AACR2

> 130   _0 $a Science and society (New York, N.Y.)

RDA

> 130   _0 $a Science and society (New York, N.Y.)

Catalogers will also still encounter the abbreviation "etc." in many access points for treaties and protocols.

AACR2

> 110   2_ $a European Economic Community. $t Treaties, etc. $g Morocco, $d 1976 Apr. 27. $k Protocols, etc., $d 1982 Mar. 11–1991 June 26

RDA

> 110   2_ $a European Economic Community. $t Treaties, etc. $g Morocco, $d 1976 April 27. $k Protocols, etc., $d 1982 March 11–1991 June 26

Aside from abbreviations, there are other changes in access points. The following sections address persons, families, corporate bodies, works, and expressions and discuss the changes in access points for each one.

Changes in the Construction of Access Points for Persons

Date of Birth and Date of Death

Both AACR2 and RDA contain instructions to add a date to a person's name if there is a need to distinguish that person from similarly named persons, and both provide the option to add the dates even if there is no need to distinguish one name from another. The Library of Congress created a rule interpretation for AACR2 that instructed catalogers always to add the date, regardless of the need to distinguish between names. That instruction was continued by an LC-PCC PS for RDA, so AACR2 headings and RDA access points will look the same with respect to dates included in access points for persons. However, there are changes with respect to the manner in which the dates are recorded.

The abbreviations "b." and "d." prescribed in AACR2 for use when just a pre-twentieth-century birth date or just a death date was present in a heading are expanded to "born" and "died" in RDA. Although RDA contains the instruction to record birth and death dates when available, it prescribes no particular convention. Examples in RDA show some birth dates with hyphens, other birth dates preceded by the word "born," and death dates preceded by the word died. LC-PCC PS for RDA 9.19.1.1 specifies that birth dates in access points should be followed by a hyphen and death dates should be preceded by a hyphen, and that the terms "born" and "died" are not to be used. For the recording of birth dates after the nineteenth century, there is therefore no change between AACR2 and RDA.

Date of birth

AACR2

    100   1_ $a Beverly, Winchell, $d 1940–

RDA

    100   1_ $a Beverly, Winchell, $d 1940–

There is, however, a significant change with respect to recording birth dates in the nineteenth century and earlier, in those cases where no death date is available.

AACR2

    100   1_ $a Camp, Joseph, $d b. 1811

RDA

    100   1_ $a Camp, Joseph, $d 1811–

Date of death

Similarly, there is a significant change between AACR2 and RDA in the recording of death dates in access points in the cases where no birth date is available.

AACR2

    100   1_ $a Alcanyís, Lluís, $d d. 1506

RDA

     100   1_ $a Alcanyís, Lluís, $d -1506

Fuller Form of Name

Both AACR2 and RDA contain instructions to add the fuller form of name only if needed for distinguishing between people with identical names, but both allow the option of adding the fuller form regardless of need to distinguish. The Library of Congress rule interpretation for the AACR2 rule advised the cataloger to add the fuller form of name, even if the person's name was sufficiently distinct without the addition. This policy of always adding the fuller form of name was not carried over into RDA. Instead, LC-PCC PS for 9.19.1.4 calls for the addition of the fuller form of name only if needed for distinction or identification. The new MARC field 378 may in any case be used for recording the fuller form of name. With RDA and the LC-PCC policy statement, there will likely be fewer instances of access points containing fuller forms of a person's name.

AACR2

     100   1_ $a Powers, Xavier M. $q (Xavier Mitchell)

RDA

     100   1_ $a Powers, Xavier M.
     378      $q Xavier Mitchell

Period of Activity and/or Profession or Occupation

When neither birth and/or death dates nor a fuller name are available to distinguish one person's name from another, the next choice given in RDA is *period of activity* or *profession or occupation*.

With respect to *period of activity*, there are two changes from AACR2 to RDA. The first involves the term "flourished." In AACR2, the time during which a person was active was represented by the abbreviation of the word "flourished": "fl." In RDA, the spelled-out term is used, but RDA gives an alternative term that could be used: "active." The LC-PCC PS for RDA 9.19.1.1 specifies use of the word "active" rather than "flourished." This change from AACR2 to RDA with respect to *period of activity* can be seen as follows:

AACR2

     100   1_ $a Albertus, $c de Parma, $d fl. 13th cent.

RDA

     100   1_ $a Albertus, $c de Parma, $d active 13th century

The second change involving *period of activity* is, as with birth dates, the difference in treatment of people born before and after 1900. AACR2 instructed the cataloger not to use "fl." for dates within the twentieth century. This guideline was not carried over into RDA, so *period of activity* can also be used for persons active in the twentieth century and later, if necessary to distinguish one person from similarly named people.

AACR2

~~100   1_ $a Williams, John, $d fl. 1916–1943~~

RDA

100   1_ $a Williams, John, $d active 1916–1943

Profession or Occupation

The option for adding a term describing profession or occupation to a heading was severely restricted in AACR2. The AACR2 section on "Distinguishing Terms" permitted the addition of a "suitable brief term" just to those headings consisting entirely of a given name, although this limitation was mitigated to some exent by a Library of Congress rule interpretation. RDA 9.19.1.5, by providing the option of adding a term describing a profession or occupation to any personal name, lifted this AACR2 restriction and, interestingly, restored a practice that had been accepted under earlier cataloging codes.

Other Term of Rank, Honor, or Office

Although RDA had initially omitted the AACR2 provision for adding "a term of address, title of position or office, initials of an academic degree, initials denoting membership in an organization, etc.," a provision for adding *other term or rank, honor, or office* was added to RDA in 2013. RDA 9.19.1.6 restores the AACR2 provision for adding terms such as "Captain" or "Sir" to a name if the other elements listed in the earlier sections of this chapter are not available. Finally, RDA 9.19.1.7, also added to RDA in 2013, authorizes "an appropriate designation" if nothing else is available.

100   1_ $a Lang, John $c (Brother of Andrew Lang)

Words, Etc., Indicating Relationship Following Surnames

Among the terms mentioned in the AACR2 section on "Distinguishing Terms" was "Jr." RDA 9.2.2.9.5, *Words, Etc., Indicating Relationship Following Surnames*, calls for recording terms such as Jr. and Sr., or numbers such as II and III, that appear with the name as part of the preferred name. This instruction is a significant change from AACR2, which did not treat these words as an integral part of a person's name and permitted their inclusion in a heading only if no other differentiating elements were available.

AACR2

>   100   1_ $a Reynolds, Shelby Z., $d 1942–

RDA

>   100   1_ $a Reynolds, Shelby Z., $c Jr., $d 1942–

Fictitious Characters

In the AACR2 environment, fictitious characters attributed with creating or contributing to a resource were not given access points to represent their relationship to the resource. They were allowed to be represented as subjects of works, but not as creators or contributors. Thus, the names of fictitious characters were established as topical subjects. In contrast, RDA explains at the beginning of Chapter 9, "Identifying Persons," that persons "include fictitious entities, such as literary figures, legendary figures, etc." Thus, fictitious characters can now be treated as creators and contributors, and name authority records should be created for them.

At the time of this writing, the following matter relating to fictitious characters was still under discussion: while RDA 9.19.1.2. f) appears to specify that fictitious or legendary persons are one of the categories of name to which titles or other designations associated with the person are always added, RDA 9.6 suggests that such titles and designations are to be added, except for spirits and Christian saints, only when such a designation is needed to distinguish one person from another person with the same name.

>   100   0_ $a Miss Piggy

OR

>   100   0_ $a Miss Piggy $c (Fictitious character)

Changes in the Construction of Access Points for Families

Families were not considered to be potential authors in the AACR2 environment, so no name authority records existed for them. Families could, however, be treated as the subjects of works, so there were subject authority records for family names. In RDA, families can now be considered creators of or contributors to works, and RDA contains an entire chapter on how to construct access points for families and record relevant authority data for these entities. Thus, name authority records can be created for them.

>   100   3_ $a Romanov (Dynasty: $d 1613–1917)

Changes in the Construction of Access Points for Corporate Bodies

"Dept. vs. Department"

Most of the differences between AACR2 and RDA with respect to the names of corporate bodies can be seen in the access points for conferences, which will be detailed shortly. The one major difference for corporate bodies that are not conferences involves the abbreviation of the word "Department." Technically, this difference does not reflect a change from AACR2 to RDA, but rather a change in cooperative cataloging policy. AACR2 never actually contained an instruction to abbreviate the word "Department" in headings. In fact, AACR2 examples show the word "Department" in its spelled-out form, which was a departure from pre-AACR2 practice. Automation was in its infancy when AACR2 was implemented, and making the change from "Dept." to "Department" in primarily paper files and card catalogs was held to be impractical. Therefore, the Library of Congress issued a rule interpretation that instructed catalogers always to use the abbreviation "Dept." for "Department" in headings. This directive was not carried over into RDA, in large part because automated means are available to make global changes to files that are now primarily digital and online.

AACR2 as interpreted by the Library of Congress

      110   1_ $a United States. $b Dept. of Health and Human Services

RDA and AACR2 as written

      110   1_ $a United States. $b Department of Health and Human Services

Conferences, Etc.

There are several differences between AACR2 and RDA with respect to names of conferences. AACR2 made a distinction between "conferences, congresses, meetings, etc." on the one hand and "exhibitions, fairs, festivals, etc." on the other. RDA does not make this distinction, conflating the two categories into one category referred to as "conferences, etc." For conferences, AACR2 called for omission from the name of a conference words that denote its number, its frequency, and the year in which it was held. RDA, however, calls for omission from the preferred name of a conference, exhibition, or fair the indication of its number and its year of convocation, but not its frequency. This difference means that catalogers will see more access points for conferences that include terms like "annual" and "biennial."

AACR2

      111   2_ $a Symposium on Sea Turtle Biology and Conservation

RDA

> 111   2_ $a Annual Symposium on Sea Turtle Biology and Conservation

The fact that RDA calls for the omission of the year of convocation from the names of exhibitions and fairs as well as from conference names represents a change from AACR2, which never called for omission of year from the names of exhibitions and fairs, but only of frequency. Since the year is omitted from the preferred name, it is treated as an addition to the preferred name and is recorded in the qualifier.

AACR2

> 111   2_ $a Polyurethanes Expo '96 $c (Las Vegas, Nev.)

RDA

> 111   2_ $a Polyurethanes Expo $d (1996: $c Las Vegas, Nev.)

Another difference of note is the manner in which locations are recorded in the access point when there are more than two. For conferences held in more than two locations, AACR2 instructed the cataloger to record only the first listed place, followed by the word "etc." RDA makes no restrictions on the number of places to be recorded and instructs the cataloger to include the name of each place in the access point.

AACR2

> 111   2_ $a Danish-Swedish Analysis Seminar $d (1995: $c Copenhagen, Denmark, etc.)

RDA

> 111   2_ $a Danish-Swedish Analysis Seminar $d (1995: $c Copenhagen, Denmark; Lund, Sweden; Paris, France)

RDA, reflecting the digital environment in which it was written, has an instruction that says to record "Online" for the location of a conference that is held over the Internet.

> 111   2_ $a Electronic Conference on Land Use and Land Cover Change in Europe $d (1997: $c Online)

The most significant change in conferences is that in RDA each instance of an ongoing conference can now have its own authority record. In AACR2 this happened in rare cases, such as when a particular instance of a conference was being used as a reference for another conference. Thus, in the RDA environment, a cataloger will see a substantially greater number of authority records created for individual instances of ongoing conferences.

For the benefit of serials cataloging workflows, the cooperative cataloging community made a policy to allow the creation of authority records for unqualified ongoing conferences, separate from the authority records for each individual instance. Thus, catalogers searching in the LCNAF may find authority records for both types of record. The LC-PCC PS for RDA 11.13.1.8 instructs catalogers to add a standardized note to the authority record for the ongoing conference alerting users of the authority record to the possibility that records exist for individual instances of the conference.

Ongoing conference

> 111   2_ $a ILCLI International Workshop on Cognitive Science
> 667 $a See also related access points for individual instances of this conference which include specific information about the number, date, or place of the individual conference.

Individual instance of a conference

> 111   2_ $a ILCLI International Workshop on Cognitive Science $n (10th: $d 2010: $c San Sebastián, Spain)

Changes in the Construction of Access Points for Works

There are a few major changes between the uniform titles formulated under AACR2 and the preferred titles for works and expressions constructed according to RDA For preferred titles of works, one of the changes involves the spelling of "*Qur'an*" in RDA, which was spelled "*Koran*" in AACR2.

AACR2

> 130   _0 $a Koran

RDA

> 130   _0 $a Qur'an

RDA also introduced changes in how access points involving the Bible are constructed. First, *Old Testament* and *New Testament* are spelled out rather than abbreviated.

AACR2

> 130   _0 $a Bible. $p N.T.

RDA

> 130   _0 $a Bible. $p New Testament

Also, books and groups of books in the Bible are recorded directly as subheadings of *Bible*, rather than indirectly through their associated testament.

AACR2

> 130   _0 $a Bible. $p N.T. $p Peter

RDA

> 130   _0 $a Bible. $p Peter

AACR2

> 130   _0 $a Bible. $p N.T. $p Gospels

RDA

> 130   _0 $a Bible. $p Gospels

Finally, RDA differs from AACR2 in how it constructs preferred titles for portions of a person's works. In AACR2, the uniform title for a portion of a person's works was the term "Selections." RDA prescribes that the term "Selections" be preceded by the term "Works," which is what is referred to in RDA as a "conventional collective title." In both AACR2 and RDA, the authorized access point for the work begins with the preferred access point for its author.

AACR2

> 100   1_ $a Maugham, W. Somerset $q (William Somerset), $d 1874–1965. **$t Selections**

RDA

> 100   1_ $a Maugham, W. Somerset $q (William Somerset), $d 1874–1965. $t Works. **$k Selections**

Changes in the Construction of Access Points for Expressions

Aside from spelling out abbreviations like "arr." ("arranged"), the changes from AACR2 to RDA with respect to expressions have mainly to do with how languages are added to access points for manifestations that embody two or more expressions. In AACR2, if a single resource contained two different expressions of a work in two different languages, then an authorized heading would have been formulated that consisted of the authorized access point for the work plus the the the name of both languages, separated by an ampersand. In RDA, an authorized access point (and its corresponding authority record if one is created) is constructed for each language expression.

AACR2

> 100   1_ $a Piave, Francesco Maria, 1810–1876. $t Ernani. $l English & Spanish

RDA

> 100   1_ $a Piave, Francesco Maria, 1810–1876. $t Ernani. $l English
> 100   1_ $a Piave, Francesco Maria, 1810–1876. $t Ernani. $l Spanish

If three or more language expressions were embodied in the same manifestation, under AACR2 one heading would have been formulated that consisted of the authorized heading for the work and the word "Polyglot." In RDA, separate access points for each language expression are created.

AACR2

> 100   1_ $a Piave, Francesco Maria, 1810–1876. $t Ernani. $l Polyglot

RDA

> 100   1_ $a Piave, Francesco Maria, 1810–1876. $t Ernani. $l English
> 100   1_ $a Piave, Francesco Maria, 1810–1876. $t Ernani. $l German
> 100   1_ $a Piave, Francesco Maria, 1810–1876. $t Ernani. $l Spanish

GENERAL GUIDELINES FOR RECORDING AUTHORITY DATA

There are seventeen new MARC authority fields that were created for recording information about persons, families, corporate bodies, works, and expressions. These new fields were created in response to RDA elements, several of which are described in chapters 5 and 6 of this book. Many of these new MARC fields have specific descriptive conventions that were nonexistent in the AACR2 environment. In order to be able to interpret authority data encoded in MARC, it helps to understand some of the specific conventions established by the Library of Congress in cooperation with the Program for Cooperative Cataloging.

There are two aspects of authority data in the MARC environment that aid in the interpretation and creation of authority records. First, it is useful to know the common authority subfields. Second, it is helpful to be familiar with the various controlled lists from which terms and phrases may be added to various parts of the authority record. The following discussion elucidates both.

Common Authority Subfields

Each field holds one or more subfields that carry information about a specific attribute of an entity. Many authority subfields serve the same purpose across all fields. The most common are the subfield $s for *start period*; the subfield $t for *end period*; the subfield $u for *uniform resource identifier*; the subfield $v for *source of information*; and the subfield $2 for *source of date scheme, term, or code*.

The subfield $s is used for recording the starting date for an attribute associated with the entity, while the subfield $t is used for recording the ending date. Examples of dates can include the year a person started or ended at a place of employment; the dates the person entered or left a field of activity or occupation; the year a family or corporate body was founded or terminated; or the range of dates within which a person, family, or corporate body are associated with a geographic place. The following are examples:

046	$s 1972 $t 2006
	years that a corporate body began and ended
370	$e Brazil $s 2000
	year that a person started living in Brazil
373	$a Aalborg University, Denmark $t 1994
	date a person stopped working for a university
374	$a Teacher $s 1978 $t 2010
	start and end dates of a teacher's career

Subfield $u is used for recording the uniform resource identifier of the resource used to justify data within the field. The subfield $u is always used in conjunction with and must be preceded by the subfield $v in the new MARC fields (the subfield $u can appear alone in the 670 field). The subfield $v is used for citing the source consulted for justifying data within the field. Information in subfield $v is recorded in the same form that it would be recorded in the MARC 670 (Source Data Found) subfield $a. For most fields—except the 1XX, 4XX, 5XX, and a few others—subfield $v can be used in lieu of or in addition to the 670. The following example shows how the subfields $u and $v might be used in an authority record.

| 372 | $a Speech perception $v Wernicke's Corner WWW site, viewed October 29, 2012 $u www.wernickescorner.com |

Subfield $2 can hold several types of information, all under the general theme of "source." The source encoded in subfield $2 varies depending on the MARC field in which it appears. For field 046 (Special Coded Dates), subfield $2 is used for recording the *source of date scheme*, typically when the EDTF scheme is being used. For field 368 (Other Attributes of Person or Corporate Body), subfield $2 is used simply for recording the *source*, which would generally be a controlled list. For fields 370, 372–376 (various attributes of Group 2 entities), and 380–382 (Form of Work; Other Distinguishing Characteristics of Work or Expression, Medium of Peformance), subfield $2 is used for the *source of term*. This term can come from a controlled list, such as a subject heading list or a name authority file.

Each field has a specific set of lists from which the term can be taken. For example, Field of Activity (field 372) and Profession or Occupation (field 374) terms can be taken from a subject heading list, such as the *Library of Congress Subject Headings* (LCSH) or the *Medical Subject Headings* (MeSH). In contrast, Associated Group (field 373) terms can be taken from name authority lists, such as the Library of Congress Name Authority File (LCNAF). Finally, for field 377 (Associated Language), subfield $2 is used for the *source of code*, referring to the language code source used when the term is taken from a source other than the *MARC Code List for Languages* (http://www.loc.gov/marc/languages/).

Some fields can have all of these subfields, whereas others have only one or several. Whenever a field has one or more of these subfields, there is a preferred order in which the information should be recorded: $2, $s, $t, $v, $u. Following is an example of a field that comprises all five subfields, recorded in the preferred order.

373      $a University of California, Irvine $2 naf $s 1985 $t 1999 $v Jay
         Arthur WWW site, viewed November 15, 2012 $u www.jayarthur.
         university.edu

Controlled Lists

Some terms, phrases, and proper names can be recorded in natural language, but for many fields, the preferred convention is to use terms, phrases, and proper names from controlled sources such as LCSH and LCNAF. If the term comes from a controlled list, then the source must be cited in subfield $2. In some cases, the form of the term in the controlled list is in the plural. In such cases, that term is recorded in plural form in a 3XX field, but if it is used as a part of an access point, the singular form of the term is used.

100   1_ $a James, Michael $c (Physician)
374      $a Physicians $2 lcsh

Most of the 3XX fields are repeatable. In addition, many subfields are repeatable within the same field. The preferred convention within the cooperative cataloging environment is to repeat subfields within the same field rather than repeating the entire field.

374      $a Poet $a Singer $a Actor

However, in some cases, it might be clearer to repeat the entire field rather than stringing a series of subfields together.

> 373 $a University of California, Los Angeles. Department of Sociol-ogy $2 naf
> 373 $a University of Wisconsin—Madison $2 naf
> 373 $a University of California, San Diego $2 naf

Terms, phrases, and proper names that are taken from the same controlled vocabulary can be repeated within the same field.

> 372 $a Philology $a Romanian literature $a Arts, Romanian $2 lcsh

However, when terms, phrases, and proper names are taken from different controlled sources, they must be recorded in separate fields.

> 372 $a Health Disparities $2 mesh
> 372 $a Health—Social aspects $a Social medicine $a Women's health services $2 lcsh

Information that requires the addition of a subfield $s, $t, $u, or $v needs to be recorded in its own subfield.

> 373 $a University of California, Los Angeles. School of Law $2 naf
> 373 $a University of California, Los Angeles. Department of Sociology
> 373 $a University of New Mexico $2 naf $s 2005 $t 2010

THE NEW AUTHORITY FIELDS

Now that we have discussed some general conventions for how to record the data, we can focus on the data and which fields are used for recording the data.

Field 046—Special Coded Dates

Special coded dates are recorded either in the ISO Standard 8601 format or the EDTF date scheme. The ISO Standard 8601 format is used for certain dates, and the basic format is *yyyymmdd*, *yyyy-mm*, or *yyyy*.

> 046 $f 1851
> 046 $g 1945–02
> 046 $s 20050505 $t 20050509

The ISO Standard 8601 format also instructs catalogers to record centuries in the two-digit form and to subtract "1" from the absolute value. Thus, the eighteenth century would be recorded as

> 046 $s 17

B.C. dates are preceded by a negative sign and are also recorded by subtracting "1" from the absolute value. Thus, 502 B.C. would be recorded as

    046      $s -501

The EDTF date scheme is used for probable, uncertain, and estimated dates. Whenever it is used, a subfield $2 must be added at the end of the field with the code "edtf."

    046      $g 1915? $2 edtf   *probable date*
    046      $f [1801,1802] $2   edtf *uncertain date*
    046      $s 1783~ $2 edtf   *estimated date*

There are six main subfields within the 046 field: the subfield $f for *birth date*, the subfield $g for *death date*, the subfield $k for *beginning or single date created*, the subfield $l for *ending date created*, the subfield $s for *start period*, and the subfield $t for *end period*. The 046 field is valid for every type of authority record, but not all subfields are valid in every type. Some subfields are valid in certain records, while other subfields are valid in others. The following delineates which type of subfield can occur in which type of authority record.

Field 046 Subfield $f—Birthdate

Subfield $f is used in records for persons only to give their birth dates.

    046      $f 1906? $2 edtf   *estimated year of birth*
    046      $f 19501104   *certain date of birth*

Field 046 Subfield $g—Death Date

Subfield $g is used in records for persons only to give their death dates.

    046      $g 1976–01   *month and date of death*
    046      $f 1889 $g 19861124   *year of birth and date of death*

Field 046 Subfield $k—Beginning or Single Date Created

Subfield $k is used in records for works and expressions only to signify the beginning date of a work or expression or the date the work or expression was created.

    046      $k 2004   *year a work was created*

Field 046 Subfield $l—Ending Date Created

Subfield $l is used in records for works and expressions only to signify the termination date of a work or expression.

```
046    $l 2009              year a work ended
046    $k 1953 $l 2005      start and end of a serial run
```

Field 046 Subfield $s—Start Date

Subfield $s is used in records for families and corporate bodies only to signify the date those entities came into existence.

```
046    $s 1986              year a corporate body was founded
```

Field 046 Subfield $t—End Date

Subfield $t is used in records for families and corporate bodies only to signify the date those entities ceased to exist.

```
046    $t 2009              year a corporate body ended
046    $s 1883 $t 1958      range of years a family existed
```

Field 336—Content Type

Field 336 is used for recording the content type. Content type is an expression-level element, so it can be added only to an expression-level authority record. Field 336 has the same meaning in authority records as in bibliographic records and uses the same terms, codes, fields, and subfields.

In practice, field 336 may be utilized less often in authority records than in bibliographic records. In the cooperative cataloging environment, institutions are given the choice to create "differentiated" or "undifferentiated" authority records. If FRBR were applied to the fullest degree, a separate authority record would need to be created for every expression that differed in content type, language, or some other aspect. These separate records are referred to as "differentiated" authority records. For example, one English translation of a work would have a separate authority record from a different English translation of the same work. An English translation would also have different authority records if it were written in text, rendered in braille, or narrated in the spoken word. However, it is possible to create an authority record that represents *all* English translations of a given work. Such an authority record is referred to as an "undifferentiated" authority record. Thus, to make authority files less unwieldy and cumbersome, cooperative cataloging policymakers have given authority record creators the choice to create either differentiated records or undifferentiated records. Content type can be added to a differentiated record, but must be omitted from an undifferentiated record.

Following is an example of content type data recorded in the 336 of a differentiated expression record. As in the bibliographic format, subfields $a and $2 are required, while subfield $b is optional.

```
336    $a performed music $b prm $2 rdacontent
```

Field 368—Other Attributes of Person or Corporate Body

Field 368 was created to hold information about persons and corporate bodies that may be useful for identification of the entity; it may later be added to an access point if needed to differentiate a given entity from similarly named entities or to convey the idea of a corporate body. Field 368 has four main subfields: subfield $a for the *type of corporate body*, subfield $b for the *type of jurisdiction*, subfield $c for *other designation*, and subfield $d for the *title of person*. All subfields are repeatable.

Field 368 Subfield $a—Type of Corporate Body

Subfield $a is used exclusively for corporate bodies for recording their type. Related to the RDA subelement "Names Not Conveying the Idea of a Corporate Body" (under the general element "Other Designation Associated with the Corporate Body"), this subfield holds the type of information typically added to the access point of a body whose identity as a corporate body is not clear. However, even if the body's name conveys the idea of "corporateness" and does not require the term to be added to the access point, the term can still be added in field 368 subfield $a. Any term that might reasonably be added to a corporate body access point can be recorded in the 368 field, but convention may favor use of a controlled vocabulary source, such as LCSH.

```
110   2_  $a Johann Traeg (Firm)
368       $a Firm
```

```
111   2_  $a Marine Awareness Workshop for Beqa Lagoon $d (1996: $c
          Pacific Harbour International Hotel)
368       $a Meetings $2 lcsh
```

Field 368 Subfield $b—Type of Jurisdiction

Subfield $b is related to the RDA subelement "Type of Jurisdiction" (under the general element "Other Designation Associated with the Corporate Body"). This subfield can be used for holding the type of term that may later be added to an access point of a jurisdiction in order to distinguish the jurisdiction from a similarly named place.

```
151       $a Cork (Ireland: County)
368       $a County
```

Field 368 Subfield $c – Other Designation

Subfield $c is used for both persons and corporate bodies and is based on the RDA element "Other Designation Associated with the Person" and the subelement "Other Designation" (under the general element "Other Designation Associated with the Body").

Subfield $c can be used for recording, for example, the words "Spirit" or "Saint" or some other designation for a person.

    100 1_ $a Garland, Judy $c (Spirit)
    368      $c **Spirit**

    100 0_ $a Sava, $c Saint, $d 1169–1237
    368      $c **Saint**

    100 0_ $a Budd, Henry $c (Cree indian)
    368      $c **Cree indian**

Subfield $c can also hold the type of information typically added to the access point of a corporate body to distinguish that corporate body from similarly named bodies.

    110 2_ $a World Cup (Cricket)
    368      $c **Cricket**

Field 368 Subfield $d—Title of Person

Related to the element *title of the person*, subfield $d is use exclusively used for persons for recording designations of nobility, royalty, term of address for a person of religious vocation, or ecclesiastical office or rank.

    100 1_ $a Deutsch, Abraham, $c Rabbi, $d 1902–1992
    368      $d **Rabbi**

Field 370—Associated Place

Field 370 is for recording information about a geographic location associated with an entity. It has six main subfields: subfield $a for recording *place of birth*, subfield $b for recording *place of death*, subfield $c for *associated country*, subfield $e for *place of residence/headquarters*, subfield $f for *other associated place*, and subfield $g for *place of origin of work*. Field 370 can be recorded in any type of authority record involving the Group 1 and Group 2 entities. However, not every subfield can be included in every type of record. The following discussion delineates which types of records can contain which subfield.

Generally, the associated place is recorded in the form in which it is found in the qualifier of an access point. This means following the names of smaller jurisdiction with the names of larger ones (where appropriate), abbreviating according to RDA Appendix B (where applicable), and usually employing a comma for punctuation instead of parentheses. These conventions are based on the form in which the geographic name would be established in the LCNAF. If the associated place is in a form taken from a list other than the LCNAF, then that source needs to be indicated in a subfield $2.

> 370 $a Los Angeles, Calif. $c U.S. $f Westwood, Los Angeles, Calif.

Field 370 Subfield $a—Place of Birth

Subfield $a is used only for persons and is used for recording their town, city, province, state, or country of birth.

> 370 $a Boston, Mass.

Field 370 Subfield $b – Place of Death

Subfield $b is also used exclusively for persons and is used for recording their town, city, province, state, or country of death.

> 370 $b N.S.

Field 370 Subfield $c—Associated Country

Subfield $c can be used in records for persons, families, corporate bodies, and works for recording the country with which those entities are identified. Because an entity can be identified with more than one country, it is a repeatable subfield.

> 370 $c Australia $c U.S.

Field 370 Subfield $e—Place of Residence/Headquarters

Subfield $e can be used in records for persons, families, and corporate bodies for recording the town, city, province, locale, state, or country in which that entity lives or has its headquarters. It is also a repeatable subfield.

> 370 $e Phoenix, Ariz. $e England

Field 370 Subfield $f—Other Associated Place

Subfield $f can be used in records for persons, families, corporate bodies, works, and expressions for recording some other town, city, province, state, or country associated with that entity that was not covered by the previous subfields. This can include a person's place of employment, a geographic locale (other than its headquarters) with which a corporate body is extensively associated, or some other place. It is also a repeatable field.

> 370 $e New York, N.Y. $f Japan
> *corporate body based in New York, extensive involvement with Japan*

Field 370 Subfield $g—Place of Origin of Work

Subfield $g is used exclusively for works and is used to record the country or other territorial jurisdiction in which they originated. It is a repeatable field.

> 370 $g New York, N.Y.
>   *place of origin for the serial publication entitled* Science and society

Field 371—Address

Field 371 is used for recording the address of a person's residence or a corporate body's headquarters. It has six main subfields, including subfield $a for *address*, subfield $b for *city*, subfield $c for *intermediate jurisdiction*, subfield $d for *country*, subfield $e for *postal code*, and subfield $m for *electronic mail address*. Only the subfield $a and the subfield $m are repeatable. The subfield $a can include information such as street address and suite numbers. If both are given on the resource, they should be recorded in separate subfields. Unlike field 370, in field 371 the names of towns, cities, states, provinces, and countries can be recorded as they appear on the source. The following is an example of a 371 field in which every subfield except the subfield $m is present:

> 110   2_ $a Center for Global Studies
> 371 $a Suite 400 $a 157 Haddock Lane, $b Houston $c TX
> $d USA $e 77041

For reasons of privacy, catalogers contributing to the LCNAF are discouraged from including a residence address for a living person in an authority record. As a result, authority record users may see very few instances of a fully fleshed-out 371 field in an authority record for a person. They are more likely to find only a subfield $m in the record, which will contain the person's e-mail address. Following is an example of a 371 field added to the name authority record for a person.

> 100   1_ $a Richards, Madeline.
> 371 $m mrichards@university.com

Field 372—Field of Activity

Field 372 is used for recording information about the field of endeavor or area of engagement for persons or corporate bodies. It has one main subfield, subfield $a, for *field of activity*, which is repeatable. A person or body's field of activity can be described in natural language terms or in terms of a word or phrase taken from a controlled subject list. If a term is taken from a subject heading list, a subfield $2 should be added with the code for the specific list. A term from a controlled list such as LCSH can be described as a main heading or as a precoordinated string. If recording the latter, conventional preference is to capitalize the first word of each component and remove spaces from between the main heading and subdivision, separating the components with dashes.

> 372　　　　Europe—History $a Europe—Intellectual life $a Europe—Civilization $2 lcsh

Field 373—Associated Group

Field 373 was created to accommodate the RDA elements "affiliation" (an attribute of persons) and "associated institution" (an attribute of corporate bodies). It has one main subfield, subfield $a, for *associated group*, which is repeatable. RDA gives specific instructions to "[r]ecord the name of an associated institution by using the preferred name for the institution." If the name is taken from the LCNAF, then a subfield $2 containing the code "naf" should be added.

> 373　　　　$a University of California, Los Angeles. Department of Sociology $2 naf

Field 374—Occupation

Field 374 was created to accommodate the RDA element *profession or occupation*, and it is used exclusively in personal name authority records. It has one main subfield, subfield $a, for *occupation*, which is repeatable. As with the 372 field, the 374 field can contain natural language or controlled vocabulary terms, and the main heading can be precoordinated with a subdivision, if applicable. Whenever a term is taken from a list, a subfield $2 should be added in order to specify which list.

Occupation can be related to *field of activity*, but it differs in two important ways. First, *occupation* is often described in terms of persons (e.g., "nurses"), whereas *field of activity* is described in terms of disciplines or areas of endeavor (e.g., "nursing"). Second, *occupation* can be added to an access point if needed to distinguish the person's name from similarly named persons. If a term is added from a controlled list, such as LCSH, the term may often be in the plural. If that is the case and the term is being used as part of an access point, it should be converted to its singular form when placed in the qualifier of the access point. The following example shows a 374 field along with a 100 and 372 field for the same person.

> 100　1_　$a Smith, Michael $c (Architect)
> 372　　　　$a Architecture $2 lcsh
> 374　　　　$a Architects $2 lcsh

Field 375—Gender

Field 375 is used exclusively for persons, to describe their gender. It has one main subfield, subfield $a, for *gender*, which is repeatable. RDA contains instructions to use the options *female*, *male*, or *not known*, but it allows the cataloger to record another suitable term or phrase as appropriate. If a person's gender changes and the relevant dates are known, these dates can be recorded in the subfield $s and $t of each field as appropriate.

375 $a male $s 1947 $t 2001
375 $a female $s 2001
670 $a ... $b (born in 1947; from birth to 2001, used George Freeman; on November 14, 2001, changed name to Georgette Freeman)

Field 376—Family Information

Field 376 was created exclusively to accommodate RDA elements that are attributes of families. It has three main subfields (all of which are repeatable): subfield *a* for recording *type of family*, subfield $b for recording *name of prominent member*, and subfield $c for recording the *hereditary title*.

Field 376 Subfield $a—Type of Family

Type of family is an element that must be recorded in an access point for a family. In addition, it may also be recorded in the 376 subfield $a and should follow the same form in which it would appear in the access point.

100 3_ $a Tāmhanakara (Family)
376 $a **Family**

Field 376 Subfield $b—Name of Prominent Member

Name of prominent member is core only if needed to help distinguish one family from a similarly named family. It can be added to an access point, encoded in 376 subfield $b, or both. When added to the subfield $b, it should be recorded in the form in which it would appear in an access point.

100 3_ $a Denney (Family: $g Denny, Anthony, 1501–1549)
376 $a Family $b **Denny, Anthony, 1501–1549**

Field 376 Subfield c—Hereditary Title

Subfield $c can be used for recording the hereditary title of nobility associated with a family. It is always recorded in the plural.

100 3_ $a Cholmley (Family)
400 3_ $a Cholmondeley (Family)
376 $a Family $c Marquesses of Cholmondeley

Field 377—Associated Language

Field 377 can be used in records for persons, families, corporate bodies, and expressions for recording the language associated with those entities. It has two main subfields (both of which are repeatable): subfield $a for *language code* and subfield $l for *language term*.

Field 377 Subfield $a—Language Code

The language with which an entity is associated is generally recorded using a three-digit code taken from the *MARC Code List for Languages* (http://www.loc.gov/marc/languages/). When taken from this list, there is no need to add a subfield $2. However, if it is taken from another list, then a subfield $2 must be added in order to indicate which list is being used.

> 377 $a eng $a fre
> 377   _7 $a en $a fr $2 iso639–1

Field 377 Subfield $l—Language Term

Sometimes the language associated with an entity cannot be found on an authorized list. When this is the case, the code for the general language under which the more specific language falls should be recorded in the subfield $a, and the natural language term for the more specific language should be recoded in the subfield $l.

> 377 $a nya $l Chewa

If there is more than one language associated with an entity, any of the languages that requires the use of a subfield $l should be recorded in a separate field.

> 377 $a fre
> 377 $a bnt $l Lenje

Field 378—Fuller Form of Personal Name

Field 378 is used only for persons and is used to record a variant of the name that is fuller in form than what has been chosen as the preferred name. It is the form that is typically found in the subfield $q of an authorized access point, which is why the letter "q" was chosen to demarcate the field's only subfield: subfield $q, for *fuller form of personal name*. The 378 subfield $q holds the same information that would appear in the qualifier of the authorized access point for the person. The subfield $q is not repeatable.

> 100   1_ $a Shore, C. A. $q (Cecil Alan)
> 378 $q Cecil Alan

As noted in a previous section of this chapter, catalogers following AACR2 and Library of Congress rule interpretations always added the fuller form of name, even when it was not needed to distinguish one person's name from another. In the RDA environment, this is no longer true. Instead, catalogers following RDA and the associated LC-PCC policy statements have the option of adding the fuller form if it is judged to aid in identification or to omit it. Even if the fuller form is not added to the access point, catalogers contributing to the LCNAF are encouraged to record this information in the subfield $q of the 378 field.

> 100 1_ $a Russell, Benjamin N., $d 1947–
> 378 $q Benjamin Nelson

Field 380—Form of Work

Field 380 was created to accommodate the RDA element *form of work. Form of work* is the class or genre to which a work belongs and can be added to the access point of a work if needed to distinguish that work from similarly named works. It has one main subfield, subfield $a, for *form of work*, which is repeatable. As with the other fields already discussed, the 380 field can contain natural language or controlled vocabulary terms. Whenever a term is taken from a list, a subfield $2 should be added in order to specify which list.

> 130 _0 $a War of the worlds (Television program)
> 380 $a Television program

Field 381—Other Distinguishing Characteristics of Work or Expression

Field 381 was created for use in authority records for works and expressions only. It carries information about a work or expression that can be used for distinguishing the entity from other similarly named entities but that does not fall into the other defined categories of elements used for those purposes. It has one main subfield, subfield $a, for *other distinguishing characteristic*, which is repeatable.

> 130 _0 $a Genesis (Old Saxon poem)
> 381 $a Old Saxon poem
>
> 130 _0 $a Bible. $l English. $s Authorized. $f 2004
> 381 $a Authorized

Field 382—Medium of Performance

Field 382 is the first of three new MARC fields that were added specifically for attributes of musical works and expressions. These fields can be used in bibliographic as well as in authority records. Field 382 encodes the RDA element *medium of performance for musical content. Medium of performance* can under certain circumstances be a core element and is sometimes added to the preferred access point for a work or expression. (Detailed instructions are found in RDA 6.28.) The field is repeatable.

> 382   0_ $a orchestra

Field 383—Numeric Designation of Musical Work

Field 383 is another of the three new MARC fields that were added specifically for attributes of musical works and expressions. It encodes the RDA element *numeric designation of a musical work. Numeric designation of a musical work* can under certain circumstances be a core element and is sometimes added to the preferred access point for a work. (Detailed instructions are found in RDA 6.28.) The field is repeatable, as different sources can assign different identification numbers to the same work, and contains subfields for serial number (subfield $a), opus number (subfield $b), thematic index number (subfield $c), thematic index code (subfield $d), and publisher associated with opus number (subfield $e).

> 383 $a op. 3 **$e** André

Field 384—Key

Field 384 is the third of the three new MARC fields that were added specifically for attributes of musical works and expressions. Field 384 encodes the RDA element *key*. Like *medium of performance*, *key* can under certain circumstances be a core element, and is sometimes added to the preferred access point for a work or expression. (Detailed instructions are found in RDA 6.28.) The first indicator specifies whether the key is the original key (first indicator has value "0") or is transposed (first indicator has value "1").

> 384   1_ $a D major

AUTHORITY RECORD EXAMPLES

Now that the new MARC authority fields have been elucidated, we will analyze eight records created using RDA instructions, LC-PCC policy statements, and PCC guidelines, noting the differences between AACR2 and RDA. In these examples, we will see how the various MARC fields are typically used to encode attributes of persons, families, corporate bodies, works, and expressions that correspond to RDA elements.

Case 1: Person

In the first example, we see an RDA authority record for a person: *Jones, Judd, $d 1931–2011*. Elements that are different from or would not have been present in an

AACR2 record are in **bold**. The 008 field byte 10 (byte 008/10), or the "Descriptive cataloging rules" byte, is coded "z," which stands for "Other." This byte would have been coded "c," representing "AACR2," in an authority record created using AACR2. Also of note is the presence of "$b eng" and "$e rda" in the 040 field. The designation of "rda" in the subfield $e is mandatory and is the way to identify the record as an RDA record. The addition of the "$b eng" represents a new practice in cooperative cataloging, where the language of cataloging is included in the record and falls in between the $a and the $e subfields of the authority record.

Although the 670 field is not new with RDA, and *could*, under either AACR2 or RDA, have contained a wealth of information, the ability to translate this information into coded form has inspired many catalogers to populate the 670 fields with much more data than previously. In addition, the pre-RDA practice with respect to 670 (and 675) fields was to keep them minimal, including just the information necessary to justify or explain the contents of the 1XX, 4XX, and 5XX fields. Let us look now at how the information contained in the 670 fields has been encoded in the new MARC fields.

The 046 field includes the birth date ("19310817") in subfield $f and the death date ("20110309") in subfield $g. The record also has a 370 field, which encodes the person's place of birth ("Ala."), his place of death ("New York, N.Y."), and his associated country ("U.S."). The record encodes the information about his field of activity ("performing arts") in field 372 as well as his profession or occupation as an actor, singer, dancer, and model in field 374. Finally, it encodes information about his gender ("male") in field 375 and the language he used in his performing career (English) in field 377. All of this specific encoding makes it possible, for example, to do precise searches for persons in the field of performing arts who were born in Alabama. The specific encoding of these data also has the potential for advanced applications that would enable the user of a catalog to find, for example, the works of male dancers born in the twentieth century.

Case 2: Family

The next case is an authority record for a family: *Calder (Family: $d 1757–1959: $c N.C.)*. Here, we have not identified any data elements in **bold** because, prior to RDA, family records were not added to the name authority file. We first see byte 008/10 coded with "z" for "Other" and the 040 that includes "$b eng" and "$e rda." Next, we see a beginning date for the family ("1757") in the 046 subfield $s and a termination date ("1959") in the subfield $t. The authorized access point for the family includes the family's name ("Calder"), the word "Family," the date range of the family ("1757–1959"), and the associated place ("N.C."). The record has a 370 field showing the associated country in the subfield $c ("U.S.") and the other place associated with the family in the subfield $e ("Wilmington, N.C."). It also has a 376 field showing that it is simply a family, as opposed to a dynasty or clan. One thing to note in the record is the presence of a 667 field with the text "SUBJECT USAGE: This heading is not valid for use as a subject; use a family name heading from LCSH." Name authority records for families entered into the name authority

Case 1. Authority Record: Person

LDR 01159cz a2200241n 450

  001   4141128
  005   20121228073943.0
  008   971025n| azannaabn n aad c
  010 __ |a n 97842073
  040 __ |a ___ |b eng |e rda |c ___
  046 __ |f 19310817 |g 20110309
  100 1_ |a Jones, Judd, |d 1931–2011
  370 __ |a Ala. |b New York, N.Y. |c U.S.
  372 __ |a Performing arts |2 lcsh
  374 __ |a Actors |a Singers |a Dancers |a Male models |2 lcsh
  375 __ |a male
  377 __ |a eng
  670 __ |a Judd Jones papers, 1952–2011: |b (Judd Jones was an African-American actor, singer/dancer and director whose career was centered in New York City. At the beginning of his career he also modeled for various magazine advertisements)
  670 __ |a IMDb WWW site, Nov. 21, 2012 |b (Judd Jones (1921–2011), actor; Born: 1921 in Alabama, USA; died: March 9, 2011 (age 89) in Manhattan, New York City, New York, USA; Filmography: The Scarlet Letter (1995), Malcolm X (1992))
  670 __ |a Ancestry WWW site, Dec. 6, 2012 |b (Jude Jones, b. 17 Aug. 1931, Alabama; d. 9 March 2011, New York, New York)

Case 2. Authority Record: Family

LDR 00611cz a2200169n 450

  001   8969097
  005   20120420160506.0
  008   120420n| aznnnabbn |n ana
  010 __ |a n 2012026835
  040 __ |a ___ |b eng |e rda |c ___
  046 __ |s 1757 |t 1959
  100 3_ |a Calder (Family: |d 1757–1959: |c N.C.)
  370 __ |c U.S. |e Wilmington, N.C.
  376 __ |a Family
  667 __ |a SUBJECT USAGE: This heading is not valid for use as a subject; use a family name heading from LCSH.
  670 __ |a NUCMC data from Amer. Jewish Archives for Its Family papers, 1757–1959 |b (Calder family; residents of Wilmington, N.C.)

file must always have this text to distinguish them from subject authority records for families entered into the subject authority file.

Case 3: Corporate Body

The next case is an authority record for a corporate body: *Cato Institute*. The exclusively RDA elements of the record are in **bold**. We know it is an RDA record because of the presence of the "z" in the 008/10 byte and the "$e rda" in the 040 field. Other RDA elements in the record include a 368 field describing the type of corporate body ("research institutes"), a 370 field that gives information about its associated country ("U.S."), and a more detailed 371 field that gives most of the address of the body ("1000 Massachusetts Avenue, N.W., Washington, D.C."). The record also encodes the Institute's field of activity ("public policy") in a 372 field and the language of its publications ("eng," the code for "English") in a 377 field. Note the use of the subfield $v and $u in the 371 and 372 fields of this record to give the precise source of the data in the subfield $a of each of these fields.

Case 3. Authority Record: Corporate Body

```
LDR 01181cz a2200253n 450
  001   1409489
  005   20121106074728.0
  008   780217n| azannaabn |a ana
  010 __ |a n 78006519
  040 __ |a ___ |b eng |e rda |c ___
  110 2_ |a Cato Institute
  368 __ |a Research institutes |2 lcsh
  370 __ |c U.S.
  371 __ |a 1000 Massachusetts Avenue, N.W. |b Washington |c D.C. |v
         Cato Institute, WWW home page, viewed Nov. 2, 2012 |u http://
         www.cato.org/about.php
  372 __ |a Public policy |v Cato Institute, WWW home page, viewed Nov.
         2, 2012 |u http://www.cato.org/about.php |2 lcsh
  377 __ |a eng
  410 2_ |a Institut Katona
  670 __ |a Inquiry, Nov. 21, 1977 (a.e.) |b p. 1 (Cato Institute, San Fran-
         cisco, CA)
  670 __ |a Plant closings, c1982: |b verso of t.p. (Cato Institute, Washing-
         ton, D.C.)
  670 __ |a Ot plana k rynku, 1993: |b t.p. (Institut Katona)
  670 __ |a 2011 state legislative guide, 2011?, via WWW, viewed Novem-
         ber 2, 2012: |b PDF cover page (Cato Institute)
  670 __ |a Cato Institute, WWW home page, viewed Nov. 2, 2012: |b about
         Cato (The Cato Institute is a public policy research organization)
```

Case 4: Conference

The next case is an authority record for a conference: *Joint Meeting of the FAO Panel of Experts on Pesticide Residues in Food and the Environment and the WHO Expert Group on Pesticide Residues $d (2012 : $c Rome, Italy)*. As in the previous records, the exclusively RDA elements are in **bold**, and the RDA record can be identified by the "z" byte in the 008/10 byte and the "$e rda" in the 040 field. This record also has a 046 field encoding the starting date of the conference in the subfield $s ("20120911") and the ending date of the conference in the subfield $t ("20120920"). The record has a 368 field, describing the type of corporate body ("meetings"). It has a 370 field giving information about the location of the conference ("Rome, Italy"). It has a 372 field providing information about the field of activity ("pesticide residues in food"). Because it is the joint meeting of two different corporate bodies, there is a 373 field citing the associated corporate bodies ("FAO Panel of Experts on Pesticide Residues in Food and the Environment" and "WHO Expert Group on Pesticide Residues"). Finally, there is a 377 field describing the language associated with the meeting ("eng," the code for "English"). Note the absence of 411 fields in this record. The references from variant names for the conference are now found in the unqualified record for the ongoing conference, *Joint Meeting of the FAO Panel of Experts on Pesticide Residues in Food and the Environment and the WHO Expert Group on Pesticide Residues.*

Case 5: Work (Graphic Novel)

The next case is an authority record for a work: *Card, Orson Scott. $t Ender in exile (Graphic novel)*. As in the previous records, the exclusively RDA elements are in **bold**, and the RDA record can be identified by the presence of the "z" in byte 008/10 and the "$e rda" in the 040 field. The record contains a 046 field giving the date of the work. According to RDA, the date of work *may be the date the work was created or the date the work was first published or released*. In this case the date of publication ("2010") serves as the date of the work, and so this is recorded in the 046.

The RDA record has a 380 field describing the form of work ("graphic novel"). This incidentally is the same term used in the authorized access point to distinguish this work from a similarly named work. As *could* have been true in an AACR2 authority record, the RDA record has a 500 field containing the authorized access point for the related work, but this 500 field contains additional information that serves to specify the nature of the relationship between the two works. The work represented by the authority record is a graphic novel, *Ender in*

Case 4.   Authority Record: Conference

LDR 0093nz a2200193n 450
```
001    9203082
005    20130222050907.0
008    130221n| azannaabn |n ana
010 __ |a nb2013003652
035 __ |a (UK)008687049
040 __ |a UK |b eng |e rda |c UK
046 __ |s 20120911 |t 20120920
111 2_ |a Joint Meeting of the FAO Panel of Experts on Pesticide Residues in Food
       and the Environment and the WHO Expert Group on Pesticide Residues |d
       (2012 : |c Rome, Italy)
368 __ |a Meetings |2 lcsh
370 __ |e Rome, Italy
372 __ |a Pesticide residues in food |2 lcsh
373 __ |a FAO Panel of Experts on Pesticide Residues in Food and the Environ-
       ment |a WHO Expert Group on Pesticide Residues |2 naf
377 __ |a eng
670 __ |a Pesticide residues in food 2012: |b t.p. (Joint Meeting of the FAO
       Panel of Experts on Pesticide Residues in Food and the Environment and
       the WHO Core Assessment Group on Pesticide Residues, Rome, Italy,
       11-20 September 2012)
```

Case 5.   Authority Record: Work

LDR 00565cz a2200169n 450
```
001    8477900
005    20120701122634.0
008    101117n| azannaabn |a aaa c
010 __ |a no2010187846
040 __ |a ___ |b eng |e rda |c ___
046 __ |k 2010
100 1_ |a Card, Orson Scott. |t Ender in exile (Graphic novel)
380 __ |a Graphic novel
500 1_ |w r |i Adaptation of (work): |a Card, Orson Scott. |t Ender in
       exile
670 __ |a Ender in exile, 2010, ©2010.
678 __ |a Graphic novel first published in 2010 based on Card's novel
       Ender in exile.
```

Exile, which is a derivative work of the original eponymous novel. To explain this, the relationship designator "Adaptation of (work):" (from RDA Appendix J) is recorded in the subfield $i, which precedes the access point for the related work in the 500 field. Also, to convey that relationship data are present elsewhere in the 500 field, a subfield $w with the designation "r" is included. The 678 field, which could also have been present in an AACR2 record, provides a summary that contextualizes this work in natural language.

Case 6: Work (Series)

The next case is an authority record for another work, but this time it is a series: *Alphabeta*. As in the previous records, the exclusively RDA elements are in **bold**, and the RDA record can be identified by the "z" in byte 008/10 and the "$b eng $e rda" in the 040 field. This record has a 046 field giving the beginning publication date of the series in the subfield $k ("2011"). In the case of this particular series, there is actually a termination date ("2012"), which is recorded in the subfield $l. In addition, a 380 field has been added to describe the form of the work ("series").

Case 7: Work (Musical Work)

The next example is an authority record for a musical work, Dmitri Shostakovich's 6th symphony: *Shostakovich, Dmitriĭ Dmitrievich, 1906–1975. Symphonies, no. 6, op. 54, B minor*. Again, new RDA elements are in **bold**, and the presence of the "z" in

---

Case 6.　Authority Record: Work (Series)

LDR 00679nz a2200217n 450
```
001   9101372
005   20120925074550.0
008   120924n| azaaaaaan |n ana c
010 __ |a no2012127469
040 __ |a ___ |b eng |e rda |c ___
```
046 __ |k 2011 |l 2012
```
130 _0 |a Alphabeta
```
380 __ |a Series
```
642 __ |a 2 |5 DPCC |5 UPB
644 __ |a f |5 UPB
645 __ |a t |5 DPCC |5 UPB
646 __ |a s |5 UPB
643 __ |a Malvern East, Victoria, Australia |b Electio Editions
670 __ |a If not in paint, 2011: |b cover page 4 (Alphabeta two)
```

Case 7. Authority Record: Work (Musical Work)

```
LDR 01020cz a2200241n 450
 001 4275690
 005 20130410085334.0
 008 840229n| azannaabn |a aaa
 010 __ |a n 82243132 |z no 98010916
 040 __ |a ___ |b eng |e rda |c ___
 046 __ |k 1939
 100 1_ |a Shostakovich, Dmitriĭ Dmitrievich, |d 1906-1975. |t Symphonies, |n no. 6, op. 54, |r B
      minor
 380 __ |a Symphonies |2 lcsh
 382 __ |a orchestra
 383 __ |a no. 6 |b op. 54
 384 0_ |a B minor
 400 1_ |w nnaa |a Shostakovich, Dmitriĭ Dmitrievich, |d 1906-1975. |t Symphony, |n no. 6, op.
      54
 670 __ |a His Sinfonie Nr. 6 h-Moll op. 54 [SR] 1980: |b labels (Sinfonie Nr. 6 h-Moll op. 54)
 670 __ |a LC manual cat. |b (hdg.: Shostakovich, Dmitriĭ Dmitrievich, 1906-1975. Symphony,
      no. 6, op. 54)
 670 __ |a His Shestaia sinfoniia, 1941: |b t.p. (Shestaia sinfoniia; op. 54)
 670 __ |a Grove music online, March 22, 2013 |b (op. 54, Symphony no. 6, b, 1939)
```

byte 008/10 and "$e rda" in the 040 field signify that the record has been cataloged using RDA.

The 046 subfield $k gives the date of the work, which in this case was taken from a reference source (Grove music online).

The form of title in the 100 field ("Symphonies" in the plural, with the serial and opus numbers in the subfield $n and the key in the subfield $r) may seem strange to those not accustomed to music cataloging, but the conventions have not changed a great deal from AACR2. Abbreviations are allowed for numeric designations of a musical work (see RDA B.5.4).

Adding the form of work in a 380 field is a new RDA practice.

As mentioned previously, unique to music are the 382, 383, and 384 fields. The 382 field represents the medium of performance—the instruments and/or voices required to perform a piece of music. In this case, the medium of performance is "orchestra." The 383 field is the numeric designation of musical work. The subfield $a encodes a serial number ("no. 6") and the subfield $b encodes an opus number ("op. 54"). The separate subfields parse information that would otherwise all be in subfield $n of the 100 field, or, depending on the type of title, not recorded at all except in a 670 field. Finally, the 384 field is for key, and the 1st indicator "0" specifies that B minor is the original key of this piece.

Case 8: Expression

Our last case is an authority record for an expression: *Beauvoir, Simone de, 1908–1986. Works. Selections. English. 2012.* As in the previous cases, the exclusively RDA elements are in **bold**, and the RDA record can be identified by the "z" in the 008/10 byte and the "$e rda" in the 040 field. Note that this is a "differentiated" authority record, as it is specific to the 2012 expression; the authorized access point includes the date.

The 046 field in the record contains a subfield $k that encodes the date the expression began. The case is similar to that of the graphic novel (Case 5). The date in the 046 subfield $k can be based on the "earliest manifestation embodying the expression" if the date of expression is unknown.

The 100 field (subfields $t and $k) contains the conventional collective title, as described earlier in this chapter: "Works. Selections." Note that the AACR2 form of the title is found in a 400 field subfield $t, with the coding of the subfield $w indicating that the form found in the 400 field was an earlier authorized form of the access point for this expression.

The 377 field contains the language of the expression ("eng," the code for "English"), not the language of the original ("fre," the code for "French").

Case 8.   Authority Record: Expression

```
LDR 00541cz a2200169n 450
  001  8881701
  005  20130327071803.0
  008  120119n| azannaabn |a aaa
  010 __ |a n 2012004156
  040 __ |a ___ |b eng |e rda |c ___
  046 __ |k 2012
  100 1_ |a Beauvoir, Simone de, |d 1908–1986. |t Works. |k Selections. |l
         English. |f 2012
  377 __ |a eng
  400 1_ |a Beauvoir, Simone de, |d 1908–1986. |t Political writings
  400 1_ |w nnea |a Beauvoir, Simone de, |d 1908–1986. |t Selections. |l
         English. |f 2012
  670 __ |a Political writings, c2012
```

CONCLUSION

This chapter provided a detailed discussion of the changes related to authority records in the new RDA environment. It first highlighted the major differences between AACR2 and RDA with respect to access points, so that the reader will know how to search for familiar headings that underwent changes in the move to RDA.

It then focused on authority records, looking at the new variable fields and their respective conventions for recording data. Because many libraries and other agencies rely on authority data from the national authority file—whether they participate in the creation of these data or not—it is important to know the cooperative cataloging policies that govern the way that information is recorded in authority records. It is hoped that this chapter provided a basic explanation so that the reader can better understand, if not create, authority data using RDA.

Bibliography

Except for the "Selected Readings" at the end of this bibliography, all of the entries are for resources that are available primarily online. The *RDA Toolkit* requires a subscription; the remaining online resources are, at the time of this writing, freely available. Dates are omitted for those resources, such as the *RDA Toolkit*, that are updated on a regular basis.

CATALOGING TOOLS AND STANDARDS

Library of Congress Network Development and MARC Standards Office. *MARC Standards.* http://www.loc.gov/marc.

RDA Toolkit. http://www.rdatoolkit.org/. This is published by the American Library Association, the Canadian Library Association, and CILIP (Chartered Institute of Library and Information Professionals). It includes *Resource Description and Access, LC-PCC Policy Statements, AACR2*, and additional resources and tools. Note that access to the *LC-PCC Policy Statements* does not require a subscription to the *RDA Toolkit*.

POLICIES, GUIDELINES, AND TRAINING MATERIALS

ALCTS (Association for Library Collections & Technical Services, a division of the American Library Association). *Cataloging and RDA Webinars.* http://www.ala.org/alcts/confevents/upcoming/webinar/cat. This webpage contains links to the recordings, and frequently the slides, from webinars presented on RDA and other cataloging topics. Several of the webinars are individually cited in chapter 9 of this book. Recordings of many of the webinars are available through the ALCTS YouTube channel (http://www.youtube.com/user/alctsce).

International Federation of Library Associations and Institutions. *Names of Persons: National Usages for Entry in Catalogues.* 4th ed. München: K.G. Saur, 1996. Available as a PDF document at: http://www.ifla.org/node/4953

Library of Congress. Catalogers Learning Workshop. *RDA: Resource Description & Access Training Materials.* http://www.loc.gov/catworkshop/RDA%20training%20materials/index.html. This webpage includes links to detailed training materials, webcasts, and sample RDA records.

Library of Congress. Network Development and MARC Standards Office. *RDA in MARC.* October 2012. http://www.loc.gov/marc/RDAinMARC-10-12.html.

OCLC. *About RDA.* http://www.oclc.org/rda/about.en.html. This webpage contains links to general "RDA resources" and also links to "RDA-related resources from OCLC."

OCLC. *OCLC RDA Policy Statement. Effective March 31, 2013.* http://www.oclc.org/en-US/rda/new-policy.html.

Program for Cooperative Cataloging. *PCC Guidelines for the Application of Relationship Designators in Bibliographic Records.* http://www.loc.gov/aba/pcc/rda/PCC%20RDA%20 guidelines/Relat-Desig-Guidelines.docx.

Program for Cooperative Cataloging. *PCC RDA BIBCO Standard Record (BSR) Metadata Application Profile.* http://www.loc.gov/aba/pcc/scs/documents/PCC-RDA-BSR.pdf.

Program for Cooperative Cataloging. *Provider-Neutral E-Resource MARC Record Guide: P-N/ RDA Version (January 1, 2013).* http://www.loc.gov/aba/pcc/scs/documents/PN-RDA -Combined.docx.

Program for Cooperative Cataloging. *RDA and PCC.* http://www.loc.gov/aba/pcc/. This is a section of the PCC (Program for Cooperative Cataloging) website that contains links to some of the PCC-generated documentation regarding RDA.

Program for Cooperative Cataloging. Cooperative Online Serials Program. (CONSER). *Serials Cataloging Issues. Resource Description and Access (RDA).* http://www.loc.gov/aba/pcc/conser/issues/index.html. This is a section of the *Serials Cataloging Issues* page of CONSER. It contains links to RDA-related documentation for serials.

Program for Cooperative Cataloging. Name Authority Cooperative Program. (NACO) *Documentation & Updates.* http://www.loc.gov/aba/pcc/naco/. This is a section of the NACO website that contains links to some of the NACO-generated documentation regarding RDA and authority records, for example: *MARC 21 encoding to accommodate new RDA elements 046 and 3XX in NARs and SARs.*

RDA Toolkit. Teaching and Training. http://www.rdatoolkit.org/training. This page of the *RDA Toolkit* contains links to a number of training resources from a variety of institutions, including some institutions outside the United States.

SELECTED READINGS

Hitchens, Alison, and Ellen Symons. "Preparing Catalogers for RDA Training." *Cataloging & Classification Quarterly* 47(2009): 691–707. doi:10.1080/01639370903203234

Maxwell, Robert L. *FRBR: A Guide for the Perplexed.* Chicago: American Library Association, 2008.

Oliver, Chris. *Introducing RDA: A Guide to the Basics.* Chicago: American Library Association, 2010.

Index

About the Authors

Chamya Pompey Kincy was a librarian at UCLA until her untimely passing in 2013. She earned three degrees from UCLA: a BS and MS in physiological science and an MLIS. She worked in the UCLA Library for sixteen years, first as a student assistant, then as a library assistant, and finally as a librarian, serving most recently as the life and social sciences cataloger in the Cataloging & Metadata Center. She was active in several professional organizations, including the Medical Library Association (MLA), the American Library Association (ALA), and the Program for Cooperative Cataloging (PCC). In the Medical Library Association, she chaired the Technical Services Section and was MLA's liaison to ALA's cataloging rule-making body, Committee on Cataloging: Description and Access. In the Program for Cooperative Cataloging, she served as cochair of the Standing Committee on Training. She was active in local, regional, and national efforts to prepare catalogers for implementation of the cataloging rules Resource Description and Access (RDA), teaching workshops all over the country.

Sara Shatford Layne was a librarian at UCLA until her retirement in 2013. She earned a BA (English literature) and an MFA (drama: costume design) from Stanford University and an MLS and PhD (library and information science) from UCLA. After earning her MLS at UCLA, she worked as a cataloger of early children's books at the Pierpont Morgan Library in New York City. She then worked as a librarian at UCLA for almost thirty years, serving most recently as principal cataloger in the Cataloging & Metadata Center. She has been active in the American Library Association, at one point chairing the Cataloging & Classification Section of ALCTS. She has taught cataloging courses at UCLA and through the distance learning program

332

of the Library and Information Science Department at San José State University.
She has published in several areas, but primarily in access to images, and coauthored
Improving Online Public Access Catalogs with Martha Yee (Chicago: American Library
Association, 1998). She currently serves on the editorial board of *Cataloging & Classification Quarterly*.

DATE DUE

NOV 2 2017			
18			
			PRINTED IN U.S.A.